Time and the Artist in Shakespeare's English Histories

UNIVERSITY OF DELAWARE PRESS AWARDS

General John Burgoyne (Richard J. Hargrove, Jr.)

Time and the Artist in Shakespeare's English Histories (John W. Blanpied)

Time and the Artist in Shakespeare's English Histories

John W. Blanpied

Newark: University of Delaware Press
London and Toronto: Associated University Presses

Associated University Presses, Inc.
440 Forsgate Drive
Cranbury, NJ 08512

Associated University Presses Ltd
25 Sicilian Avenue
London WC1A 2QH, England

Associated University Presses
2133 Royal Windsor Drive
Unit 1
Mississauga, Ontario
Canada L5J 1K5

Library of Congress Cataloging in Publication Data

Blanpied, John W., 1938–
Time and the artist in Shakespeare's English histories.

Bibliography: p.
Includes index.
1. Shakespeare, William, 1564–1616—Histories.
2. History in literature. I. Title.
PR2982.B52 1983 822.3′3 82-40387
ISBN 0-87413-230-4

Printed in the United States of America

Man has in fact no past unless he is conscious of having one, for only such consciousness makes dialogue and choice possible. Without it, individuals and societies merely embody a past of which they are ignorant and to which they are passively subject; they merely afford to the outside observer a series of transformations, comparable to those of animal species, which can be set out in a temporal series. If men have no consciousness of what they are and have been, they do not attain to the dimensions proper to history.

Raymond Aron, "Relativism in History"

. . . a second dimension of historical thought [is] the history of history: the discovery that the historian himself . . . is part of the process he is studying.

R. G. Collingwood, "The Historical Imagination"

Man is a history-making creature who can neither repeat his past nor leave it behind; at every moment he adds to and thereby modifies everything that had previously happened to him.

W. H. Auden, *The Dyer's Hand*

Contents

Acknowledgments

Of all the friends and colleagues who have read, discussed, criticized, and otherwise given me help with various parts of this book throughout its long gestation, I especially want to thank Richard Abrams, James L. Calderwood, and Kirby Farrell. To my wife, Pamela, for her patience, faith, and editorial skills, my debt is beyond account.

Earlier versions of Chapters Two and Ten appeared in *Studies in English Literature* (Spring 1975) and *English Literary Renaissance* (Spring 1975).

Introduction

> There is a history in all men's lives
> Figuring the nature of the times deceased . . .

By the time he gave this speech to Warwick in *2 Henry IV*, Shakespeare was in the midst of his eighth English history play in about that many years. Within a year he would cap off the series with *Henry V*. Even setting aside the quality of the plays, the feat remains unmatched. Not only did he fashion an entirely new kind of drama, but he developed it through a uniquely coherent sequence of plays. In the process he may have become the most truly serious historian of his time—not as a theorist, of course, but as one who both felt the need and devised the means to read the past most deeply, and who undertook to test the extent of its claims upon the present; which is to say, upon his age in general, and upon his own dramatic art in particular.

Of course, Shakespeare was writing other plays and poems during the 1590s, but the histories make up fully half of his output during that first decade of his career. I do not mean that he produced them in hermetic detachment from his other work. But their sheer number, the range and variety of his sources, and the complex consciousness expressed by the sequence itself, all suggest an extraordinary interest in history as a special domain of experience, presenting special opportunities and problems to the dramatist, and making special and rigorous claims upon him.[1]

The idea of a nine-part sequence is central to my argument in this book—not as a mere succession of plays, but as a fundamental imaginative category. I would never argue that the plays were meant to be read, performed, or witnessed as such a sequence, or that Shakespeare executed them as such. But I do argue that they are bound by an essential and distinguishable coherence, and that this coherence is not finally a matter of genre, theme, or subject, but of the peculiar sustained note of attention, on the dramatist's part, to the evolving relationship of subject to medium, history to drama. The rhythm of succession, in other words, is the rhythm of a mind actively at work in its almost overwhelming wealth of materials, shaping and releasing, imposing and revealing form—in short, "figuring the nature of the times deceased."

Taken as a sequence, then, the history plays show Shakespeare generating a vision of the past and developing, as he goes, the means of ordering its complexities onstage. In the process of exploring the effects of drama upon history, he redefines both "history" and "drama" and makes far-reaching discoveries about both his medium and his subject. History grows from an external and passive object of scrutiny into a living connection between dead past and seething present. Simultaneously, drama grows into an imaginative power dangerously alive, uniquely capable of both recreating and consuming the past.

More specifically, in *Time and the Artist* I contend that Shakespeare necessarily approached his historical materials as an artist (rather than as an ideologue or as "dramatizer" of given material); that alone among his contemporaries this compelled him to be equally serious about subject and medium; that "history," though it clearly fascinated him for many different reasons, had finally to be something more than a body of terrific story-stuff; and that "drama" could never be simply a way of packaging a frozen and inalterable reality. The plays show us that Shakespeare was profoundly concerned with the *idea* of history—that is, as a category of experience with a distinctive nature, simultaneously implacable and ghostly, undeniable and elusive; and that he was determined to find the dramatic form that most truly expressed this special kind of reality.[2]

Let me lay out my argument as a narrative structure. Shakespeare, I suggest, sets out in the earliest plays with a fairly conventional view of history as a more or less established body of facts and events, capable of assuming more or less direct expression. Very soon he discovers a sort of "indeterminacy principle" at work, the presence of his own increasingly powerful imagination distorting the image of supposedly preexistent material. He is then faced with an artistic and epistemological problem: how to get a clear and unimpeded view of history. Shakespeare's handling of this problem is typically Elizabethan in its aggressive inventiveness; what makes it brilliantly unique is the nature of the problem he insists on addressing, which requires nine complex plays to resolve. Rather than try to ignore or evade the presence of the artist in his own work, Shakespeare incorporates that presence and uses the figure as a focus of energy that he can both control and observe. But the introduction of this artistic dimension into his historical material enormously complicates his view of what "history" is. Eventually he comes to understand that given the imperatives of his art, "history" cannot be conceived except dramatically; that to render its ontological integrity he must first accept it as dramatic in its very heart and soul, not only in its original, mythic "performance," but as it is continuously recreated before, and by, a presumptive audience. Gradually, then, he is able to diffuse the energy of art from its focus in the artist figure outward into the world of the drama itself, and from that world into the present world of the audience.

In short, this book is concerned with the ways the playwright *acts* in his historical material—how he manages to transform his own inevitable presence in the histories into the means of sounding out their huge and elusive energies.

The central device is certainly the king (or would-be king). Whatever else he is in myth and history, in Shakespearean drama, particularly the history plays, he is the most immensely efficacious and powerful of figures. He focuses and reflects the dramatist's deepest concerns, even—or perhaps especially—when they conflict. For he stands at the center of any given play as the figure in whom the tensions of the play, as history and as drama, are concentrated. His symbolic functions extend both inward, into the historical world, and outward, into the dramatic occasion—toward the audience, to whom he "carries across" the living drama. In his former capacity he is preoccupied with legitimacy and the consolidation of power, and, increasingly, with the means of exercising power both at the center and throughout a rousing and multiplistic realm. In other words, he expresses the dramatist's concern with the integrity and coherence of the historical world. But in his dramatic capacity, as the agent through whom that world is brought alive in the present, he expresses the dramatist's concern with the play's credibility, the suitability of its form to the explosive form-seeking pressures it embodies. So the king is both a character in the constituted world of the play and its interpreter, even its shaper—in other words, its surrogate playwright.

As the dramatist's own presence in the sequence becomes a pressing issue (in the "king-centered" middle plays and later), I make use of two terms that, though I will have more to say about them later, merit a brief explanation here.[3] As I use them, *antic* and *machiavel* do not refer to conventional roles or archetypes. They are names for competing types of dramatic energies that come to be focused, with ever-increasing vividness, in the king and other power-figures.

Thus, as a plotter, a manager of appearances toward a future revelation, a manipulator of others' perceptions and expectations, a weaver of designs, the king functions as the machiavel. He is an actor, in both senses of the word, but his deepest motives are to bring all mere "acting" to an end. He cultivates disorder, but in the interests of a broader order. He resides in the historical world, shaping it internally, plying the skills of a playwright: timing, indirection, self-restraint, disguise. His aim is to carry forward the historical action, and therefore no single moment is completely real. The final truth is that of the fully formed design.

But the king is also a performer, singular and strange in his own realm, strangely at home in the theater as opposed to history. In this capacity, he functions as the antic, thrusting the play's live energy outward to us, rupturing the fabric of time and continuity, revealing all the machiavel's works as theatrical illusion. Self-delighting, he plays for the sake of playing, residing only in the drama. His truth is that of the performer who vanishes or reverts to chaos the moment he is out of sight or we have turned our backs.[4] There is no past, he insists, and therefore no future, only this passing moment. Jester to the machiavel's sobriety, outsider to his historical centrality, the antic in his purest form is the fool, materialized from a blurred background of anarchic energy, of the chaos always just beyond the little human clearing.

Neither type exists in a pure form in the histories, and every power-figure embodies both kinds of energy, because the power to shape the plot inevitably carries with it the power to destroy the plot by explosive performance. Jack Cade, in *2 Henry VI*, is the most radical form of the antic in the histories, but he is the monstrous parody of York, the original machiavel in the sequence and father of Richard III. Yet Richard is surely the antic performer par excellence, his nihilist energies joyful in their destructiveness, until he subsides into the historical world he has been busy mocking down. It is a pale world compared to him, and he has an easy time opposing it for most of the play. But in later plays the world acquires strength and density, and the machiavellian fiction of temporal continuity becomes tenacious and compelling. And then the antic proposition—that there is no god but the god of the play—must swell with terrific force if it is not to be brushed aside as mere escapism. And here comes Falstaff.

If there is a fundamental motive in the histories, it is the need to make a future. To this need everything else is subdued, though in Falstaff it also meets its authentic opposition. Ultimately, of course, the future is us, now—Falstaff's natural constituency. In the chapter on the final play, *Henry V,* I entertain the notion that as audience to the entire outward-spiralling sequence, *we* are the final generation of the histories.

Time and the Artist in Shakespeare's English Histories

Part I

Breaking Ground: *The* Henry VI *Plays*

1
The Artist as Adventurer

Almost everyone who knows the *Henry VI* plays would agree that they are confusing. Allowing for obvious differences, I imagine the original audience would have found them confusing too, and indeed I sometimes suppose Shakespeare himself must have gotten lost in them. Usually, though, I picture an exuberant young dramatist grandly taking on a half-century's worth of sprawling chronicle history, determined to hammer it into heroic shape, and in the process making discoveries about that material, and about his craft, that go far beyond what he originally intended. And I think that in the confusion of *Henry VI* we may read, if we can, the record of those discoveries.

But first, I want to explain why my objective is not to clear up the confusion of the plays, but to make the confusion clear. This sounds like a quibble, but it really is not. I mean that it is less accurate to say that the *Henry VI* plays are confusing than that confusion is their medium. And this amounts to saying that the essential action, and therefore the dramatic experience of the plays, consists of a movement not out of, but into, the heart of the confusion.

For a long time the plays suffered under the assumption of aesthetic inferiority. We knew the subject matter was civil disorder and that (for all their occasional virtues) the plays only helplessly mirrored it. Then a series of literary historians led by E. M. W. Tillyard discovered a sophisticated principle of order: intentional form in the service of a philosophical orthodoxy (the "Tudor Myth," "Mirrors of Elizabethan Policy"). They made it possible to think of all Shakespeare's English history plays as a distinctive and coherent group, though they located the principle of order outside the plays themselves. After the historicists, the prevailing disposition toward the plays has been the one implied in the title of J. P. Brockbank's influential essay, "The Frame of Disorder." In this view the emphasis falls upon the formal strength of the plays: Shakespeare had clearly discovered ingenious and original ways of giving order to his theme of disorder. This argument was launched in 1951 by H. T. Price; in 1972 it was sweepingly reaffirmed by Robert Ornstein. Indeed, by now the case for formal order and unity in the plays has been so convincingly argued that it has become a virtually reflexive presumption, upheld *faute de mieux* by critics far less imaginative than Price or Ornstein. I do not intend to dispute the formalist thesis. But I do think that the presumption of order in the plays has deflected attention from the experiental quality of the disorder. I want to argue that we are meant to experience that disorder with some immediacy, and not necessarily with any assurance of its coming clear.[1]

In *A Kingdom for a Stage* Ornstein finds the achievement of Shakespeare's histories to be greater than that of the comedies because of their greater originality. Shakespeare, after all, had to invent the form as he went along, and he did so triumphantly. Thus Ornstein sharply repudiates the historicists like Tillyard and Lily B. Campbell who presume a traditional guiding form for the histories, either in a previous line of plays or in a readily available pattern of thought. To imagine Shakespeare as discovering new forms for new kinds of drama naturally suggests a process full of risks and adventure. Of course such a spirit is to be found in the comedies too; if it figures more keenly in the histories it may be because they somehow preserve the authentic record of discovery.

In the early comedies—*A Midsummer Night's Dream, The Merchant of Venice, Love's Labor's Lost, As You Like It*—Shakespeare is clearly fascinated with the experience of confusion, instability, transformation; with the sudden dizzying loss of seemingly assured ground: "Here I am, and wood within this wood." In manifold ways, we are urged to participate in this "amazement," and yet the sense of an underlying design is never utterly absent. (What makes *Measure for Measure* and *All's Well That Ends Well* "problematical" is the disappearance of trust in subsurface order.) In the festive comedies, part of our delight is to feel that underlying design grow into the final, revealed form of the play: we could not have said what it was, but something that we felt all along to be in control emerges by the play's end.

The point is that the design does emerge—we do not have the sense of the playwright waiting in the wings to discharge our confusions and amazements. At the end of *As You Like It*, Rosalind, in the guise of Ganymede, promises everyone in turn the fulfillment of their desires "tomorrow," though to satisfy everyone would seem to involve impossible contradictions. To resolve the built-up paradoxes, she conjures up an imaginary uncle-magician, "Obscurèd in the circle of this forest," as her tutor. This is more than a mere trick, however. In a real sense the senex figure is herself in the role of the playwright she has become in the course of the play. She is *enabled* to enact the play's implicit design wonderfully by virtue of her residence in the woods of Arden—her own obscurity "in the circle of this forest"—during the course of which she has acquired and in the end employs dramatic powers that are part skillful, part marvelous. The situation in *Merchant of Venice* is similar in some respects. Portia has been released from her casket-prison by Bassanio, who wins her by hazarding all, foregoing conventional tests of valuation, and letting the casket metals "speak" to him of the difference between real worth and false gold. Once released in this manner, Portia acquires (presumably from her "holy" old father and from the offstage senex, "Dr. Bellario") a specifically dramatic power to break the impasse into which Shylock, in Venice, has driven the plot. Then she goes on to dramatize a comic reaffirmation of lovers' and social bonds generally back in Belmont.[2] As in other cases, the crucial feature in all this is the enabling process, what I would call immersion: the agent of the design's emergence has been naturalized in the dramatic woods. If Rosalind and Portia are dramatists (and perhaps priestesses) at the end of their plays, it is because they are also, and have first been, victims and lovers, "mere" characters. They have had to acquire the transforming festive power by the process of immersion.

This process tells us something about Shakespeare's way of working. Attentive to his materials, he seems ever willing to hazard control of conventional, or intentional, design; to immerse himself, relying only on his ability to tell real worth from false gold when the test is put to him. Were he over-anxious about his play's design, he might not be willing to let it emerge from his materials, but would want to hold to a predetermined form instead. Were he unwilling to let the material develop in unpredictable directions, to let its subtler strands seek out their own nourishment, he might still have turned out a dazzlingly complex and intricate structure, but he would never have come to that point of crisis, that "wild of nothing" (as Bassanio puts it) when deliberate design is transformed into something rich and strange.

If we can accept that Shakespeare is willing to hazard control in those plays whose superb control we rightly admire, what can we say of the early history plays, where instability often seems both matrix and matter of the plays, rather than merely a theme, or a "condition" to be overcome? If character after character is engulfed by confusion—like Talbot, "whirlèd like a potter's wheel"—and if a nation is, then so are we who in good faith undertake to read or see these plays; the more so if we do them all, in their own sequence. Yet unlike the comedies, these plays do not provide a reassuring sense of underlying design; they do not encourage the intuition that things will resolve themselves satisfyingly—that is, in a form that is equal to the chaos. Nor do the early history plays—at least the *Henry VI* trilogy—put forward a potent or trustworthy agent of the designer. Those few characters who aspire to that role are sucked back into the whirlpool of energy from which they had emerged. As for us, we are forced either to compose a paraplay as we go (a "Tudor Myth" play for instance, or some other historical fiction imported to measure the progress of the drama) or else, trusting ourselves to the unstable rhythms of the actual play, ride them into the whirlpool.

Of course, the "order," "unity," and "design" of the plays, their "art of construction," can be convincingly demonstrated; we may rightly admire the ingenuity by which seemingly intractable material—fifty years of turbulent chronicle history—has been forced under control. But to the extent that these approaches "explain away" the confusion, they beg the question of *what these plays are.* To argue for the ultimate cogency and coherence of the plays does not justify the retrospective assumption that Shakespeare, throughout the play, was all along in control of his material, waiting for the tempest to run its course before he disclosed its true, timeless, underlying form. The temptation to read the perception of ultimate form back into the process that yields it is understandable. But there is really no way of telling how much of a manifestly successful plot was predetermined, for it is precisely the temporal dimension that ordinarily drops out of sight. The question is, can we conceive of a structure that preserves just this dimension, the record of its own coming-into-being—which is to say, the quality of the "hazard" that the playwright takes along the way?

Every interpretation presupposes a myth of composition. I imagine the playwright, obsessed with instability and the spurious forms of stability, in pursuit of the will-o-the-wisp, the "ground"—where things start. Not surprisingly, he looks outside of his plays for the ground to mount them on, for drama itself is nothing if not the very form and pressure of instability. Therefore, he seeks the ground in time, in the "past," in origins. Inevitably he is led to that half-century of civil turbulence: a bonafide "era," meaning that though it was recent enough still to preoccupy historians, mythographers, and nervous party propagandists, it was a period officially past, finished, and apart, having clearly preceded the current era of official order. But what was its real connection with the present age? Where in the apparent chaos of that era could the playwright discern the underlying design that would, in time, reveal itself, and so become the future—that is, *his* time? Soberly, attentively, grinding no Marlovian axes, Shakespeare seeks out the true face of the troubled past: heroic? barbaric? providential? But something strange occurs. Seeking solid ground to mount his drama *on*, he is intrigued to find his materials melting under his pen, under the very pressure of their transmutation into drama. He begins to see that you cannot both assume origins and dramatize them. To dramatize is to incorporate. What he so earnestly sought outside his drama he now perceives only in losing it *to* his drama. In the very act of his seeking, perceiving, seizing and knowing it, the ground turns ghostly, like the ghost of the playwright's desire.

This, he understands, is his real subject: the power of his art, the elusiveness of his object. Working through this quandry will be his only access to the past.

2
Henry VI, Part One "Defacing monuments of conquered France"

1 Henry VI is about the decline and fall of England's heroic age.[1] Henry V is dead, the new king an infant, the realm in the hands of inept and contentious politicians. Abroad, English armies are disconcerted by the whoring French witch, Joan la Pucelle (Joan of Arc). Their chivalric captain, Talbot, is squandered by his ambitious, self-interested countrymen. A demeaning truce is struck; Henry V's legacy is wasted; omens of bloody civil war abound.

Any succinct summary of *1 Henry VI* presumes a design retrospectively understood. However well it might suggest the clutter of events and the theme of disorder and decline, it cannot hope to convey the dramatic roughness that would surely be apparent to any spectator, especially to a firstnighter. But it is exactly that roughness, that experiential quality of confusion, that I am after. If we can imagine ourselves as a firstnight audience unfamiliar with the history plays or even with Shakespeare, yet curious, intelligent, and attentive to this play as it presents itself to us, what in fact do we see?[2]

Beginning with the funeral march for Henry V, the first act or so presents a series of tableaux, alternately English and French, conveying the twin "stories" of domestic dissension, foreign erosion. Between these stories there is little narrative linkage. The shifts are rapid and clean, accomplished with little or no warning, transition, and often without apparent motivation. There is some broad humor in the mockery of the French, but there are also some startling juxtapositions and swift, perhaps sardonic, reversals. The rhetoric, with little exception, is strenuous, declamatory, heroic; the scenes are episodic, discrete, strongly marked by physical features (funeral canopy, Tower, turrets); the action is visually concrete, the images clear and self-explanatory (funeral march, combat, scaling and jumping off walls); the characters are assertive, boldly presented, poster-flat types. In general, it is a style without shadows.[3]

In act 2 we see the Wars of the Roses beginning as a private quarrel; we also see one party to the quarrel, Plantagenet, secretly laying claim to the crown. Otherwise, the play continues in its public mode. The action shifts rapidly and sharply between civil and military "stories," the pace quickening and the linkage, while still unstated, growing more obvious. And yet everything forceful in the play also seems somehow unstable. It is as if the very strategies of segmentation only hasten the momentum of breakdown. This instability infects the sturdiest formations, the ceremonial scenes most prominently. King Henry's first appearance in the play occurs in parliament, where the quarrels of his viciously wrangling barons cascade down the ranks from greater to lesser nobility and thence to their partisans among the commoners. Securing a brittle and wholly formal peace, the king then blithely stokes the coals of dissension by restoring Plantagenet to his "blood" and title as Duke of York. Later, while being crowned in Paris, Henry enforces another honorific truce between partisans of York and Somerset, then while disclaiming all partisanship, publically dons a red, Lancastrian rose.

Act 4 depicts the resistance and death of Lord Talbot as a sequence of operatic set-pieces. The mood of the final act, accordingly, is postheroic. Everything straightforward and sturdy turns doubtful and inconclusive. Joan is captured, tricked into admitting herself both whore and witch, and sent off to the stake. But even as she is led away, Suffolk appears with his enchanting captive, Margaret of Anjou, whom, to keep as his paramour, he undertakes to marry to King Henry, sight unseen. In the play's final episode the gullible young king easily succumbs to Suffolk's "wondrous rare description" over the vehement objections of Gloucester, and agrees to the match at the humiliating cost of a broken truce and, ultimately, the rest of Henry V's foreign conquests.

The play that had begun with a stately funeral march thus ends with the expectation of a royal wedding, but the irony is so heavy that even the feckless king seeks out privacy to "ruminate my grief."

As a firstnight audience we may be initially baffled by the strenuously episodic nature of the play. But we quickly learn to compose ourselves for a series of strong presentations. They seem in general to add up to a vigorous if essentially simple heroic drama, skillfully engineered around plain sturdy themes of a public and moral nature. The general drift is certainly toward the loss of heroic virtues, the disintegration of traditional forms of order, the decline into rivalries and selfish ambitions that will soon break into open war.

But for all the story's simplicity, it does not "flow" at all, but always has the quality of being presented, rather like monumental sculpture. The show certainly appeals to us in more than one way. We are moved by the imagined action, the fictive interior of what is represented for us; but we never cease being aware, either, of the sheer presentational skill, the very obviousness of the medium. We may even feel, perhaps with some annoyance, that our willingness to respond wholeheartedly to the imagined action is somehow thwarted by the way is it presented to us.

So—still as firstnighters—we may come to one of two conclusions. Either (1) the playwright is very skillful indeed, but immature; he can for instance compress forty years of history into a fast-moving two hours' traffic—hence the sheer number of individual scenes—but he has not yet learned to conceal his art. He relies heavily upon fashionable rhetorical effects and brave theatrical gestures; with time and experience he will doubtless develop more subtle skills. Or (2) the tension between the "fictive" and the presentational dimensions of the play become one of the playwright's "portals of discovery." Perhaps, far from wishing to conceal his art, he is trying to get at something else, something different. But what? Does the playwright himself know for sure at this point? We may recall how the tension shows up not only in the sharp jerky movement from one episode to another, but also in the very nature of any one of them; that a scene develops almost invariably through the disintegration of assertive postures. That is, the tension seems to reside somewhere between the shadowless clarity of the scenes and whatever it is that dissolves them. Is it time? History? The playwright? The nature of drama itself? But satisfying answers to these questions require more than firstnight speculations.

At the center of the play's idea of order stands the legendary figure of Lord Talbot. He epitomizes the heroic, chivalric, and communal values whose disintegration is the play's chief theme. But the audience responds not just to the theme, but to something in the dramatic material itself. The trouble with Talbot, frankly, is that he is the kind of hero you can only celebrate *in memoriam*. Onstage, as a character, he is something of an embarrassment—the figure bends so clearly toward apotheosis that it is hard to resent his sacrifice. In other words, to respond to Talbot "properly" we must cultivate certain responses and forbid certain others. But what if we trust our first reactions? What if the flatness of the character were *not* irrelevant to the meaning of *1 Henry VI?*

The play itself finds means to address the question of *what Talbot is*. Just after the scene of his operatic death, the English messenger, Sir William Lucy, inquires into the hero's whereabouts by naming his sixteen titles in a speech of twelve lines:

> But where's the great Alcides of the field,
> Valiant Lord Talbot, Earl of Shrewsbury,
> Created for his rare success in arms
> Great Earl of Washford, Waterford, and Valence . . .

To which Joan la Pucelle retorts:

> Here's a silly stately style indeed!
> The Turk, that two and fifty kingdoms hath,
> Writes not so tedious a style as this.
> Him that thou magnifi'st with all these titles,
> Stinking and flyblown lies here at our feet.
>
> (4. 7. 60–76)

A recent critic has argued that despite modern proclivities, there is really no place here (or throughout the play generally) for "realistic" responses, the scene and the play being too rigidly governed by its "emblematic" mode.[4] Joan, he argues, misses the mark in trying to identify Talbot with his corpse, just as the Countess of Auvergne missed it earlier in seeking to trap the heroic substance in the mere shadow, or "writhled shrimp" of a man. The name "Talbot"—and the ceremonial extensions of that name which Lucy lists—refer to a reality that (as Talbot had explained to the countess)

. . . were the whole frame here,
It is of such a spacious lofty pitch
Your roof were not sufficient to contain't.

(2. 3. 54–56)

It is clear that "Talbot" is too big for the stage as well as for the countess's room, and is represented in both only by rather feeble stand-ins—a "silly dwarf," a wooden character—neither of which is meant to be very convincing in itself. This strategy anticipates *Henry V*, whose heroic figures, the Chorus tells us, can only be very poorly represented by a few "flat unraisèd spirits" on this wooden O. But the difference is that the Chorus there asks us to make the spirits real in our imaginations, whereas the "emblematic" mode is defiantly nonillusionist. We are not supposed to "work our thoughts" to transform flat spirits into flesh and blood. The reality lies elsewhere; the play can only celebrate it. Sir William Lucy celebrates Talbot, magically invoking his offstage reality by chanting his names. The speech in which he does so, incidentally, is an almost verbatim transcription from Talbot's gravestone in Rouen. In a sense, "Talbot" is *best* represented by his absence.

It is true that the play is heavily given to the postures of "emblematic" or ritualistic celebration. But I doubt that it ever dispenses with naturalism absolutely, or that Shakespeare, even in this earliest of plays, confines himself so rigidly to a single set of conventions. If Joan were not at least partly right in deflating "Talbot" to the stinking corpse, there would be no play at all, but only ritual reenactment. In a small way her jeer does what the Chorus asks us to do in *Henry V*, it "forces a play." Rather than asserting a claim of "realism," it detaches Lucy's lapidary speech from its anchorage in an extradramatic reality. If only for a moment, by feeding our furtive desire for a "natural" response she allows us to hear Lucy's celebration as an *effort* at celebration, a "style"—a bare list of titles momentarily referring to a highly suspect ideal, and certainly nothing so dramatically present as the corpse itself. Really, though, it is not Talbot but Talbot's celebrant who is trapped here; for a moment the choric Lucy is revealed as a particular character, retorting to Joan in a shrill "could curses kill" mode:

O, were mine eyeballs into bullets turned,
That I in rage might shoot them at your faces!
O that I could but call these dead to life!

(4. 7. 79–81)

Rather than the celebrant's magical evocation by naming, this is the language of wishful magic that betrays its own impotence, and thus its user.

Lucy's gravestone style suffers the pain of being made dramatic dialogue. Something similar happens to the play as a whole. *1 Henry VI* presents a highly ritualized idea of the past. The broad morality-type characters, the relentless declamatory style, the discrete unshaded scenes, the minimal narrative linkage, all convey a stiff nonnaturalistic, nonrepresentational idea: a monumental past, a reality elsewhere, magically evoked on this wooden O by ritual reenactment of isolated and uniquely significant events from a kind of *illum tempus*—the first naming of roses, the death of Talbot, the coming of Margaret, and so on. The credibility of the drama lies in the firmness of its anchorage in that world elsewhere, outside—in the ground of the stable, original past.

Shakespeare seems to go out of his way to establish this ground. As H. T. Price and, since then, others have made clear, the effect of primitive stiffness is the result of highly aggressive dramatic decisions; Shakespeare beats and bullies his Hall and Holinshed into these seemingly stony, opaque formations.[5] It is as if he is determined to make sure of his ground before trusting it as a springboard into the future plays. Seeking recreation, he must assume origins. But he will also be watching what happens to his "ground" as he subjects it to the pressure of his dramatizing imagination.

What happens to the monumental past as it is dramatized is articulated perfectly in the beginning of the next play. Gloucester is lamenting Henry's marriage to Margaret, but the note of bitter baffled grief is appropriate generally to Part 1 (where the experience is too diffuse to be formulated at the time):

> O peers of England, shameful is this league.
> Fatal this marriage, cancelling your fame,
> Blotting your names from books of memory.
> Rasing the characters of your renown,
> Defacing monuments of conquered France,
> Undoing all as all had never been!
>
> (*2 Henry VI*,
> 1. 1. 96–101)

Timeless characters being unwritten, solid monuments dissolving, the whole heroic past decomposing at this very moment—and Gloucester, its celebrant, unable to do more than evoke it in its passing. As he speaks, the whole past of Part 1 melts into a kind of dream of the waking present. But *in* Part 1 as well, that queasy sense of instability mocks and undermines the monumental postures from the start. Stability is always in the past, it seems; the present is always the awareness of falling through space.

In Talbot's career, as in most heroic drama, we see a valued past being lost. But we should also see that it is lost in part because it does not manifest itself as living character—because it cannot command distinctive life in the dramatic present. Once gone, Talbot fades like yesterday's dream. In seeing him off, Shakespeare bids farewell not to an heroic age and heroic virtues, but rather to an *idea* of heroism—to a way of conceiving heroism, hence the past.

I do not imagine Shakespeare set out to present a dramatically weak Talbot, but he surely would have recognized what had happened during the course of the composition. In other words, the crucial point is not the relative "immaturity" of Shakespeare's poetic powers, but his attention to the real effects of whatever style he commands at the time. Let us grant, for instance, that when the highest peers of the realm, the statesman Gloucester and the churchman Winchester, erupt into one of their automatic quarrels, we are "meant" to be moved by the spectacle. The issues and consequences are serious—the squandering of Henry V's legacy, the spiraling descent into factionalism and war, the betrayal of Talbot. Yet in candor we will also hear in the wrangling the sound of squabbling children:

> —But he shall know I am as good—
> —As good? Thou bastard of my grandfather!
> —Ay, lordly sir! For what are you, I pray,
>   But one imperious in another's throne?
> —Am I not Protector, saucy priest?
> —And am I not a prelate of the church?
>
> (3. 1. 41–46)

Suppose that Shakespeare "meant" to elicit chiefly impressive effects, but then heard his own invention mocking him. Rather than suppress the mockery, he would surely have absorbed the lesson that heroic effects, of the kind he had sought, cannot simply be called up in drama without suffering some kind of transformation. Like heroic statuary, they require stable ground, discrete space, a context of fixed and unambiguous references. But drama itself is fluid, active, temporal. The scene of the quarrel is admirably structured so that the squabbling is transferred downward from the high peers to their partisans, Warwick and Somerset, thence to their servingmen. But this downward "spilling" movement, proceeding through a series of displacements, has its own dramatic logic and impulse, quite indifferent to the characters or issues. They do not *make* the movement as, say, Hal and Falstaff do, or even Hotspur, through overflowing energy. Rather, they obey the movement helplessly, as if some offstage force directed them, dragging them toward some ultimate breakdown.

Talbot is the mainstay, not only of English fortunes in France, but of the monumental mode of the play itself. But he is undone from the moment of his conception, bespeaking a myth of timeless order and stability that is conceivable in drama only in its passing. "The stage," says Jonas Barish, "specializes in change and movement, but virtue, whether Christian or secular, is a function of constancy."[6] So no cause for dissolution is offered *in 1 Henry VI.* Rather, the play itself is the cause: the generic act of dramatization, the ab-original act of separating form from formlessness.

If the quarreling of the peers, the heroics of Talbot, or the exaltations of a fabulous Henry V do not deeply interest Shakespeare, then what does?

There are three stand-out scenes in the play that almost everyone agrees are the product of Shakespeare's markedly free invention. Wherever else he may have felt bound by chronicle matter and conventional styles, there he allowed himself a sway of craft and imagination that quickens the play as a whole, and which may well have suggested to him (as it can for us) where his real interests and sympathies lay. Free, original, and therefore "playful," the three scenes seem to ring an almost formal set of changes on the relationship of "history" to "play," and therefore to constitute Shakespeare's tacit commentary upon his own processes.

The first of the three (the Countess of Auvergne's "trapping" of Talbot, 2. 3) is an "interlude" in the war as in the play. Purely gratuitous, it has no source and no consequence, though its implications resonate through the play. The second scene (the Temple Garden, 2. 4) shows us sourceless play hardening into history. And in the third (Mortimer in prison, 2. 5) we are presented with a staged metaphor of history itself, the incarnate past, materialized into the living play.

The Temple Garden scene imagines how the War of the Roses might have started in those subhistorical hollows nonexistent for the chroniclers. Carefully suspended from any sense of "source"[7]—the characters appear for the first time and come on quarreling over an unspecifled "case of truth"—the scene nevertheless yields all-too-certain and familiar consequences, as Warwick pointedly remarks at the end:

> And here I prophesy: this brawl to-day
> Grown to this faction in the Temple garden
> Shall send, between the red rose and the white,
> A thousand souls to death and deadly night.
>
> (2. 4. 124–27)

The scene develops from the free to the familiar, the unrestrained to the predictable. We witness the development as a transformation from a verbal to a symbolic drama. The language of individual men, full of motive and passion, bent on shaping the future to their wills, gives way to a wholly conventional style of speech, a purely ritual accompaniment to the unequivocal visual meanings of the "dumb significants" that they hold aloft to express their choice of faction. We watch men gravely determining a "future." But we recognize that even as they commit this "future," it has already hardened into a dreadful past. The "play" has turned to "history" in the very process of utterance.

But if the Temple Garden scene leads to the general public future—out of the play, into the shared public past of its audience—it also leads deeper into the play itself, into the interior plot through which Plantagenet (York-to-be) comes to life and begins to shape the intermediate future dramatically.

At the end of the Temple Garden scene, Somerset's taunting of Plantagenet as "yeoman" suddenly raises the "historical" issue of Plantagenet's dispossession of property and title because of his father's execution for treason under Henry V. Until this moment "Henry V" has figured in the play only as a name for a lost heroic age. Now for the first time we are invited to think of the past as made up of particular, ambiguous, and controversial events. Stung by Somerset's taunt, "Obscurèd

Richard" thus seeks illumination of that suddenly disclosed past from the man who is its living relic, intact but long forgotten. And thus Mortimer materializes in the drama, very much a dramatic creation (despite some confused "warrant" from the chronicles).[8] Ancient keeper of the secret past, Mortimer functions as a sort of window or secret passageway opening into a dimension of time that had previously existed only emblematically.

Plantagenet has come seeking a bit of family history. What he gets, amazingly, is genealogical "proof" of his right to Henry's crown (2. 5. 63 ff.). Leaving the Temple Garden, he had been one among several figures blindly fated to fulfill a public "prophecy." But now the old man's words transform Plantagenet's world from a place of formless frustration and motiveless dissension into a drama with clear temporal plot structure, and a role for himself as contender for the highest stakes of all. By the end of *this* scene he has acquired (if only potentially) a motive, a voice, a secret future: a character.

The "window" effect of the scene is enhanced by the care Shakespeare has taken to set it apart. Even in so episodic a play it is notably isolated, seeming to arise from obscure depths, dreamlike. The setting (the prison), the event (the interview), and the character of Mortimer himself are all wholly unanticipated. Furthermore, even before we learn of the coming interview, Mortimer comes forward as a distinctive and arresting character, speaking in a specially heightened style (2. 5. 1–7). Only after he has planted himself as a dramatic presence do we learn what he has to do with the Temple Garden scene just concluded. Then, of course, the tone of his disclosure to Plantagenet—sepulchrally solemn, tremulous with ancient authority—combines with the structural features to give the dramatic occasion an extraordinary emphasis in the play.

From one point of view, Shakespeare is using his considerable if unsubtle gifts to establish Mortimer as a choric figure sitting above the drama, and through experience, wisdom, and the suggestion of unearthly powers vouchsafing to his "heir" a privileged view of time's secret structure. But again, it is not a question of Shakespeare's "intention" but of what actually occurs in the course of the drama. Straining to make Mortimer transcendant, Shakespeare calls attention to what was "meant" to be invisibly functional, namely Mortimer's peculiarly self-dramatizing language:

> These eyes, like lamps whose wasting oil is spent,
> Wax dim, as drawing to their exigent;
> Weak shoulders, overborne with burdening grief,
> And pithless arms, like to a withered vine
> That droops his sapless branches to the ground.
>
> (2. 5. 8–12)

This gravity of utterance is supposed to lend oracular authority to his disclosures of the past. But the performance preempts its function. If we do not forbid outlaw responses, we will see behind the "choric" figure a sharp parodic one: a grotesque caricature of the playwright himself, fashioning a secret interior plot in which to launch his favored character. What has been displayed to us, officially, as "history" (the factual bedrock of the past), he secretly shows us to be something staged and stageable—literally, something playful: theater.

Mortimer has no life outside this scene. He lives to speak and, having spoken, to die. In his strangely sequestered performance he detaches "time" from its moorings in an extra-dramatic "history" and bequeaths it to his heir, the man of the future. As furtive playwright, he creates for York a secret past that by necessity breeds its own future—a purely dramatic logic. But the dreaminess of the scene, its isolation, its whispered intimacies, also suggest a deeper dramatic process. "Obscurèd Richard"—fatherless, powerless—comes from the Temple Garden as a vacant identity, blind disembodied energy. He encounters his senex-uncle, who endows him with name, form, character, and power. But, as in a dream, it is not really clear who breeds whom in this operation. Mortimer seems to arise, ambiguously, both from the drama generally and from Plantagenet's own intense necessity—his (one might say) parthenogenetic wish to come to life. It is easy, of course, to endow the scene with greater intent, retrospectively, than it deserves. But in its very murkiness I think we can see the gathering reflections of dramatic consciousness.

Mortimer, bequeather, disappears. And Plantagenet with his separate reality becomes the first character in the histories to have an interior life—a life, that is, separable not only from the public view of him, but from the prevailing rhetorical texture of the play's nearly uniform surface. Others' energies are declamatory; his are, potentially, those of secrecy, indirection, timing and disguise—precisely the dramatic energies that mock heroic postures.

Plantagenet has become a double man: one, public, mired in the hapless flux of present events; the other, private, more real than the first, yet existing only in a "future" that so far exists only in his head. (He is the predecessor, then, not only of Richard III but of Bolingbroke and Hal, and indeed of every historical *actor.*) In the next play his double perspective grows explicit and shapes the structure of the play itself, but here we are simply made aware of his interiority, of a man withholding, and also divided from, his true self. In the parliamentary scene where he is restored to his "blood" and title as Duke of York, the action appears to Henry and the others as recompense for "his father's wrongs." But we understand that to the double man the restoration is only a stage in the unfolding design of his destiny. For the present that sense of design remains implicit: Mortimer's counsel has been "lock[ed] . . . in my breast, / And what I do imagine, let that rest." There is nothing to do but wait, "hold his tongue," and suppress his "rancorous spite." After Henry has publicly put on a red Lancastrian rose and Warwick opines that "he thought no harm," York (as he is henceforth called) again must stifle his speech:

> An if I wist he did—But let it rest.
> Other affairs must now be managéd.
>
> (4. 1. 180–81)

He bides the drift of events, of "other affairs," waiting for the future to catch up with him.

Meanwhile, although he takes no action to bring that future about, we perceive him as an actor—no cardboard machiavel like Winchester, but as one capable of deploying public perceptions to screen his private reality, capable of performing a part, capable of using rhetorical language dramatically (in contrast, say, to Talbot or Winchester, who are innocent of using any style at all). In Part 1, indeed, York's status as "actor" rests almost entirely on this capability of seeing experience as the materials of a drama—material from which he is essentially detached and that he is therefore in a position to manipulate. But even in this limited sense he takes on a special kind of potency. From his location near the center of dramatic realities he tunes and quickens our interest in the play itself. With a sense of dawning consciousness, he assumes a potentially shaping power over the rhythms of the play he inhabits. He is

Talbot's true opposite, pointing forward from this fast-dissolving present toward a new "reality elsewhere" in the future—a future that is not merely to be suffered passively, but is to be actively created: made *drama*.

The charisma of the "double life" that York brings out of the Mortimer scene serves the same "detaching" function, vis-à-vis the play's monumental postures, as Joan's jeering of Talbot's corpse. Like the jeer, the glimpses of York's separate reality give us a locus for responses that the monumental style requires us to suppress; they bring the operations of the play a little closer to us, so we may see how much distance it "properly" demands for its heroic effects.

I suggested earlier that these middle scenes generally might serve a similar function for Shakespeare. Their freedom from chronicle sources, their isolation from the main events of the play, allow him a chance to cultivate his own artistic detachment, his passivity as observer of his own processes. Openly playing "playwright," positing fanciful "origins" of historic events in the Temple Garden scene, he watches the action branch. On one hand it leads inexorably out of the play into the "fixed future" (the accomplished public past). On the other hand it leads deeper into the play's own fictive realm, gathering its own imperatives and consequences, its own internal cogency and persuasiveness. It begins to persuade us—from our outsiders' position, secure in that fixed future—to enter the world of the play itself where the "future" looks like something that can be shaped.

This interior movement, as I have said, is mostly incipient in *1 Henry VI*. But its presence is precisely what distinguishes the work of the dramatist from that of the chronicler. The dramatist at this stage works chiefly parodically, undermining his own stony triumphs, and arranging to watch where his own "negative interests" lead him. Clearly they lead to characters with dramatic powers of one sort or another: to Mortimer, passingly, and more profoundly to York.

They also lead for a time to Joan la Pucelle, a curiously potent figure. The play's chief actor, she manipulates experience dramatically, working by stealth, deceit, and a vaguely wanton ability to excite and confuse both friends and enemies. Her "art and baleful sorcery" is also a superior use of dramatic language, as in the case of the "fair persuasions, mixed with sug'red words" by which she entices Burgundy to defect (3. 3). Yet she is endowed with none of the true actor's interiority, none of the independence that would enable her to outlast her function in the play, which is to trap Talbot. And once her powers are played out, she swiftly shrinks into a caricature of the fraudulent witch that the moralist critics like to see. But we have seen her, as a language-using character, succumb to the energetic rhythms of the play.

1 Henry VI is manifestly weak in characters who are durable or dense, and who effect consequences in the course of the play through their force or sentience. We are often told that the play's "rhetorical texture," its "ceremonial style," preempts the question of individual characters. The assumption is that Shakespeare's interest in character and dramatic utterance (as against "poetry" and literary manners) did not really develop till later in his career.

But if we assume that Shakespeare was always interested in character, then it follows that all speech in his plays is dramatic speech, even the most heavily decorated and ornamental rhetorical styles—which is to say that Shakespeare never fails to think of any kind of speech, at bottom, as human in its origins. And yet, he also clearly knows that speech is separable from its speaker—that it becomes utterance only in the act of separation. He knows, further, that as he speaks the speaker is always doing something else: consciously or not, he is negotiating some kind of relationship with his own language. And this doubleness—language being both the speaker's own and not his own—sits at the heart of drama (as opposed to ritual) and gives to Shakespeare's in particular the luminous and inexhaustible consciousness so unmistakable in his greatest plays. Here in the earliest ones we find him listening chiefly for moments and strategies of dissociation.

In other words, if we listen to the ceremonial style in *1 Henry VI* as dramatic speech, what we hear are inchoate characters, unemerged, halfborn, and somehow willingly submissive to that "web of significance" that, rather than transcending the speakers, is all the while being woven out of their very passivity. This "web" is precisely a web of language, of public or conventionalized language, in which the speakers are bound "all unawares."[9] It is a language creatively weak and impersonal, even inhuman, because the strength, the reality, the validity of its assumed public references are taken for granted.

Like the dumbly significant roses, this language presumes to point "outward," offstage, toward some stable, absolute, and indisputable "meaning." Joan exploits just this assumption of stable external referents in her seduction of Burgundy: "*Look* on thy country . . . *see* the cities and the towns defaced. . . . *Behold* the wounds, the most unnatural wounds." (Italics mine.) Now, the playwright in the role of Tudor Mythographer would assume that his audience was the repository of such indisputable "meanings." He would need only to play his roses and French witches and English heroes to strike up their reality in his countrymen's hearts. But Shakespeare discovers it to be a very ghostly reality indeed.

To resume my myth of composition: Shakespeare, pursuing the ghostly ground of "history," lets his drama sink, to find its natural resistance. Like Bassanio stalking his first arrow with the second, he attends to the critical process of disintegration in the woods, eager but patient to see what rematerializes. What he sees emerging, finally, is now a powerful image of the strange, remote, exotic. Rather, he finds himself looking into a mirror at the vague but deepening image of the artist immersed in the materials of "history," shaping them, so to speak, from inside the woods. He sees, further, that this artist is able to shape his woody matter because he perceives it to be no matter at all, but forms of desire conjured up through the human uses of language. What he has discovered, in other words, is that his drama precedes and contains "history," rather than the other way around—at least "history" as he has so far conceived it. The discovery might well dismay him. He has been pursuing the ground, after all, the otherness of the past, not the image of his own superior imagination. But the discovery would exhilarate him, too, since he has called forth life out of his stony material, where none had been before. And he has released his imagination from a kind of servitude to a shadowy reality. For a moment he is thrown into crisis, into what Bassanio (having chosen correctly, and turning from Portia's image to Portia herself) calls a "wild of nothing": there is no reality other than the play itself, no past and no future other than what it can persuasively generate by *speaking for itself*.

So *1 Henry VI* is the "bedrock" fabricated for the sake of the future. It is surely not the ground that Shakespeare set out to find. But I think Stephen Dedalus is right: Shakespeare's "errors are volitional and are the portals of discovery."[10] The ease of the play's disdain for its own stony effects is a sure sign that it has failed to enact the central issue between the dramatist and history. But in taking the measure of his own powers, acknowledging his fortunate failure, Shakespeare wins a future in which to seek a truer image of the past.

3

Henry VI, Part Two "Undoing all as all had never been"

2 *Henry VI* opens with a royal ceremony in which Henry meets his new bride; it ends with the Lancastrians in flight and the Yorkists crowing with the success of their first bloody battle of the civil war. The play enacts a cultural collapse. What holds it off is the king's Protector, Gloucester, whose tragedy occupies the first three acts; and what brings it on is Gloucester's murder by a conspiracy of ill-assorted peers, including York, whose emergence is the story of the last two acts. The articulation of this three-way relationship among Henry, Gloucester, and York gives the play its elegant structure, despite the weight and diffusion of its materials—its numerous and various characters and episodes, furious bloody action, and a far greater range of speaking styles than in Part 1.

Yet, though these materials seem at first to have been subdued by a purposeful structure, in the last analysis there is an emotional incoherence to the play, as if an almost autonomous ghost of violence rises off and escapes the clear but shrunken body.

In *1 Henry VI* the past was conceived as existing somewhere "out there," beyond the drama, in "France." But here it is sought *in* the drama, right at home, and conceived as continuous with our experience in the medium of the play itself. The advances over Part 1 are immediately obvious from a comparison of the opening scenes.

In Part 1 the opening ceremony is structured around the absence of a cohering center: Henry V is dead, Henry VI an infant. The stage is filled by characters with only legendary pasts grasping for stability, while messengers invade with names of territories lost, allies defected, a mythic hero taken. The world outside is huge, but vague and sliding; the response onstage is to dig in and loudly declaim one's presence: "Hung be the heavens with black!"

Part 2 opens with everyone already present, gathered onstage for the presentation of Margaret to Henry. They are all home from adventures abroad, returned from "out there." And they are all familiar, bearing their pasts from Part 1, though also older and graver now. The "out there" they have returned from is not just France and the disastrous loss of fortunes, but innocence, inexperience, newness generally. All these now must be performed in the context of that knowledge. That is why the ceremony seems so dazed, as if it were transpiring behind glass. Its occasion is patently inauthentic, qualified too ironically by the recent past, yet no one moves to acknowledge that fact. The mood is brittle; the careful public language seems treacherous. Suffolk has wed Margaret as Henry's "procurator" and now has come to "deliver up my title in the queen" to "that great shadow I did represent." Margaret's salutation to "mine alderliefest lord" is ceremoniously neutral, but Henry's response threatens to shatter the credibility of the occasion by sheer foolish excess:

> Her sight did ravish, but her grace in speech,
> Her words yclad with wisdom's majesty,
> Makes me from wond'ring fall to weeping joys,
> Such is the fullness of my heart's content.
>
> (1. 1. 32–35)

Reading the marriage contract, Gloucester falters, but the Cardinal moves quickly in to take his place. Esteemed French conquests of Henry V have been traded for the daughter of "Regnier King of Naples, Sicilia, and Jerusalem"—all empty titles. The scandal is painfully obvious to everyone, except perhaps Henry. Yet even he is eager to finish up the ceremony and disappear, as if embarrassed by the glassy falseness of these public attitudes and by the vacuity of his own public presence.

Henry's departure stirs the stage into life. Gloucester bitterly denounces the marriage ("Undoing all as all had never been!") and then, rather than quarrel with the Cardinal, leaves the scene. Others follow, plotting and counterplotting against their predecessors before being spun off the stage. In the end York is left alone, dramatically present, as if he had been standing all this while at the source of the commotion. The impression is proleptic. The need for public posturing over, he is free at last to flesh his private voice in his private plot, and what he tells us in his monologue is what we have just seen mimed. He will play roles in others' intermediate intrigues until Gloucester is wasted in his battles with the peers, then he will emerge to challenge directly the one figure oblivious to intrigue, yet whose failure to rule has spawned the power struggle: Henry himself.

This is a compelling structure, its dramatic energy flowing purposefully from Henry's static ceremony, through Gloucester's reckless passion, and into York's compacted monologue. It adumbrates the course of the play itself by demonstrating how power will be transferred from King to Protector to Usurper. What is more, the scene appears to unfold in an unforced harmony of historical material and dramatic control, as if the natural rhythms of drama were also the surest way of delivering up the true shape and meaning of the cultural collapse. We can feel quite free to trust our first responses now, comfortable with the sense that the play is addressing us directly. It does so most obviously, of course, through York, who not only inherits the abandoned stage, but at once lays claim to it through the authority of a charmismatic voice. In contrast to Henry's vacant ceremonial voice, York's is a distinctive mixture of lurid self-inflation and biting self-consciousness. And it is always peculiarly physical, not only in its habitual imagery but also in the pressure of a frustrated personality:

> So York must sit and fret and bite his tongue
> While his own lands are bargained for and sold.
> Methinks the realms of England, France, and Ireland
> Bear that proportion to my flesh and blood
> As did the fatal brand Althaea burnt
> Unto the prince's heart of Calydon.
>
> (1. 1. 228–33)

Where this driving pressure leads him, in his monologue as in the play itself, is to the ultimate encounter with Henry, who occupies the center of power so fraudulently:

> And force perforce I'll make him yield the crown
> Whose bookish rule hath pulled fair England down.
> (1. 1. 256–57)

The energy carried by York's voice is destructive energy, but it derives from the fraudulence of official postures and reaches out to the audience with disarming immediacy. It performs and locates the disintegrative force that invaded Part 1 mysteriously from "out there," and at the same time projects that force into a shapely and intelligible plot. Harnessing the play's own energy of "undoing," York appears to be controlling that plot. In fact he does not control it. His vivid presence is a function of a larger design that includes both Henry's gift for absence and Gloucester's position as surrogate for the disappearing king. What Shakespeare has done is to enlarge his sense of history to include all those unacknowledged ghosts of *1 Henry VI*. Silence, absence, impotence, flux itself have all been captured and enlisted in Part 2. What this means, however, is that so have we. A structure that depends for its coherence upon a tension between presence and absence, on- and offstage rhythms, clearly demands an active and attentive audience. We harbor silent continuities, sustain a character during his absence from the stage, sanction his claims of interiority by extending our emotional and imaginative credit. This is quite different from our role in Part 1, with its series of shadowless tableaux that faded to dream as soon as they were out of sight. Detached, we celebrated only what we saw, and furtively mocked it too. Here, our memory, faith, and complex sympathies become a part of the play's full design.

Henry

Henry VI's role in Part 1 was largely negative. First his youth, and later when he did appear, his insipidity, amounted only to the absence of a center of power after his father's mysterious death. But what in Part 1 was a mute structural assumption, underlying the design, in Part 2 is incorporated by the play's design, so that decomposition is analyzed in terms of character. Here Henry VI is present from the beginning—his presence *trapped* by a role he clearly dislikes, and even heightened by his attempts to evade it. To be king means, among other things, to create ceremonial occasions in which his language is presumed to carry privileged force. But Henry is always speaking and acting as if he were, or wished to be, absent. His hasty departure in the opening scene establishes the motif; in following scenes we see him vividly ineffectual as a "peace-maker" of wrangling peers (1. 3), a dupe of a transparent hoax (2. 1), and an oblivious puppet of his own Protector's enemies (2. 3).

Up to the third act it is possible to see Henry as essentially innocent in his passivity, however foolish he may appear. This is how he remains in the bad quarto of the play, *The Contention:* childish, ineffectual, pathetically misplaced.[1] But evidently Shakespeare was intrigued by the implications of a weak character caught in a strong role, because in act 3 Henry's innocence does not come so easily. In this scene he has suffered the arrest of his former Protector, friend, and uncle, on patently false charges of treason; Gloucester himself, in his parting speech, has forced Henry to acknowledge the arrest as a political plot. Yet no sooner is Gloucester taken into the "custody" of his oldest enemy, the Cardinal, than Henry addresses the conspirators:

> My lords, what to your wisdoms seemeth best
> Do or undo, as if ourself were here.
>
> (3. 1. 195–96)

Even Margaret is astonished at the ease of the abnegation this time:

> What, will your highness leave the parliament?

In *The Contention* Henry answers simply:[2]

> I Margaret. My heart is kild with griefe,
> Where I may sit and sigh in endlesse mone,
> For who's a traitor, Gloster he is none.

But in Shakespeare's Henry we can hear all the self-indulgence of his opening speech to Margaret ("Such is the fullness of my heart's content"):

> Ay, Margaret. My heart is drowned with grief,
> Whose flood begins to flow within mine eyes:
> My body round engirt with misery—
> For what's more miserable than discontent?
> (3. 1. 198–201)

But it is not just that *The Contention* sacrifices the studied quality of the self-consciousness. In that version Henry simply leaves the parliament as he says he will. But Shakespeare's Henry cannot resist a lingering portrayal of his ineffectuality in an elaborate, and grotesquely inappropriate, conceit—worth quoting in full precisely because of its excess:

> And as the butcher takes away the calf
> And binds the wretch and beats it when its strains,
> Bearing it to the bloody slaughterhouse,
> Even so remorseless have they borne him hence;
> And as the dam runs lowing up and down,
> Looking the way her harmless young one went,
> And can do naught but wail her darling's loss,
> Even so myself bewails good Gloucester's case
> With sad unhelpful tears, and with dimmed eyes
> Look after him and cannot do him good,
> So mighty are his vowèd enemies.
> His fortunes I will weep, and 'twixt each groan
> Say "Who's a traitor? Gloucester he is none." [*Exit*]
> (3. 1. 210–22)

The rhetorical fraudulence is obvious—that is, the discrepancy between the conventional rhetorical figure and the manner in which Henry uses it to dramatize his helplessness. As with Richard II later, a good deal of active art goes into the self-portrayal of victimized innocence; and as with Richard, the pathos of the performance scarcely conceals Henry's furtive pleasure in the role. Nor is the performance just a matter of self-pity, a king more aggrieved by his loss of Gloucester than by Gloucester's own misfortunes.[3] The evasion is more complex than that. By his "Do or undo, as if ourself were here," and then by underscoring his helplessness before irresistable "vowèd enemies," Henry is signaling the queen that she and her coconspirators have leave to dispose of Gloucester, so long as it does not threaten the credibility of his own helplessness.

But obviously, to dramatize one's own innocence is to acknowledge, at some level, that it has already been lost. Henry's weakness has acquired dramatic density, become psychologically interesting. What looked like a strong but simple desire not to be present has evolved into increasingly desperate attempts not to be. For two acts he can maintain effectual absence by speaking in formulas or as a naif; but by act 3 the abnegation mimed in the opening scene breaks into the play itself. Henceforth, like an actor caught playing dead, the more Henry insists upon his vacancy the more vivid he becomes in that role.

Meanwhile Shakespeare makes it clear that Henry's failure to protect his Protector and hence to forestall the tide of violence unloosed by the murder is not a matter of stars or witchcraft, but of human character. Nor is it a matter of mere weakness overwhelmed by malice and ambition. Between Henry's passivity and the chaotic rage it mirrors there is a vital connection invisible to chroniclers of "history" but brought to light by the dramatist.

York

Against the self-absenting Henry Shakespeare poses a self-aggrandizing York. They face each other across the murder of Gloucester, in which they mutually, albeit covertly, participate. Henry plays dead to his own part in the murder, fainting at the spectacle of the actual corpse, waking in a spasm of honest anger—skewering Suffolk—and then subsiding into his habit of self-pitying impotence (3. 2). York works through others: he joins his voice with the conspirators, but then is conveniently absent for the murder and its explosive aftermath. Withholding himself like the actor whose capabilities we glimpsed in Part 1, he is represented on the scene first by the Nevils, who marshal the wrath of the commoners against Suffolk, then by Jack Cade, whom he has "seduced" as his "substitute" (3. 1. 371). Riding home the "fell tempest" bred by these agents, York brings all the play's fiercely disintegrative energies to an appointed climax in the open challenge to Henry:

> Give place. By heaven, thou shalt rule no more
> O'er him whom heaven created for thy ruler.
>
> (5. 1. 104–5)

Emblematically this is a picture of self-willed pride confronting will-less innocence. Behind the picture we should also see two actors, more kin than opposite, joined in a larger design than they can realize and yet which they helplessly cooperate in advancing. Still, Shakespeare works to show this process in terms of human character. In *The Contention* York is simply dogged, robust, machiavellian, as Henry is simply pathetic and ineffectual; most of the speeches conveying their self-consciousness are cut or reduced to brisk epigraphs. But Shakespeare conceives them both as trapped in insufferable roles, reflecting each other's despair. York's strength is a version of Henry's weakness and is equally deceptive. He appears to command the structure of dramatic displacements catalyzed by Henry because he articulates the sense of his own displacement with such force. In three crucial places (1, 1. 3. 1, and 5. 1) he punctuates the play's precipitous "undoing" by his alternately cold and furious soliloquies, his rage for destruction repeatedly expressed in terms of maddened self-division.[4] What makes him compelling as a character is precisely his sense of himself as an actor focusing his skills upon the healing moment:

> Now, York. . . .
> Be that thou hop'st to be; or what thou art
> Resign to death. . . .
>
> (3. 1. 331–34)

> Then, York, unloose thy long-imprisoned thoughts
> And let thy tongue be equal with thy heart.
>
> (5. 1. 88–89)

He is able to perform himself to us only because he is barred from performing himself within the historical world of the play.

Certainly he conveys some authentic pain in his "mad-bred flaw." Nevertheless, the "madman" that we see behind the public mask is also the stagey creation of a cool politician who deploys himself as a hidden lead in a masterplot. His ability to stage himself in the various roles of his dispossession is impressive: the plundered handwringing "silly owner of the goods" (1. 1. 223), the "laboring spider" weaving "tedious snares to trap mine enemies" (3. 1. 340), the "starved snake" (3. 1. 343), the deranged Ajax (5. 1. 26), and so on. In themselves these roles are conventional, but behind them is a creative urgency. Pressured toward obscurity in his own "right," York responds by improvising workable personas. Obeying the playworld's imperative to speak or die, he gives himself voice through the dramatic images of enforced silence.

Meanwhile we credit his improvisations not because they are compelling in themselves, but because through them he gives shape to the play's cascading energies, its invigorating drive toward disclosure, its promise of a satisfying catharsis. He is our ally, our agent in the field of play. Or so we allow ourselves to believe, or half-believe. In fact we know better, even as we play along, and our responses to York are likely to be mixed with more fascination and more distrust than I have suggested. For of course he is not really playing to perfect the drama, to deliver over history as fully articulate play, to illuminate the lust for violence, or to justify the frenzied murder of Gloucester. He is not playing for us at all, but for himself; not for illumination, but for the objects, the dramatic props—sword, sceptre, gold—he has wishfully invested with magical potency; not to resolve the play, but to escape it. All his roles anticipate their own dissolution in the relief of an all-consuming role as "England's lawful king." As York approaches his climax, it becomes clear that he is as desperate in his aggressive way as Henry is in his passive, to thrash himself out of the world of playing. Ultimately the two contenders meet in the identity, not the polarity, of their desires:

> Was never subject longed to be a king
> As I do long and wish to be a subject.
>
> (4. 9. 5–6)

Gloucester

Between these mirroring opposites sits the dourly tragic figure of Gloucester, "the good Duke Humphrey." He eloquently laments that the heroic past of Henry V has been shamed by the "fatal league" of Henry's son with Margaret. But in fact the marriage is the bitter fruit of that false flowering. Heroic deeds have not degenerated into so many erasable titles, mere names and "characters," as Gloucester says; rather, in the light of the waking present, the deeds—the "monuments of conquered France"—are revealed as the illusions of wishful naming: the *story* of the past. Gloucester would keep that story alive through the sheer passion of his memory. But even as he labors, the world is sliding away from him, "undoing all as all had never been!"

This despairing phrase is echoed in Henry's betrayal of Gloucester: "My lords . . . Do or undo, as if ourself were here." The original act of the play is Henry's abnegation of power—not the marriage in itself, but his refusal to play a central role coherently, and so justify the scandal by a commanding personal presence. He is, in Suffolk's deadly phrase, "that greater shadow" whom Suffolk and others are free to "represent" "as if ourself were here." He refuses to *be* the thing *named,* and this dislocation of the name—king—from its correlative—power—epitomizes the play's world of displaced identities and meanings. He sets in motion the "undoing" action, the most prominent victim of which is the shadow-king's highly visible surrogate, Gloucester.

Like Talbot, Gloucester must be sacrificed because he obstructs the play's obsessive drive toward self-completion and disclosure. But the process is complicated because he obstructs that drive with something Talbot scarcely has, dramatic character. In the third scene, for instance, Gloucester is vehemently abused by his battery of enemies, the Cardinal, Margaret, Suffolk, Somerset, and Buckingham. The manner is familiar from *1 Henry VI.* They each attack in turn, blocklike, in order of importance; therefore, though the assault carries formidable rhetorical weight, it is also potentially laughable. Gloucester does not laugh, but rather than digging in and retorting in kind as he would surely have done in Part 1, he suddenly turns and leaves the scene without a word. A few lines later he returns:

> Now, lords, my choler being overblown
> With walking once about the quadrangle,
> I come to talk of commonwealth affairs.
>
> (1. 3. 150–52)

Shakespeare accomplishes several things at once here. He connects Gloucester's personal character with his symbolic purview, "commonwealth affairs" taking precedence over "choler." He establishes dramatic indirection as a potent device: Gloucester's withdrawal is a more commanding act than any amount of counter-rant, and shows up his enemies as essentially passive and reflexive in their aggression. Most important, he endows Gloucester with the will to separate himself from the ongoing rhetorical surface of the play. Gloucester's silence and absence, in obvious contrast to Henry's, give him an independent strength, a presumed interiority, that translates into a dramatic presence of a kind that Talbot never attains.

Gloucester's presence in the play, then, is a far more complex business than Talbot's. On the one hand, it takes three busy acts and a frightening concentration of purpose from his massed enemies to bring him down. This effort excites our complicity. On the other hand, his very powers of resistance give body to what he represents—namely, the "commonwealth," the shared cultural space of the playworld itself: all that stands between a culture-collapsing encounter between the two misplaced figures of Henry and York. And the strength of his dramatic character gives us the kind of emotional stake in his tragedy that Talbot could inspire, at best, only ceremonially.

Gloucester's tragedy is that he too is misplaced, forced to embody the play's communal values personally because Henry fails to do so himself. This was also Talbot's position, in the absence of Henry V and (in effect) of Henry VI. But unlike Talbot, Gloucester's rectitude is not an emblematic function of a morality figure, but the leading trait, both limiting and expressive, of a dramatically conceived character. When he publically abandons his wife to the law, for instance (2. 1), we are not being asked to approve this chilly display of moral consistency, but to understand it as true to Gloucester's character. This rigidity is both strength and weakness. Unlike Talbot, Gloucester inspires personal hostility, and for the same reason that he is able to resist his tormentors for so long—his cultural functions are rooted in his character. Hot-tempered and arrogant, he defends a moral order as much from stubborn pride of place as from unworldly virtue. But his fractiousness is schooled by qualities that serve him as hard-nosed guardian of a feckless king and an imperiled realm: dry wit, shrewd common sense, self-control, and above all a stubbornly narrow and naive faith that the law which he serves is sufficient to protect him from his self-serving enemies.

But he does not really serve the law, he bodies it forth by the sheer density of his dramatic presence. The law exists in him, because he makes it work—gives it body for others. "This is the law, and this Duke Humphrey's doom," he intones, sentencing the Armourer Horner and his apprentice Thump to judicial combat to determine the truth of their quarrel (1. 3. 208). The sentence turns out to be just and efficacious. Thump wins, Horner confesses treason with his dying breath, and Henry praises God who "in justice hath revealed to us / The truth and innocence of this poor fellow" (2. 3. 97–98). But in the same scene Gloucester himself is dispossessed. He will shortly be "tried," and though unassailable before the law, will nevertheless be abandoned to his "vowèd enemies" and murdered. The point is, of course, that though Gloucester bodies forth the law for others, he does so in Henry's name, as Henry's representative. Despite the passionate will of his enemies, despite his own personal toughness, Gloucester is vulnerable because Henry fails to protect his Protector by giving body to the law he represents. Without that valorization, the law is grounded nowhere, it exists nowhere within the play except in Gloucester's own articulate presence. And yet the very necessity of that lightningrod presence means that he has already been abandoned by the "shadow" he represents. Gloucester's character, vulnerable in its very strength, is not simply given in the play; like York's, Henry in effect creates it out of his own self-evasion.

The mutual dependencies of Henry, Gloucester, and York add up to the play's distinctively humanistic design: an attempt to contain the historical experience of cultural disintegration, and to understand it as a product of fathomable human rivalries, accountable motivations, and an intelligible if fateful distribution of attributes. It brings "history" into view not as the remote and haunted object of Part 1, but as the product of interwoven human actions of a kind that drama is especially suited to convey. In the humanistic design, in other words, the playworld is rendered as a harmony of psychologically interesting characters and an elegant structure of events. It is a well-balanced world, affording some genuine pleasure as it unfolds, despite the grimness of its theme and action. For all its sprawl, rhetorical excess, and Byzantine intrigue, the world of the play is sustained by a rhythm of cooperation between the audience and a dramatist who, presumably, stands behind his design, and can be expected to resolve its conflicts, both human and formal, in a satisfying way.

The conflicts come to a head in act 3, where the transition from Gloucester's story to York's occurs. We feel intensely engaged in the action here, our sympathies torn not so much between Gloucester and York as between Gloucester and the necessity for his removal. We are implicated in the characters, in the credibility of Gloucester, therefore in his sacrifice—but we are also committed to the fulfillment of the action to which Gloucester's murder is, as he says himself, the "prologue."

The murder itself is muffled—"two or three running over the stage, from the murder of Duke Humphrey," as the scene direction has it (3. 2). This business mimes a powerful Shakespearean perception: murder will out, not as a moral but as a dramatic fact. Performed by hirelings (surrogates) not wholly controlled by those whose will they enact, the murder cannot be contained; as deed it is uttered like language and spills over the stage until it is "reported" to the offstage world. Yet the impact of revelation is delayed by Margaret's and Suffolk's attempts to muffle Henry's reaction to the news—strained operatic performances (Margaret at one point goes on with prima donna virtuosity for over sixty lines) that blunt the point of crisis and leave us awkwardly detached.

But then the scene is roughly invaded. The Nevils and a few townsmen representing the many that can be heard outside burst in, Warwick bringing back the "report" of Gloucester's death from "the commons" who,

> . . . like an angry hive of bees
> That want their leader, scatter up and down
> And care not who they sting in his revenge.
>
> (3. 2. 125–27)

This is a strongly cathartic moment. We have not only been suffering the cloistered intrigues of the conspirators, but like Henry have been silently sanctioning them as necessary to the forward motion of the play. Suddenly the anger and clamor of "the commons," mobilized against the onstage manipulators, locates and gives voice to our suppressed "natural" feelings. Now Suffolk literally is encompassed by York's agents, the Nevils, and by extension that wider participating audience, the enraged commoners. Suddenly the drama is drastically enlarged—the "commonwealth" comes to life—and we are powerfully reengaged in its fate.

This enlargement is necessary to contain our conflicting sympathies—to justify the fraudulence that we have assented to in the interests of fulfilling the play's design. Now, despite some tortuous moments of doubt, the design seems to be holding. Now at last the destructive force is out in the open, and the "undoing" rhythms should inevitably deliver the play to its climax and catharsis in the open clash between king and usurper.

But in fact the design fails to hold. The outward rush of violence that follows from the murder has sources more obscure, and generates more spontaneous power, than the artful vision of control can accommodate. The stage (as one critic puts it) "grows slippery with the gore of decapitated bodies and impaled heads gloried over by their killers."[5] The Cardinal dies "raving and staring as if mad" (3. 3. SD), Suffolk is banished and lynched in the "bloody and barbarous spectacle" that serves for justice once Gloucester is gone; his head turns up later, hugged by a grieving Margaret as her distracted husband receives news of Jack Cade's rampages. Cade, by the logic of the design, is York's surrogate and front-runner. But when York at last steps forth from behind his screen to declare his "real" identity, it is clear that he lays claim to a dramatic authority he no longer has. Somewhere during the long transition of power the play has changed course—been taken possession of, so to speak, by a deeper and more disturbing purpose. Its disintegrative energies, when York tries to take them up, have swollen far beyond the "control" imagined in the opening scene and projected through the humanistic design.

Shakespeare as usual leaves signs of his discoveries. Act 4 is dominated by the Cade scenes—surely the most memorable and remarkable achievement of the play. It is here that we should look to see where, and perhaps how, power changes purpose.

Consider Cade's inception—it is a development, I think, from that of Mortimer's in *1 Henry VI,* though what is shadowy and inchoate there (the suggestion that Mortimer was bred by York's own need to come into dramatic life) has grown articulate in York's soliloquy in act 3 now. Dispatched to Ireland just at the point of Gloucester's removal, York finds himself at a critical moment in his plot: "Now, York, or never, steel thy fearful thoughts." Out of his "thoughts"—

Faster than springtime show'rs comes thought on thought,
And not a thought but thinks on dignity—

he conjures up his surrogate:

And for a minister of my intent
I have seduced a headstrong Kentishman,
John Cade of Ashford,
....
This devil here shall be my substitute. . . .

The language is that of a dramatist bringing to life a character so vital that he appears full-blown, with an energy seemingly endowed by nature:

In Ireland have I seen this stubborn Cade
Oppose himself against a troop of kerns,
And fought so long till that his thighs with darts
Were almost like a sharp-quilled porpentine;
And in the end being rescued, I have seen
Him caper upright like a wild Morisco,
Shaking the bloody darts as he his bells.

(3. 1. 331–66)

This, as C. L. Barber shows, is a figure of holiday misrule.[6] But his origin in the play is crucially ambiguous. On one hand he is the product of nothing but the zeal and effort of York's necessity-inspired "thought," woven *ex nihil* from his "laboring spider" brain. That is the dramatic reality, and in that sense Cade is more willfully derived than Mortimer in Part 1. On the other hand, fictively speaking Cade already "exists" and has already been conscripted by York. The point is, at this crucial moment York focuses intensely excited "thought" upon inert *potential* energy—unquickened matter—and gives it its particular shape. The Irish campaign will furnish him with the "men I lacked," but in the soliloquy these "men" also become the ground of popular support he will appropriate through Cade, and by means of which he will "stir up in England some black storm / Shall blow ten thousand souls to heaven—or hell."

The ambiguity of Cade's genesis—he is both natural and fabricated, derives from both inside and outside the play—parodies dramatic creation. York "creates" Cade, but as soon as he does the monster, like Frankenstein's, buds off from his creator's control. (Accused of having learned his royal genealogy, as "Mortimer," from York, Cade sneers in an aside, "He lies, for I invented it myself.") The scenes of rampage—like the character of the antic psychopathic rebel himself—are far freer in their vitality, less convention-bound and more spontaneous, than York's self-dramatizations. Their undeniable power comes from their ambiguity: they are menacingly real, but also playful; horrible but also funny; macabre, but a welcome relief from the turgidly distended performances by Margaret and Suffolk that we have just endured. The creature certainly has more raw and disquieting power than the master. In 4. 6, having taken London Stone, Cade's first two decrees as lord mayor are that "the pissing conduit run nothing but claret wine this first year of our reign" and that "it shall be treason for any that calls me other than Lord Mortimer." In true holiday-slapstick fashion, a soldier runs in calling "Jack Cade" and is promptly killed on Cade's orders. These two gestures show the combined absurdity and horror of Cade, the quality of sheer unrestraint that makes him both ultimately safe and also menacing. Though he can only exhaust himself, he nevertheless generates anarchic energy that out-runs sources and original controls. As "holiday" he surely goes beyond York's control.

This may not be immediately apparent. As Cade's power shrinks, York's begins to swell. The holiday figure, having purged authority's corruption, ushers in the potent figure of "England's lawful king." The visceral power of the Cade scenes flows into that "Army of Irish, with Drum and Color" with which York makes his triumphant reentry in act 5:

> From Ireland thus comes York to claim his right
> And pluck the crown from feeble Henry's head.
> Ring bells aloud, burn bonfires clear and bright,
> To entertain great England's lawful king.
>
> (5. 1. 1–4)

York is "lawful" because he has absorbed Gloucester's original grounds of authority into himself: he *is* the law, he *is* the realm. And now he has also consumed the very thing, Cade, that had bodied him forth, and yet was his own conjuration. York would seem to come on at this moment as a figure of extraordinary power.

Several kinds of climaxes seem possible: explosive illumination, appalling irony, or even Tamburlanian heaven-storming ("Ah, Sancta Majestas! who would not buy thee dear"). But whether it is to be hot or cold, thrilling, chilling, soberly sorrowful, or just plain didactic, we have been prepared, through a momentum of enlarging expectations, for a synthesis, a resolution: the satisfaction of an ending addressed to us.

What we get is something unexpected: a stiffened distancing of the action, "history" presented with the fake dignity one might expect of someone, on the morning after, trying to brave out a postorgiastic depression.

First, York's long-withheld challenge to Henry in act 5, scene 1 ("Give place!") precipitates an archly symmetrical declaration of opposing powers: the summoning of supporters on both sides, the assertion of ritual identities through heraldic family crests, the exchange of bitter vaunts and threats. The Battle of St. Albans follows (5. 2), presented as a sculptured series of tableaux reminiscent of the style of Part 1. York meets Old Clifford, exchanges chivalric courtesies, and kills him; Young Clifford, finding his father's body, dedicates himself as scourge of the House of York; Richard meets and silently dispatches Somerset, his father's oldest rival; Henry, for the first time in the play preferring *not* to leave a scene, is carried off by Margaret and Clifford to the relative safety of London. In the final scene (5. 3) the Yorkists regroup, exchange compliments, and resolve to pursue their advantage to London. Warwick has the final word: "Sound drum and trumpets, and to London all: / And more such days as these to us befall!"

Not that this final act is not exciting enough. It sweeps the play's disintegrative action to its "natural," perhaps inevitable, conclusion, and certainly it yields a dire vision of a world willfully consuming its own restraints and careening toward chaos. Yet the excitement, the momentum, the vision, all seem somehow gratuitous. The movement as a whole lacks either the full emotional punch or the humane comprehension of the action that we have expected. In its climactic scenes, the play seems to have withdrawn from us.

In the confrontation scene (5. 1), watching power mass into its brute reflexive forms of opposition, Henry's voice rises to lament the passing of loyalty and faith. It is another "fain would I," but what is chilling is not just the impotence of Henry's appeal, but its impertinence to the particular forces that have brought about this moment. The point is precisely the abstraction of human motives, the draining of individual wills and identities into ritual postures and speeches that have nothing vital to do with the events that produced them. The sense of design triumphant is absolute, but not that of the "humanistic design" that seemed to govern the play. All the complex and evasive intrigues, the will to violence and dissolution, have been distilled to a point of open and direct opposition, motiveless and "pure." But the point is reached through the shift of focus and the transfer of dramatic energy onto new, unknown, and strangely abstract characters.

We can almost feel the dramatist's gaze grow cold on York and leave him, abandoned like a posturing puppet, to his own resources. His climactic moment of self-assertion turns out to be his self-dissolution. Fully possessed by the myth of the true king, York lacks the autonomous dramatic resources of his separate reality. Then, he could work his thoughts and conjure up Cade; now, unable to avouch himself, he can only call up his sons as his "bail," his "surety": "I'll warrant they'll make it good." In the moment of his assertion he breeds, as it were, the future that will consume him; his will goes out into its agents, who materialize with full preemptive force. He who has worked his way outward, through so many surrogate roles and plots to this "real" moment, is abruptly out-pointed by an unknown son for whom *he* is the frontman, the surrogate. It is Richard, in his sardonic exchange with Young Clifford, who has the last word in the scene.

The battle scene itself is not the natural culmination of an action building from the past; it is controlled instead by the logic of a future that has yet to show its face. The humanistic design of the play has depended on scenes (like those focused on Gloucester, or those showing the progressive hardening of Margaret from ambitious lover to harridan) fluidly organized around characters conceived as having interior lives that might be manifested in a variety of perspectives, public and private.[7] Scenic structure and language, however conventionalized, were coherently derived from this primary conception of character, which in turn presupposed our active credulity. But the formal tableaux of the battle scene are governed by no such sense of underlying continuity. York and Old Clifford are not meaningful as adversaries except formally, as fathers in the process of being superseded by distinctly unchivalric sons.

Clear and implacable, the violence of the final act proceeds without audience involvement. We do not "know" these new characters, they do not speak to us, they have no interior life, and hence require no emotional sanction. Most unsettling, they do not even pretend to bid for it as, say, Talbot did, or as York continues to do by insisting on his destiny, his nature, and incidentally, England's welfare. But the voices of Richard and Young Clifford, who enter the play without precedent of character, suggest the authority of a fated future that will become "real," "historical," quite without our participation. Finding his father's corpse, Clifford articulates his acquiescence into a role that, as he speaks it, seems prefabricated. His voice expresses an extraordinary passion, yet it is programmatic, detached, abstract:

> Even at this sight
> My heart is turned to stone; and while 'tis mine,
> It shall be stony. York not our old men spares;
> No more will I their babes. Tears virginal
> Shall be to me even as the dew to fire;
> And beauty, that the tyrant oft reclaims,
> Shall to my flaming wrath be oil and flax.
> Henceforth I will not have to do with pity.
> Meet I an infant of the house of York,
> Into as many gobbets will I cut it
> As wild Medea young Absyrtus did.
> In cruelty will I seek out my fame.
>
> (5. 2. 49–60)

And after dispatching Somerset Richard aphorizes about himself as an agent of history: "Priests pray for enemies, but princes kill" (71). The detachment of voices from the action conveys the sense of sinking, eyes opened, into "history" as the fixed future. These characters see themselves bound into roles far more clearly than do York and his fighting bears, the Nevils; but there is no pretense, no struggle, and no regret. Somehow the will has been cut loose from any motive center, from any of the humane modes of consciousness or feeling imagined by this play. And yet the incoherence itself is willful.

In the moment when Young Clifford and Richard step out as the dramatized wills of their parties, something new crystallizes. A drama in the background of this present action comes into view, still vague but larger than anything the contention between York and Henry is sufficient to express. In *Richard II,* the rival kings in their encounter will embrace between them the implications and meaning of a massive cultural breakdown, chiefly because Richard II insists on dramatizing the exchange of power, and so brings some clarifying light to an otherwise obscure moment. But the contention that climaxes the humanistic design in *2 Henry VI* sheds no such light, gives off none of that large intelligibility. Instead, the main characters have dwindled to puppetry, playing out automatic roles in a little play that itself inhabits the larger drama, now emerging from the ruins of the humanistic design. Since that greater drama has not been delivered in this play, but will need a new one, we may tautologically call it the "future," as Young Clifford does:

> But that my heart's on future mischief set,
> I would speak blasphemy ere bid you fly,
> But fly you must. Uncurable discomfit
> Reigns in the hearts of all our present parts.
>
> (5. 2. 84–87)

But the point of this future is that it is unknown, unfeatured, lacks language, and remains, therefore, ghostly. There is no model in *2 Henry VI* for the future; rather, the play itself provides the grounds for its fabrication.

And yet the ghostly future drama has been present, in one sense, all along, as a kind of veil separating characters from their own experience. To the extent that we perceive them as unconscious instruments of an impersonal "historical" violence, we will feel uneasy with the humanistic design. In retrospect, that design is in trouble from the beginning. Recall the opening scene—everyone home from adventures abroad where innocence was lost and honor squandered, the embarrassed pretense of starting anew. All the grisly "undoings" that flow from this scene express the fundamental undoing, that of the operative myth of Part 1, the myth of a ground of reality (the name and fame of England) existing "out there," secure from the play's instabilities and yet authenticating its postures. This is the homecoming play, where painful truths are brought home to their sources. What Suffolk brings home to the "shadow" Henry is a monster born from the strenuous displacements of energy abroad, energy warped and misspent in carrying out monumental acts in distant places.

These "acts" are presented in Part 1 as heroic myths: the stuff of stories wonderfully free of fabrication. In other words, the play enacts an impulse to present its works as those of an authorial god, whose first book is nature itself. The impulse is doubtless Shakespeare's own, but it is countered at once by another, which is to expose the first as spurious. Thus Part 1 breathes by wasting its own monumental acts. But now in Part 2 it becomes apparent that the fabricator of monuments was all the while playing dead at home. What astonishes is the vehemence with which this discovery is pursued, the relentless fury with which the hapless king, caught in the act of leaving the scene, is hunted down. For above all it is the king who embodies the consciousness through which the realm of the play, "England," will cohere if it ever will. To refuse responsibility for the constitutive act, to cast himself as helpless looker-on, is to abandon the realm to chaos. But he will no longer be allowed to disavow that chaos. Like an outwitted heir, cajoled and exiled, the monument-making energy comes rushing back to its sources, packed with violence and retribution and purpose, a recoil of aggression upon the dissociated self. This is the ghost that haunts the opening scene. The reunion is initially suspended in embarrassment: a state ceremony hastily concluded, its forms intact but threatened, its language dangerously neutral, a shadow king eager to vanish with his foreign gift—precisely as if he were being stared at (as he is, we may now understand) by an eye slowly focusing with comprehension.

The king exits; but his foreign gift is a curse. Through Margaret, as we hear in Gloucester's bitter eulogy, is unleashed a pitiless force, the backlash of violated nature. Gloucester protects a spurious center of power; he must be removed. Henry is no longer safe behind his blank ceremonial naiveté; if he will not *be* king by acknowledging as "mine" the constitutive act that distinguishes form from formlessness, he will still be held accountable for the exertions by which he maintains his "innocence." He will be hounded mercilessly, stripped of all his protectors, until he is skewered in the end by his furious queen: "What are you made of? You'll nor fight nor fly" (5. 2. 74).

The question will remain unanswered in this play. The homecoming energy has much further to go before reaching the center and disclosing its true features in its true language. What has become quite clear, however, is that these plays bear

Henry's name because they bear his image and that they are parodies of power because they cannot be generative powers in themselves, which is to say, successful recreations of history. Before that can happen, Henry must be made answerable by his true opposite, Richard.

The silence of the ending is not that which comes after all has been said. It is the silence of functional incoherence, the loss of connection between speaker and speech, and between speech and action, by which fictive integrity is conveyed dramatically to us. And that, perhaps is what civil war really is to Shakespeare. He has looked for sources of corruptibility in human experience and found himself looking at the corruptibility of his medium. Hazarding control, he lets the rhythms of his drama play themselves out. Against the emerging presence of the larger undelivered drama, the humanized design of the inner play fades into a dream of artistic control. Unlike York he lets it go, relinquishing control rather than trying to enhance its draining credibility. He lets the play disintegrate in hopes of finding out the sources of disintegration; abandons the artist's role of making chaos humanly intelligible, and follows it into the sodden depths of Part 3.

4
Henry VI, Part Three "To make a bloody supper in the Tower"

Part 3 opens on an anticeremony. Making a new beginning out of Part 2's ending, the Yorkists re-report their battlefield successes like this:

EDWARD
Lord Stafford's father, Duke of Buckingham,
Is either slain or wounded dangerous;
I cleft his beaver with a downright blow.
That this is true, father, behold his blood.
[*Shows his bloody sword.*]

MONTAGUE
And, cousin, here's the Earl of Wiltshire's blood,
Whom I encount'red as the battles joined.

RICHARD
Speak thou for me and tell them what I did.
[*Throws down Somerset's head.*]

YORK
Richard hath best deserved of all my sons.
But is your grace dead, my Lord of Somerset?

NORFOLK
Such hope have all the line of John of Gaunt.

RICHARD
Thus do I hope to shake King Henry's head.

(1. 1. 10–20)

Gangster humor from Renaissance princes. As "ceremony" (and it is followed by York's ascent of the empty throne) this scene repudiates the pretenses of those that opened the first two plays. But the realism is reductive: people reduced to heads and blood—not blood as pedigree, that stubborn fiction, but lifeblood, the synecdoche collapsed to the literal: here *is* the noble Duke of Buckingham, *here* is my Lord of Somerset. Later, before *his* head is severed and set upon the gates of the town of York, York is taunted with a napkin bloodied by his murdered boy, Rutland, and with a paper crown. They are both symbols and both props. Later, Clifford's head will replace York's on the town gates. Like oaths, alliances, battles, and kings, heads are multiple in this play, and interchangeable. Chivalric pretenses, ceremonial distinctions, are stripped down to the brute realities of the war, and what is disclosed at the bottom is a brute play, proliferating props and dramatic occasions with a kind of rampant mechanical energy, yet with little transfiguring power.

York's martyrdom (1. 4) may be moving, but only as a performance keyed to the insular dramatic situation. His certain death is forestalled by Margaret so she may taunt him with sadistic eloquence. York at last is moved to vent his rage and grief in a manner that provokes Northumberland to tears and Clifford to slaughter. Northumberland transmits the scene's passion to us, but we do not sympathize from any sense of intimacy or of justice, nor does the sympathy carry over in any way to the Yorkist cause. In fact, the scene is an echo of the faded assumptions of the preceding play—that there is a natural connection between character, speech, and scenic structure, and that what induces our belief is this organic coherence of the elements. But here there is no such coherence, and the scene "persuades" through its very gratuitousness, through the extraordinary rhetorical feat required to carry it off, as if to announce the end of the convention it relies on: This sort of outright emotional appeal is henceforth no longer credible.

The presumption of a natural dramatic coherence had been exhausted in the previous play; the scene of York's martyrdom locates us in the chill realities of the waking present, just as Gloucester's moving eulogy for the heroic past located the waking realities of his play. But by the end of Part 2 the issue between artist and his material had not been truly joined. The ground—the past as other than his wishful fabrication—eluded the artist still, bedeviling his best efforts to disclose it through the natural processes of drama. So now, in his third attempt, he forgoes the myth of drama as a "naturally" intelligible form of human experience. Earlier I referred to the phenomenon of characters lapsing into predetermined roles, into what I have called the fixed future, the "future" that we look back upon as "history." Curiously, this sense of "lapsing" is strongest as the characters become most furiously aggressive. We have the apparent paradox that war, or at least (to borrow Ulysses' phrase) the "mere oppugnancy" of war in *3 Henry VI*, represents the most thoroughly passive idea of history.[1] Coherence in Part 2 was maintained by an implicitly active faith in the distinctiveness of experience: Gloucester's murder would reap clear and "natural" consequences. Now it is as if that faith had been withdrawn from the material, the drama allowed to succumb to the hopelessly passive "structure" of its chronicle sources. And indeed critics often tax Shakespeare with a weary acquiescence to the mechanically strung-out pattern of events in the chronicles. But the "pattern" of the chronicles, the image of history they present, is only a dreary reflection of an underlying chaos. Hall could not imagine the source of this chaos, nor could Shakespeare in Part 2. But he sees by now how it mocks inherited conventions, not only of historical knowledge, but of dramatic order as well. So now he is willing to let his drama sink through the spurious ground of its own coherence, in the hopes of discovering how it is that inchoate human experience, by the time we perceive it as "history" (by the time, that is, it is dramatized) has grown into something that looks so solid, inevitable, fated. Part 3, in other words, takes a plunge into that chaos. "Naturally coherent" dramatic elements dissolve into grotesque realizations of underlying impulses; and here these realizations are divested of the humane distinctions afforded by "civilized" imagination. Thus the essential shapelessness of the seemingly fated material is allowed to declare itself.

The Towton "molehill" episode (2. 5) at first seems to contradict this view of a landscape abandoned by shaping consciousness. The scene, heavily stylized, falls into two parts. First Henry, withdrawing from "the equal poise of this fell war" (13), speaks a wishful, mournful pastoral monologue. Then he is audience to a "death masque" of the son who has killed his father and the father who has killed his son, both unknowingly. As a whole, the episode seems to afford a privileged view of the play from the vantage of an external ground.

But if Shakespeare thus makes a choral commentary on his chaotic material, how can I claim that he has allowed it to sink toward the critical "wild of nothing" where it must contrive to speak for itself?

Rather than shaping, the scene projects the play's helplessness. Given the clear truth of what Henry "chorically" says from his molehill—that the oppositions in the war have become pointless in mindless savagery—his own withdrawal would generate sympathy and thereby shaping power if it were not so slack itself. The wistful pastoral may be moving as a set piece, but the stunned wishfulness that *makes* it a set piece—

> O God! methinks it were a happy life
> To be no better than a homely swain;
> To sit upon a hill, as I do now,
> To carve out dials quaintly, point by point,
> Thereby to see the minutes how they run—
>
> (2. 5. 21–25)

points back to that pattern of needful innocence developed in Part 2. Henry's desire to escape the drama mires him in it; the radical incoherence of the war is the mirror image of his wish, the death masque a projection of his own failure to give cohering shape. Nor will Shakespeare rescue him. Henry's will to nonbeing has stiffened into paralytic parody; the energy that in Part 2 went into disguise and evasion here has subsided into puppetry,[2] and the dramatic forms it takes are correspondingly lifeless. As Henry's withdrawal mirrors the "mere oppugnancy" of the war, so his static monologue mirrors the static masque, and the glazed immobility of the entire scene is answered by the equally helpless frenzy of the retreat that follows (125 ff). The scene boldly proffers itself as a comprehending drama, containing and transfiguring the exhausted drama of the war; it pointedly fails, falls into its elements, generating images only of its own futility.

The extremes of the molehill scene suggest the nature of the play's dissociations generally, which were forecast in the final act of Part 2. Throughout Part 3 the action is what Ronald Berman calls a "furious recapitulation of crime":[3] excitement in a nondramatic mode, visceral and spectacular, but without sustained fictive energy. The greater the fury, the more helplessly it repeats earlier actions that, for all their original doubtfulness, seem in retrospect authentic by comparison. Battles, murders, vaunts, and cajolings, the making and breaking of oaths, the alignment and realignment of "loyalties," all are carried forth with "sodden concentration upon self-interest" (Berman), and all lead only to futility. The mood is well caught in the confrontation scenes (as in 1.1, or 2.2) where the hostile parties are able neither to give their words the weight they obsessively mean for them to have, nor to extricate themselves from the sluggish verbal battle (e.g., 2. 2. 95–177). Through it all runs the bleary, enervating sense of déjà vu. The record of the past that sanctions York's claim on the crown, for instance, is originally advanced by Mortimer, in Part 1, in a resonant hush suggesting the disclosure of potent truths; in Part 2 it is functionally recited by York in conscripting the Nevils to his cause; in Part 3 it has become the gratuitous but obligatory form of argumentation, repeated in the "debate" of the first scene, and again in the opposing bids for French support in 2. 3. That sequence becomes a miniature history of the way "history" itself, conceived as an objective and orderly "record of the past," grows shapeless and impertinent when bleached of dramatic authority.

Shakespeare is sometimes said to be "embarrassed" by the disorder of his historical material. Tillyard finds him in all this to be rather wearily and dutifully touching chronicle bases, trapped by his obligation to Hall's system of causes and effects. He evinces the "factious" ease with which York breaks his oath to allow Henry undisputed reign during his lifetime.[4] But the ease may be just the point. Playing clown to his father's heavy, Richard argues York out of his oath through a little satirical "proof" that has no need to be convincing (1. 2. 22ff). Father and son are playing out parts in a parody become so predictable it requires only the glibbest of gestures.

There is little energy, and less need, for maintaining credible dramatic conventions of any sort. Scene after scene enacts the dissolution of language itself into one or another form of puppetry. On one side oratorical performances are less credible, more hermetic, often more extensive than ever, relying on possibilities of emotional responsiveness all but exhausted. On the other side the dialogue increasingly sheds the defunct forms of meaning and declares itself with almost childishly helpless candor:

Be Duke of Lancaster; let him be king.
(1. 1. 86)

Let me for this my lifetime reign as king.
(175)

. . . . I will be king or die.
(1. 2. 35)

EDWARD
Richard, I will create thee Duke of Gloucester;
And George, of Clarence . . .

RICHARD
Let me be Duke of Clarence, George of Gloucester.
(2. 6. 103–6)

The idiom (which occurs *ad nauseum*)[5] is that of children fighting over parts. Dukedoms and kingships are mouthed till they have become bare objects, props, like paper crowns—infinitely interchangeable because fundamentally meaningless. The theatrical sense of *being*, implicit in Part 2, surfaces into the starkness of a playworld from which imagination has withdrawn. So might an Elizabethan playhouse have looked to a cynical spectator: an insular world of intense activity and no meaning, and no force at work to carry that activity across to him *as* meaning. The characters, far from being the semiautonomous mediators between the audience and the "past" they inhabit, have become outcroppings of their context, powerless to know, let alone transmit it. Detached, we watch with growing coldness the play's passive matter receding in ever-diminishing circles. But we also feel that the dramatist watches with us, attentive, willing to hazard all to see what might appear.

The risk is that nothing will appear. In that case we might account for the confusion, the exhaustion, by writing off the play as a medieval relic in which the fictive credibility, the mimetic will or integrity, is drained off in the institutions of some such machinery as the Wheel of Fortune, Providential Justice, or the travails of Respublica. All are morality concepts that gain plausibility chiefly in the absence of strong, resistant characters. Or the failure of mimetic will, of strong centrifugal force in the play, might simply be attributed (à la Jan Kott) to a ruling concept of history as Juggernaut.

But something does appear that preempts all such rationalizing efforts to rescue the play from its own collapse. What the dramatist sees emerging from the chaos is not some stern didactic form, not some I-told-you-so, much less the triumph of the Tudor clerk, the Hall-and-Holinshed So-what, but rather himself: a profoundly ambiguous and misshapen version, but indubitably a version of himself nonetheless.

The abrupt emergence of the "new" Richard in 3. 2 has been variously accounted for—in one view as the revival of Shakespeare's waning interest in his material.[6] My own view is that Shakespeare "loses interest" volitionally—that is, willingly risks intelligibility in the interests of discovery. Thus from its own "thorny woods" the play calls forth its own shaping consciousness. As the embodiment of disorder, Richard, in effect, is tempted into being.

From his first appearance in Part 2 Richard's potential self glints from behind its future-mask in puns, asides, and a glibly vigorous idiom. He regularly undercuts Edward's more conventional attitudes and expressions in Part 3. But not until the wartime show of unity (the brothers as "three glorious suns") reaches its culmination in Edward's assumption of the crown, does Richard stir into life behind the mask. Edward in his first action as king is stupidly absorbed in stalking Lady Grey, only—predictably—to become the hunted object himself. By this point in the sequence of plays we have witnessed the assertion and submersion of so many characters, most of them unable to stay coherent for more than an act or two, that we are scarcely surprised to find Edward consumed by the role he thinks he commands, nor to feel the energy flowing toward Richard, growing correspondingly vivid in his detachment. But we cannot have been prepared for the force and style of Richard's eruption when he is left alone on the stage. The effect is that of self-creation, the first authentically new thing to occur in this dreamscape since York bespoke himself in the beginning of Part 2. In antic joy of self-recognition, "Richard" bursts fully-malformed and richly decked into life:

> Why, love forswore me in my mother's womb;
> And, for I should not deal in her soft laws,
> She did corrupt frail nature with some bribe
> To shrink mine arm up like a withered shrub;
> To make an envious mountain on my back,

Where sits deformity to mock my body;
To shape my legs of an unequal size;
To disproportion me in every part,
Like to a chaos, or an unlicked bear-whelp,
That carries no impression like the dam.
And am I then a man to be beloved?

(3. 2. 153–63)

Richard dramatizes the myth of his own beginnings. For the truth of this view of the past he avouches himself, now. No one will be able to say it better or more directly than he, and no one will have the same mastery of language that he gains from this forthright seizure of the grounds of his own being. From the "beginning" he goes on to appropriate the past, not helplessly, but with utter awareness.[7] He repeats with inflected clarity the metadramatic rhythms that brought forth York in the earlier play. What remains inchoate in York's self-creating will Richard brings into articulate sharpness; what is sentimental he cauterizes. Though Richard yearns, too, for the "golden time," the crown "Within whose circuit is Elysium," he associates it from the beginning with "all that poets feign of bliss and joy" (1. 2. 30–31). "Feign" probably bears both of its senses here, "to make" as well as "to make up." Richard sees "heaven" as something not to achieve but to "make." Like York he sees himself as cast for the role of king, not, however, as natural hero, but as fabricating freak; birthright is not a destiny to be entered into, but a future to be seized and wrought:

I'll make my heaven to dream upon the crown
And, whiles I live, t'account this world but hell
Until my misshaped trunk that bears this head
Be round impalèd with a glorious crown.

(3. 2. 168–71)

And unlike York's, Richard's capacity for playing is unimpeded by rationalization of his motives. The prerogatives of birth, concern for England's welfare, the self-evident necessity of mythic fulfillment, insofar as they color his will at all, are more or less efficacious conventions. Unlike York's images of Ajax and Achilles, Richard's very choice of models (the Wily-Heroic) acknowledges the irony of the heroic image consciously used, hence collapsed, in a dramatic context:

I'll play the orator as well as Nestor,
Deceive more slily than Ulysses could
And, like a Sinon, take another Troy.
I can add colors to the chameleon,
Change shapes with Proteus for advantages,
And set the murderous Machiavel to school.

(188–93)[8]

In Richard, also, York's ontological torment is heightened into articulation:

For many lives stand between me and home;
And I—like one lost in a thorny wood,
That rents the thorns and is rent with the thorns,
Seeking a way and straying from the way,
Not knowing how to find the open air
But toiling desperately to find it out—
Torment myself to catch the English crown;
And from that torment I will free myself
Or hew my way out with a bloody axe.

(173–81)

Renting and being rent, seeking and straying, not successively but simultaneously—a better image of the dramatist-as-actor, both born of and opposed to the play-matter, both naturalized and naturalizing the "woods," has so far not been available in the histories. Though gruesomely distorted (he desperately toils, and hews with bloody axe), this is the dramatist we have been pursuing, who above all seeks through his woods to "catch the English crown," meaning the symbolic appropriation of "England" through her past. Now Richard audaciously assumes that role. In creating himself he will recreate the play itself—so this radical new consciousness implies. To be sure, York provides an ominous precedent whereby the continuous fabrication of "self" as so many dramatic roles turns out to be self-sacrificial. Tellingly, what Richard envisions at the end of all his vigorous versatile playing is the "open air"—freedom from the struggle of action, the heavenly peace of the "golden crown." But unlike York, whom this vision turns into cold news, a dream of the past, Richard is ready to play through the ambiguities of his predicament, accept the absurdities, and command the role he is destined to play.

It is Richard, not York, who is destined to confront Henry

openly and force him to declare himself as he would not in Part 2. For York, the contention was a matter of character; he meant to supplant Henry within the historical context that they shared, but no more than Henry would he assume responsibility for the context. "King" remained constant, an ideal; only the occupant of the name would change. But Richard seeks Henry not personally, but as the embodiment of that will-to-nonbeing configured as "history" in these plays. He seeks him not as a character at all, but both as the symbol of "the world of England under Henry VI" and as the world itself, *Henry VI.* In other words, it is Richard who finally pins upon the king the plays that bear his name.

At the end of the play and his life, Henry, with all the satisfying authority of the dying-seer convention, prophesies—for the play's purposes, creates—the known destiny, the fixed future of "Richard," specifically by linking future to the myth of beginnings:

> The owl shrieked at thy birth, an evil sign;
> The night crow cried, aboding luckless time;
> Dogs howled and hideous tempest shook down trees;
> The raven rooked her on the chimney's top,
> And chattering pieces in dismal discords sung.
> Thy mother felt more than a mother's pain,
> And yet brought forth less than a mother's hope,
> To wit, an indigested and deformèd lump,
> Not like the fruit of such a goodly tree.
> Teeth hadst thou in thy head when thou wast born,
> To signify thou cam'st to bite the world . . .

Suddenly Richard stops his mouth:

> I'll hear no more. Die, prophet, in thy speech.
> [*Stabs him*]
> For this (amongst the rest) was I ordained.
> (5. 6. 44–58)

Then taunting, then restabbing the corpse, Richard manages to cap the long sum of atrocities in the play; but as Edward Berry points out, it is not the action but the articulation of motives that sets Richard outside the context of the play.[9] Thus, seizing his destiny by preempting Henry's oratory—*making* that "fixed future" his own—Richard signals the end of the convention whereby "losers may have leave to chide" (3. 1. 185). This convention had allowed to farewell performances, regardless of their dramatic context, a margin of gratuitous credibility. Gloucester, Suffolk, Lord Say, York are all allowed a hush in the drama, as if to complete themselves impressively. This is one of the amiable theatrical pretenses that Richard, hewing his way through the thorny woods, declares henceforth defunct.[10]

> I, that have neither pity, love, nor fear.
> . . . .
> And this word "love," which greybeards call divine,
> Be resident in men like one another,
> And not in me. I am myself alone.
>
> (68–83)

The implications of Richard's audacity are huge. What Richard claims is nothing less than the ability to shape "history" to his liking, in his own image. He promises, that is, what the molehill vision so signally fails to do, to completely transfigure this passive landscape of the play. Richard's appearance is such a relief that we may not be inclined to challenge the presumption. Out of silence he steps forward to renew a sterile language—to restore to drama the potency of its salient conventions of pretense, disguise, and indirection. He can promise this renewal because his claim is so radical. In the course of the plays all "divine" or privileged meanings have been exhausted; Richard willingly, willfully embodies the exhaustion. Having created himself he will also create the future (his "heaven") by an act of radical definition: "I am myself alone." Thus, Myself against the World. There is nothing *but* this "world" of exhausted possibilities, and yet Richard stands against it, forcing the entire natural world to declare itself his woods, not only able to rend with its thorns, but rendable, subject to the impression of *his* consciousness. The world really is his stage, and nothing is exempt from his creative powers. Abjuring all ties (specifically the distinctive family ties of the histories, fathers, brothers, sons) and hence any extradramatic origin, Richard distinguishes self from world by assuming the "residence" of language *in* the world. Henry must resort to a language of mythological portents to declare the "truth" of Richard's birth and future; but for Richard there are no such native truths, and language is utterly instrumental. So he identifies the very matrix of the play itself, the source, ground, mother nature, as his opposition, and so subject to his recreation. All that is not "myself" he names as ground, and so he makes the world of the *Henry VI* plays "mine."

When the implications of Richard's posture are extracted from the ambiguities of his protean presence, it is clear what an outrageous parody of the artist he is, claiming the power to recreate the known world of the past in his drama. If my reading has been correct, however, Shakespeare has been guided through these early history plays in part by wondering, if not whether the past could in fact be recreated by drama, then at least why it could not. He has been seeking that precreative condition before dramatic conception and dramatic matter have separated. Since that condition is hypothetical and irrecoverable, he seeks an image of it, proceeding "downward" through increasingly more radical forms of disintegration, decreation. Richard provides the image. At the point of crisis, the force of his hyperbolic posture within the play carries over to the audience outside the play in such a way as to credit, temporarily, the hyperbole. Richard rescues the play by breaking out of its diminishing circles of repetitions, redelivering it to us as the promise of a future—a promise not abstract, but anchored now, in the replenished present moment of the drama itself. For the moment of that possibility the "future," though assured, is yet to be. The known past—so thrives the illusion—may yet be recreated.

At Tewkesbury (5. 5) the "three glorious suns" of York take turns stabbing to death Henry's son, Prince Edward, before the eyes of his mother, Margaret; Richard would kill Margaret, too, since "Why should she live to fill the world with words?" (44). This is exactly what she does in *Richard III,* but Edward forestalls Richard's sword. Edward is conventional. Told a moment later that Richard has gone "to make a bloody supper in the Tower" (to eat up Henry), Edward nods, "He's sudden if a thing comes in his head" (86). And then he says he hopes that in his absence his wife has borne him a son (who will also, of course, be called Edward, and be cannibalized by Richard).

No restoration seems imaginable until he who would eat his bloody supper wide awake has freely had his fill. To "identify" Richard, morally, as diabolical is beside the point unless one comes to terms with the implications of his preemptive ability to identify himself. For in that ability he appears to confront us, at long last, with the bodily form of the plays' bedevilling dissociations. And we are teased with the prospect of a nightmare comedy in which this palpable embodiment is actually allowed to run his harnessed absurdities to their real conclusions. At this point it is not so clear just what those conclusions must be, nor how far Richard, for whom there is no distinction between dramatic and historic power, might make good on his promise to recreate history in his own image. In the next play, Shakespeare can test out the terrific temptations of such a promise. For now it is enough that there will be a next play. He has still not encountered the real ground of his material; instead he has flushed out a deeply parodic, tenacious, charming, and forceful image of himself. He has acknowledged him "mine," located and bodied him forth; now he must either exorcise or comprehend him.

Part II

From Parody to Passion: Richard III, King John, Richard II

5
The Antic and the Machiavel Revisited

The three middle plays of the historical sequence seem only marginally concerned with historical processes. Certainly readers and audiences have long found them—especially the first and third of the triad—powerfully self-contained. In many ways they resemble Shakespeare's tragedies to come more than his histories completed. As in the tragedies, a powerful central figure, through the logic of his own personality, provokes the forces that restrain him. His actions generate a plot—which is to say, the otherwise obscure and abstract "force" acquires shape and definition. Fate, nature, providence, humanity—whatever we call it, it shows itself as structure. It comes across to us as living form.

In the histories, Shakespeare is stalking time—not as an abstraction or a disembodied force or process, but as it intersects with character and becomes an organic part of human destiny. By now he understands that "history" is not just the past, but is the human connection between the past and the present. He has learned in *Henry VI* not to seek time past apart from the present time of his dramas, and he has learned not to seek the past as a distant object undistorted by the vigor and ingenuity of his own seeking. But he has yet to test the real implications of that distortion. In the king-centered plays he begins this process, searching out the meaning of history in the very art and artistry of his own plays. But before going further, let us look at those artist-kings in illuminating moments of action.

Richard III

King Edward on his deathbed orchestrates a show of unity among squabbling kin and courtiers. With glib decorum they swear perfect and heartfelt love, embrace old enemies, vow lasting harmony. The king—sloth and brutality having given way to sentimentality—is pleased. "There wanteth now our brother Gloucester here / To make the blessèd period of this peace." On cue, Richard bursts in. There is a moment of suspense—one never knows what he will say, what mask he will be wearing. Luckily, he is in a peace-loving mood befitting the occasion. Indeed, he so swells with benignity that "I do not know that Englishman alive / With whom my soul is any jot at odds / More than the infant that is born tonight." And then the virtuoso touch: "I thank my God for my humility" (2. 1. 73).

No one laughs or scoffs; there are no clowns, wits, no guiltless, honest, or deep-feeling men in the company. To laugh or scoff would be to acknowledge the postures Richard mocks. His style is open and palpable mimicry, carried out with his victims' consent. Once they are overextended—like a carnival crowd having heard the whoosh of the rocket and now watching the sky for the flare—Richard explodes it in their midst. "Who knows not that the gentle Duke [Clarence] is dead?" Everyone is seized by obscure dread. An evil is loosed, but no one can contemplate Richard. "Look I so pale, Lord Dorset, as the rest?" whispers Buckingham. "Ay, my good lord; and no man in the presence / But his red color hath forsook his cheeks." The pallor, says Richard, incriminates the queen's kindred; to the king, bitter and grieving, *all* present are guilty for having failed to plead against his "brutish wrath" for the life of Clarence. Richard shakes his head sorrowfully, a good man helpless in a malicious world. For all his conspicuous presence, no blame, no agency, attaches to him. He is invisible, working through others' dispositions, making manifest what lies latent and potential, moving easily among their hypocrisies, guilts, and self-deceits. He appears among his victims in mockingly transparent roles that they cannot or will not penetrate. Because we recognize the roles, we feel that he shows his true self to us alone.

King John

After a seemingly endless day of debate between John and his enemies in Angiers—a timeless day of implacable public posturing, of self-righteous rhetoric only too thinly masking the brutal wills beneath—at last all gives way to the furious blood-letting so deeply desired. King John comes up victorious: his enemies are overawed by the speed and power with which he asserts his "strong possession" of the English crown. But abruptly, in the very flush of victory, John pulls to one side his new henchman, Hubert, and the wide formal scene gives way to a strangely private one (3. 3. 19). Suddenly we become eavesdroppers; or, it is as if the Bastard, dispatched to England, had turned back and inadvertently overheard his king, in a new and heavy-breathing language, making love to Hubert's loyalty and ambition. "Give me thy hand," whispers John. "I had a thing to say, / But I will fit it with some better tune." John wishes it were midnight, he wishes they were meeting in a churchyard, he wishes that Hubert felt more drowsy and melancholy; he wishes him to understand his intention "without thine ears, and make reply / Without a tongue, using conceit alone." Hubert is made to understand that the "very serpent" in John's way is his captured nephew, the boy Arthur. "I'll keep him so," says Hubert, "That he shall not offend your majesty."

KING JOHN
Death.

HUBERT
My lord?

KING JOHN
A grave.

HUBERT
He shall not live.

KING JOHN
Enough.

With this John fires a series of crisp orders all around, and the secret scene closes over. It is as if the public crust of the play had shifted to reveal, as in a crevass, grotesquely discontinuous, the outcropping of yet-more-deeply buried motivations. Yet what we have glimpsed, though painfully intimate, does not quite seem like *John's* private life: the moment is private, but he remains indistinct within it. Our hunger is teased for privileged perception, a privileged relationship, but no one steps forth to gratify it. John is incoherent, the Bastard is gone, and we are on our own.

Richard II

Unable to resolve his subjects' quarrel out of court, Richard II presides over a trial by combat. Conventions are most scrupulously carried out—ritual identifications, accusations, vaunts, and vows—and the king impeccably enacts his role as impartial instrument of a divinely sanctioned process. Not a hint as to the strangeness of the occasion is admitted, not a word of dissent is heard, no role could be more secure than that of the king's. The ceremony is relentlessly impersonal: the combatants, the actual grounds and content of their quarrel obscure, seem glad to consign lives and honor to an institution whose justice is represented by an ideally faceless king, a king without personality. What is he thinking? No one could possibly know, and indeed it is a meaningless question: the ceremony seems to guarantee that he has no hidden, no interior thoughts or character. Finally everything prescribed and necessary has been said, the combatants' desire to close in battle about to be fulfilled, the charge is begun. But "Stay!" calls the Marshal. "The king hath thrown his warder down"—and in midcharge the antagonists are brought to a halt. Everyone suffers a moment of shocked confusion. The king's act is completely baffling—and yet he is the *king,* and his most inexplicable act is Law. But as the general frisson wears off, a new clear-sightedness takes hold. A splendid edifice has been shivered, and amidst the rubble stands a wry, distinctive, mocking, vulnerable, and above all a decidedly strange figure, the king himself.

Richard III's mockery is self-protective, Richard II's self-destructive. Richard III's excesses are cool, calibrated perfectly to his victims' dispositions; Richard II's are hot, he pursues propriety to the breaking point, where it becomes grotesquely inappropriate to ordinary sensibilities. Richard III remains invisible among his works; Richard II in his becomes glaringly visible, even freakish. Between these two a world opens up. *Richard III* culminates an old parodic mode of theatricality, *Richard II* initiates a new, more deeply sentient one. But just in their centripetal theatricality, the obsessive strangeness of their central figures, the two plays call to each other. Between them, in a chasm of style and sensibility, sits the eloquently tortured *King John,* embarrassing both its king-centered kin with its awkward fraternal resemblance. *King John,* alas, is not centered at all—or rather it distributes its center, and splits the king-power, between John and the Bastard. John, a manipulator like Richard III, is also self-destructive like Richard II in his use of power. But the destruction is inadvertent. The theatrical self-consciousness through which the Richards center themselves is relegated to the Bastard, who is cleared from the stage at John's first self-revealing moment. John understands and commands only one kind of theatrical power, the machiavellian. He does not understand the more private uses of performance and so, unlike Richard II, he does not command the collapse of his powers. The collapse reveals John as shrinking, dodging, panicky, and incoherent.

Both Richards (and for half the play the Bastard) give off a self-congratulatory quality in their acting styles. Richard III of course crows quite openly, Richard II more furtively but just as surely, even when his performances become overtly self-destructive. Unlike John, but like the Bastard, both Richards take, and both offer, pleasure in their distinctive powers. It is a gratuitous and aesthetic pleasure, sometimes an almost sexual response to the medium of drama itself (though in that response Richard II is willing to waste himself, and Richard III is not). Over and above their roles as kings or would-be kings or surrogate kings or anti-kings in the worlds of their historical fictions, they have a peculiar and specific life at the leading edge of the whole field of play—that is, where the play touches us. Shakespearean kings generally are such doubly charged figures, representatives of their fictive worlds but also their subverters. As leading actors they manifest traditional bodies of meaning, define and protect an inhabitable cultural space. But they are also actors in the most immediate theatrical sense, improvisers, self-delighters, strange rather than familiar, radically at odds with the patterns of order they represent. In other words, antics as well as machiavels.

In the archetypal relationship of the king and his fool, the fool (according to William Willeford) evokes a "germinal wholeness" that has been necessarily sacrificed at the inception of the realm—when form, in other words, was wrested out of chaos. In normal circumstances the fool's privileged presence at the side of the king insures a healthy equipoise between form and formlessness, order and anarchy. But the exercise of folly may be untimely, excessive, or wrongly directed, and, as

Willeford says, may "prove as unwelcome as any other incursion of chaos upon the established order; then the fool may have to suffer the king's revenge." But "this danger to the fool, one of his occupational hazards, is merely a reflection of his danger to the king."[1]

Shakespeare's kings tend to embody this tension in their competing functions as antic and machiavel. Always there are moments when the king appears to have balanced these energies in himself and in his rule, but such moments are necessarily ephemeral. Richard III, no less than Henry VI, King John, and Richard II, is ultimately self-destructive. None of them is merely a victim; all are driven to *perform* their own folly. Subverting the machiavellian fictions they inhabit, they deliver the plays to us as live actions, taking intelligible forms in the very process of decomposition.

Yet in the end of each one of these plays the driving question about the meaning of history in human affairs—a question that has been three-quarters submerged in the tragic or mock-tragic action—rises to the surface. Oddly enough, part of the "intelligibility," in each case, is the clear sense of irresolution, the sense of history still undigested, even by these richly innovative dramatic forms. As in the *Henry VI* plays, each play in this trio ends by showing the way into the future, not only in English history, but in the dramatic sequence itself.

6
The Dead-End Comedy of *Richard III*

Richard is a great role, as Richard himself was the first to discover in his coming-out soliloquy in *3 Henry VI.* All his predecessors—in Shakespeare, Marlowe, More, and elsewhere—are superseded by the way theatricality is built into his character. He is "sent" into the "world," incomplete: he is not of it, has no fixed identity, no "character" but the unique freedom of the self-creating actor. It is painful—he can see that the world that rejects him is not worth having, that worldly power is a sham and worldly attachments worse than nothing—but it is also exhilarating because he alone stands undetermined by that world's laws and rhythms. In fact, he can create himself by mocking down the world. That will be his plot, the action through which he will become a character. He is not born into this plot, this role; he creates them. He creates "history" by showing how lifeless and manipulable, how insubstantial it is in the hands of a mocking artist.

His first soliloquy in *3 Henry VI* is the *locus classicus* of machiavellian theatrics: energetic performing power, the proliferation of selves through dissembling roles, in the service of an ultimate goal, the crown. But the machiavel itself is a role in *Richard III.* It is played by Buckingham, Richard's "other self," who has mastered the "deep tragedian's" arsenal of effects as a means toward the end of worldly power. In his opening monologue Richard himself does not allude to the crown; he mentions it only glancingly after meeting Clarence, and not at all in his exuberance after seducing Anne. For two acts he scarcely considers the ends of acting. Foremost in the dramatic persona comes the self-delighting antic, for whom the world is so corrupt and stupid that the satisfactions to be gained in mocking it cannot compare with those of regarding himself, his own audience, in a glass, and descanting on his own deformity. With Buckingham, then, he begins to play for power; but even then we watch the antic playing the machiavel:

> My other self, my counsel's consistory,
> My oracle, my prophet, my dear cousin,
> I, as a child, will go by thy direction.
>
> (2. 2. 151–153)

The self-delighting antic is invisible to Buckingham. In Richard he really sees himself.

The antic thrives on absolute antithesis. Richard would "undertake the death of all the world" (1. 2. 123), wants "the world for me to bustle in" (1. 1. 152), "all the world to nothing!" (1. 2. 237). It is idle to wag a finger at this anarchic individualism as if it were an embarrassment. It is his study, his pride, his art, to create himself in radical opposition to the world—meaning "history," the sum-total of everyone else's experience; to perfect himself in opposition to everything that is not himself. Such rigorous economy surely masks a powerful fantasy, bound to be exposed sooner or later, but for awhile it pleases us to be engaged by Richard's sheer performing verve. And besides, coming fresh from the clamor of *Henry VI,* we must welcome a theatrical mode that presents such deftly vivid distinctions. Probably no play was ever before pitched to its audience with such subtly knowing calculation as is *Richard III* in its opening gesture. The cool precision of Richard's rhetorical stance disavows bombast, sentimentality, vagueness; it asserts dry clarity. It gives enough of a "character" to seem fascinating, not so much as to muddy our immediate perception, or disturb the grounds of our engagement. It offers, in other words, a uniquely theatrical gratification.

The opening is a masterful tease, a great theater game; the speech is a wonderful blend of self-disclosure and self-concealment, or so it seems. Richard is bored, an unemployed actor in "this weak piping time of peace"; therefore, since he cannot have war and cannot enjoy lust, "I am determinèd to prove a villain." This is a coldly aesthetic aim, and curiously abstract, as if the nature of the villainy were unimportant. Like Iago, that other trickster, he is something of a *bricoleur,* working from available materials: if they are rotten to begin with, what can he do? At least he will make the rottenness intelligible, answerable, by shaping it as his opposition, his Not-me. He does not say "I am a villain," but "I will try myself out in the role of 'villain.' " We respond first to the fiction of intimate disclosure, privileged confidence. We respond second to the thinly hidden "self," the perhaps tortured and suffering self, seeking compensatory gratification for psychic damage, or at least a kind of suffering we can only faintly perceive. Yet the tone is cool and elegant, the theater game superb, and safe. He "reveals" a dramatic persona exclusively to us, while being sure to suggest an underlying character only slightly deployed in this action, and not accountable to it. He implies in his performing verve that his energies derive from a source other than "history," "this breathing world." He is somehow autonomous, independent, unfathomable. Yet that hidden character may be a dramatic persona, too, glimpsed "behind" the first one. Our emerging doubts about the authenticity of a "self" within these roles constitutes a third line of awareness.[1]

Tamburlaine is obviously Marlowe's darling, his speech strong because it is Marlowe's, and he consumes the world because it is so shadowy to begin with. But Richard is autonomous and self-creating (with a hint of something cogent underneath) and the world he encounters is highly organized and operates on iron and distinctive laws. Indeed, the antithesis between Richard and the "world" takes the overdetermined and fantastical form of two opposing modes of drama.

Richard's is obvious enough—a highly personal mode of aggressive mimicry, the assumption of others' voices, masks, stances, in order to mock them down. He specializes in parody—thrives on others' hypocrisy, pries open dissociations, exposes the passive will beneath aggressive language, leads his victims to the destruction, the punishment, the negation, they secretly desire. He perfects himself through furious activity, but success depends on his remaining, though Crookback and prominent, invisible. ("I would I knew thy heart," says Anne; " 'Tis figured in my tongue," he replies. Unlike Tamburlaine, his tongue is not gorgeous or Senecan, except in mockery. He is always ironic, his voice never his "own" except, perhaps, in soliloquy, though even this is a cool illusion.)

The world that Richard opposes is the radical reduction of historical experience in the *Henry VI* plays (where no such clearly defined world exists) into a Providential drama of the most static, mechanical, and impersonal kind:

> That high All-seer which I dallied with
> Hath turned my feignèd prayer on my head
> And given in earnest what I begged in jest.
>
> (5. 1. 20–22)

This is Buckingham, but it could be almost any of Richard's victims. Distinctions among them are tenuous, ghostly—feigned. What gives this world its peculiar unity, its definition as a play (that is, as shaped rather than "natural") is Margaret, who appears as its spokesman, and in a sense as Richard's rival dramatist. Not that she creates anything personally; her function is to reveal God's play, which she does through curses and prophecies. She appears only twice, the first time to announce the plot as a series of providential reprisals, the second to recapitulate and confirm the plot:

> Edward thy son, that now is Prince of Wales,
> For Edward our son, that was Prince of Wales,
> Die in his youth by like untimely violence!
>
> (1. 3. 198–200)

(Never mind that the violence is "like" only in being "untimely": her vision, like her speech, makes distinctions only between "mine" and "thine.")

> Thy Edward he is dead, that killed my Edward;
> Thy other Edward dead, to quit my Edward. . . .
>
> (4. 4. 63–64)

"Here in these confines slily have I lurked," she intones, "witness" to the "dire induction" of events inexorably coming to pass. She uses the theatrical metaphor to suggest that a superior play has fulfilled itself through Richard, the scourge-of-God. What she "witnesses" is a parodic morality play in her own image: barren (gutted by a lifetime of brutality and suffering), external, mechanical, empty of personality and motivation, its single causative principle a reflex quid-pro-quo reaction, action itself conceivable only as crime, and the past *(Henry VI)* reduced to a series of crimes to be harvested in the present. The present is All Soul's Day, Judgment Day, the day when history itself is brought to an end. Margaret, in other words, "witnesses" a play about the end of playing.[2]

What makes her so apt a rival to Richard is her very gratuitousness, her ghastly detachment, her disembodied instrumentality. Her entire character is emptied into her function as Prophet, and she is uniquely impotent as a character, incapable of acting (in either sense of the word), of withholding or deploying a "self" or of influencing any action. (All Richard's victims pay tribute to her power, but after the fact: they are all very eager to read their fates in her table of curses, to see the world in her quid-pro-quo terms. Clarence alone—whom she doesn't curse—experiences guilt and terror internally, rather than homiletically.) Margaret, in other words, is archetypal, Richard existential. She is (or has become) her function, bound to her language. But Richard, essenceless, has no language of his own, only parodies others', turning it back murderously upon them:

QUEEN MARGARET
[after sixteen lines of cursing]
thou detested—

RICHARD
Margaret.

MARGARET
Richard!

RICHARD
Ha!

MARGARET
I call thee not.

RICHARD
I cry thee mercy then; for I did think
That thou hadst called me all these bitter names.

MARGARET
Why, so I did, but looked for no reply.
O, let me make the period to my curse!

RICHARD
'Tis done by me, and ends in "Margaret."

(1. 3. 232–38)

Margaret has, undeniably, a kind of brute theatrical force, though it derives from—it consummates—the tradition of declamatory assertiveness so prominent in the *Henry VI* plays, and which we discovered to be the manifestation of the self-paralyzing will that emerged as "history": the dissociation of men from their own experience. In its helplessness, its mindlessness, and its deep antipathy toward acting, Margaret's theater-mode radically opposes Richard's, but they are yoked together. Margaret's curses have a potential power to anyone secretly sharing her outright belief in magical language—which means everyone but Richard. Buckingham, the pragmatist, knows that "curses never pass / The lips of those that breathe them in the air" (1. 3. 284–85), and yet the future ghost, witness of the inexorable justice of the "high All-Seer," admits that "My hair doth stand on end to hear her curses" (303). Richard, at this, makes a truly strange response: is it simply perverse (to keep Elizabeth and the others off balance) or is it perversely nonironic (thereby unbalancing us)? In either case, by voicing a humane sympathy for Margaret as crazed victim of the past rather than its prophet, he undercuts her authority:

> I cannot blame her. By God's holy Mother,
> She hath had too much wrong, and I repent
> My part whereof that I have done to her.
>
> (1. 3. 305–7)

Part of our pleasure comes from the obvious pretense that Richard is the underdog, triumphing against overwhelming odds, "all the world to nothing." He counts the obstacles between him and the crown. But they all come down quite readily, and in fact he never does seem to sweat until after he has the crown, never seems passionate or panicky in his operations. Not only is he not an underdog, but even the scrupulously overdetermined structure of antitheses, of matched opposites, is spurious: the manifestation of a fantasy of power. It is not just that his victims are willingly victimized, though that is true, but also that their willingness traps Richard into a reflexive role of easy mastery that gradually hardens into a kind of slavishness. In working the ironic fulfillment of the peers' dissembling vows—"So thrive I mine!" and so forth—Richard seems to fulfill his own role in Margaret's program as "hell's black intelligencer; / Only reserved their factor to buy souls / And send them thither" (4. 4. 71–73). It is precisely the pallid ease, however, with which these "souls" first dissemble and then, reflexively, suffer their reversals, that as characters makes them so shadowy, such parodic play figures, and hence such contemptible victims. Richard knows this—that is why the machiavel, who values the world he scorns, is a second-rate role. One may even imagine a Richard nauseated by his victims' compulsive will to be used, to be "shadows."[3] Just this kind of puppetry provoked his dramatic insurgence in the first place (in *3 Henry VI,* 3. 2), and now it appears that all his fiercely cool manipulating energy is bound to the ultimately futile activity of making shadows of shadows.

But the play's structure is so clear, so welcome, and so brilliantly exploited for three acts by Richard that it frees our responses for pleasure in his nimbleness, and we accede to fictions we would find suspect anywhere but in a comedy. *Richard III* is not quite a comedy, but neither is it a tragedy. Typically a Shakespearean comedy proliferates confusion of plot and character with the implied promise of a wondrous resolution that delightfully enlarges the field of play in the end. *Richard III* generates the confusions, the contradictions, and through the dazzling con-man artistry of Richard seems to promise (like Falstaff, caught between his wit and his grossness) a marvelous payoff. But it is a pseudocomedy, dead-end comedy. Behind the fiction of Richard versus the World lies the myth of Richard's centrality, a center of power. The struggle is a fantasy; Margaret is a fantastic opposite, Richard's victims are ghosts, and the scenes of encounters are setups, discrete occasions for Richard's mastery of shadows all-too-willing to disappear.

> This is the day wherein I wished to fall
> By the false faith of him whom most I trusted.
> (5. 1. 16–17)

Behind the antithetical structure is a solipsistic need for full control.

I do not speak of *Richard's* need, for that would presume a psychologically complete character, whereas I think we are merely teased by the theatrical gestures of one. But through Richard—through the myth of his centrality and coherence—a fantasy of power is played out. For credibility, it needs the pseudocomic antithetical structure. Yet this structure, and hence Richard's control, are twice severely threatened. The first occasion is Clarence's account of his dream (1. 4). Unlike Stanley's dream of the wild boar (3. 3) with its obviously flat significations, and certainly unlike Richard's ghostly visitation before Bosworth, Clarence's dream narrative gives form to an unrestrained and continuous flow of feeling. It takes its form not from a convention of moral allegory—the homiletic acceptance of one's guilt because one is found out by the cosmic polygraph—but as images vulcanized from a psyche beset by guilt and terror. The sea-vision is wondrous and ambiguous, and the stifled soul rendered with bodily directness:

> often did I strive
> To yield the ghost; but still the envious flood
> Stopped in my soul, and would not let it forth
> To find the empty, vast, and wand'ring air,
> But smothered it within my panting bulk,
> Who almost burst to belch it in the sea.
>
> (1. 4. 36–41)

Temporarily the speech is the speaker, just as the dream was the dreamer and not a discrete part in a morality. In its organic unity, and consequently in its dramatic potency, this language opposes itself both to Richard's parodic style and to the rhetorically demonstrative styles of his victims. This alternative is the rare and momentary surfacing, into haunting lyrical images, of a flow of dramatic energy that usually lies concealed within the forms it empowers, but which here, under pressure of obliteration, reveals itself. In other words, the dream narrative suggests a kind of recreative power language might have, but which is systematically smothered in *Richard III.* It does not recur. Clearly it is a kind of language that Richard cannot pervert through parody, and so it makes an independent bid for our attention and engagement that must be suppressed. Richard had warned the murderers not to let Clarence talk; now he must be both stabbed *and* drowned. The need to suppress him speaks for itself.

Clarence personally makes no special claims on us—only his voice—and Richard in the next scene performs upon Edward and the court politicians—newly "reconciled" in peace and love—with such brilliantly extravagant virtuosity that the threat seems to be turned aside. The other challenge to his control of the comic structure comes later: the murder of the young princes. Here, the play's chief way of dealing with the threat of emotional impact is to distance us from the murders. Tyrrel is hired by Richard and in turn hires Dighton and Forrest, whose account of the murder Tyrrel relays in a highly mannered monologue. This comes at a time when Richard's control, both over his own persona and over others, is disintegrating, and it shows him, now king, insulated from the world rather than bustling in it. It presses in on him, visible and immobile at the center, and his agents enact his will badly or not at all. In short, though the play maneuvers to intercept the threat of our engagement in the pathos of the princes, it also pulls away from Richard. In serving his interests—in responding to the need for central control—it exposes the nature of those interests. As in the *Henry VI* plays, but with much steeper articulation, we are disengaged and left to look with chill regard upon the helpless course of the last two acts.

It is not the "success" of Margaret's play of retributive justice—nothing due its power or authority either as drama or as idea—that leads to the debacle of the ending, but the failure of Richard's play: its internal collapse. His compulsive drive toward individuation, the clear antithetical form, has been a continuing testament to his control, but it leads ironically to a high degree of visibility. He uses up the "world"—that is, those shadows who would rather succumb to Margaret's "justice" than incriminate Richard by acting a shrewd audience. He wins the crown, that symbol of the summit of individuation. But then as a Self, rather than an exploiter of others' self-abnegations, Richard turns out to have very little force or coherence. To act directly, visibly, through one's agents, is quite different from acting invisibly through the secret wills of others.

The interview with Queen Elizabeth crystallizes Richard's exhaustion. The scene parodies his seduction of Anne, which of course was a virtuoso performance, brisk and graceful in its immaculate control. Never, before or after, was it clear that Richard really needed Anne for worldly ambitions; the success itself was certainly the point. By contrast stands his *need* for Elizabeth, which keeps him visible as an actor striving but unable to deploy himself in credible shapes of language, figured in his tongue. Moreover, he is (as artist) faced with disintegrating materials. Dissociated from his true object—Elizabeth's unseen, unknown daughter—he is forced to improvise, in Elizabeth, an agent. But he has already used her up; except for her daughter, she has nothing left to lose, to masquerade. Now it is he (as before it was Anne) who labors after a shifting target, while Elizabeth, relentlessly ironic, leads him through a mocking chase after a suitable "title" for his wooing. "There is no other way, / Unless thou couldst put on some other shape, / And not be Richard that hath done all this" (4. 4. 285–87). As the antic, Richard *has* been able to reshape himself convincingly, in role after role, throughout the play. But the strenuous effort of this interview brings him nothing but himself, "Richard that hath done all this"—that is, the historical Richard that presumably underlay his antic character all along. The disclosure leads directly into a display of incoherence among his followers, "songs of death" from the field, then to Bosworth and Richmond.

This progress toward dramatic exhaustion, the drama's mortification by the "fixed future" of history, magnifies that in *2 Henry VI* where York bid to refashion "history" in his own image and ended up as its fodder. When men fail to re-create they become creatures of the chaos that, in the histories, wears the face of an orthodoxy that is both blindly aggressive and profoundly passive. Margaret's confidence is born out by the clanking machinery of the final act: the parade of ghosts declaiming Richard's outstanding debts, the reflex-insurgence of a faceless Richmond (Henry Tudor, materializing from overseas—i.e., "out there" again), the colorless correct oration of this blank hero to his troops (which exactly reverses the bookkeeping logic of Margaret's play, as in "If you do fight against your country's foes, / Your country's fat shall pay your pains the hire"), and finally the summary perfection of his closing choric speech. In other words, though Richmond thematically supersedes Margaret as the Nemesis figure, dramatically the last act recapitulates the salient features of her world-theater: strictly sequential, reactive, depersonalized, boasting off-stage authority, asserting no intrinsic force or presence. Such drama depends upon the validity of an orthodox context of belief; it would cast *us* as upholders of such a convention, repositories of its authority. If we are even half-willing to play such a role, it must be because Richard as a credible dramatic force has failed. The paralysis of his waking soliloquy shows this. It is not just that he suffers despair, but that he has no means to express his terror other than the frantic manipulation of conventional tropes:

> What do I fear? Myself? There's none else by.
> Richard loves Richard: that is, I am I.

> Is there a murderer here? No. Yes, I am:
> Then fly. What, from myself? . . .
>
> (5. 3. 183–86)

His charismatic resurgence of energy in the end—his colorfully vicious oration and the dead-end heroics in battle—only underscores the way he has lapsed into the predetermined, the "historical" role as villain.

Richard's dramatic style, by which he remains invisible among his fellows, binds him to them as a parasite on shadows. For three acts he draws blank checks on our all-too-willing credulity. He "stays alive" theatrically so long as he does not succumb to that "historical" character that lies waiting for him like a net under an aerialist. We sustain him with our credulity, hoping that he will dance something new into being, trying to forget the dreary net beneath. The net is the orthodox providential structure of the play; Richard defies it and we cheer, but at last there is nowhere to go, no real risks have been taken and nothing new been produced, and it claims him. Curiously, the historical figure he becomes in his fall is a denial of history, at least of a meaning to history that Shakespeare has been seeking. His fall proclaims the triumph of the More-Holinshed-Tudor myth of history—of that monolithic image of the providence-driven past that Shakespeare has been resisting. Now it looks as if Shakespeare has, like Richard, been operating on the ghostyly Providence all along, as his secret security, and so has been binding his powers to it.[4]

Peter Brook, writing of Grotowski, states that "the act of performance is an act of sacrifice, of sacrificing what most men prefer to hide—this is [the actor's] gift to the spectator."[5] All the signs of such a sacrifice are in Richard's attitudes toward us—the seeming disclosure of original pain, the teasing possibility of a "moral sentience" that in defeat would make him tragic.[6] Like any actor, but magnified, Richard seems powerful because he seems to fetch some "terrific" energy from outside the play's fictional domain and his function in it. Such an "outside" is, paradoxically, an "inside"—an interior and independent "self" that sets him apart from his fictive fellows (to whom this "self" is a ghost, invisible), and that brings him thrusting directly into our presence, a delight and a menace. When it becomes clear that Richard's is only an illusion of such energy, that it is reflected from the fictive world he mocks, that he is its antitype, and that he has no reservoir of secret strength to spend in our presence—that "he" has never been among "us" at all—then he loses his privileged power of ghostliness and becomes an interesting dramatic fiction: netted, and now either edible or analyzable. And indeed, Richard's sacrificial gestures in our direction have been ruses; the parody of intercourse enacted with Anne has been enacted with us as well. He does offer, however, no small attraction—the fantasy (which we may share for a while) of ever-expanding power exercised from an ever-unbroached, unimplicated center, requiring no relinquishing of the gratified self. It is the child's Superman vision projected into a real political world (and no doubt the idea of the artist as superman tempted Shakespeare no less than Marlowe in the brave new theater world of the early 1590s). At the center sits a hypothetical "self," extending control through murderous performance, sustaining itself on our consenting credulity, meanwhile acting to cancel all bonds, to sedate all live engagement, to gather an emptied world all to himself to bustle in. When Richard does disintegrate he discloses no hidden "self," but a set of stunted potentialities: a lack of bustle. Nothing has been sacrificed, and nothing, no "self," created.

What of our role in all this? We are flattered perhaps to analyze our responses in terms of a double-gratification: we enjoy a moral holiday in Richard's antics, and then, William Toole writes, "as the play progresses this faculty [moral judgment] is reawakened and we find the appropriateness of what happens to Richard appealing to our moral instincts."[7] But I suspect our participation in the play is more complicated than this; that this is a kind of rationalized fiction of what really happens. The play inescapably mirrors its audience. The offer of a "sacrifice" by an actor to a spectator is obviously a two-way gesture, frightening as well as exhilarating to the spectator. Something is being required of us too, taken from us in exchange. At the most obvious level we are put under an obligation to think and feel in certain ways, to care, to pay attention, to keep a trust; our freedom is restricted, we are fixed and identified in a special relationship. More profoundly, it is likely that such an exchange in the theater activates its primitive powers to disturb us fundamentally. If we look we lose ourselves because we see something magical. Like Pentheus in *The Bacchae* we both want to look and are afraid, afraid perhaps that looking in itself will entail *our* sacrifice.[8]

We mirror Richard's sham sacrifice, his sham openness. As he pretends to reveal, we pretend to look, to protect what we see. The play becomes a screen where we and Richard are immensely pleased to enact a restricted fiction about history. We reflect his disengagement, his self-protectiveness; in the end, our cover blown, we are expelled from the fictional space, the place of spurious magic. But we leave secretly relieved, glad not to have been asked to be more deeply moved. On the other hand, neither have we been bedazzled by the claims of the theater, and we may be sorry after all to have gotten off so well intact. Richard's own refusal to relinquish control of the play's action has kept us, in turn, free of any real responsibility of feeling for him. When he does at last lose control, he does not gain new power, there is no release of energy (as in *Richard II*, or in any of the tragedies) because there has been nothing growing and seeking the sacrificial action. In the fantasy of control that we share with Richard and with the latent performing mode of the play lies a fear of being changed, of participation in the other, the Not-me. In this mode, the object of acting is to stop others' acting; to murder the bonds of breath as Richard instructs Buckingham to "murder thy breath in middle of a word."[9] Buckingham acts (in 3. 3) to conjure support from London crowds for the murder of Hastings. In truth *we* are the prize, to control us the object of the larger performance. But we are approached by a villain, the machiavel's instructor, smiling, with murder figured in his tongue: we must be sedated. Yet moral recoil is hardly warranted here, for we have shared in the process, playing our own self-protective, hence manipulating part, aggressive in our nodding passivity, refusing to mingle breath, to recreate; smiling back at the dancing clown while holding tight to our net.

7
Stalking "Strong Possession" in *King John*

King John is the "morning-after" play[1]—cautious, suspicious, coldly analytical. It opens vigorously enough—nothing like Richard's boldly knowing wink at the audience, but still, with John speaking in a naturally strong public voice that, say, York would admire in a king. But in private John suffers the nagging of his mother. Then he must adjudicate a quarrel between brothers, and while he waxes magisterial, one of those brothers—the Bastard—begins to swell and fill the stage with mocking, charismatic presence. The upshot is that though John acquires a loyal lieutenant to defend his "strong possession" of the crown, he has been upstaged. He exits, but the Bastard remains behind to expand in his new role of resident satirist. John's swift momentum, his bid to impose a shaping power upon the play, has been fatally interrupted.

The effect thereafter is of dissipated strength, a division of power into two centers, neither of which can last. John's force splatters against its opposition in Angiers; the Bastard maintains his antic vigor for two more acts, but then succumbs to the general collapse that overtakes virtually all aspects of the play. It is a play in which nothing seems able to take root. There are erratic patches of passion that have, indeed, made it occasionally attractive in the theater: the pathos of young Arthur, the histrionic grief of Constance, the feverish death of John, the patriotic fervor of the Bastard's late speeches.[2] But these are strained or gratuitous; they do not feed into the unreceptive body of the play nor grow out of it. Even most of the play's violence—and it is more fundamentally preoccupied with violence than *Richard III*—seems frozen under glass. Perhaps it is this sense of obstinacy, of Shakespeare's refusal to do what we know he could do with this material, that is so frustrating. Consider this burst of nostalgia that a nineteenth-century critic, Edward Rose, permitted himself after a patient demonstration of Shakespeare's improvement upon his source play, *The Troublesome Raigne of John:*

> Shakespeare has no doubt kept so closely to the lines of the older play because it was a favourite with his audience, and they had grown to accept its history as absolute fact; but one can hardly help thinking that, had he boldly thrown aside these trammels and taken John as his hero, his great central figure; had he analyzed and built up before us the mass of power, craft, passion, and devilry which made up the worst of the Plantagenets; had he dramatized the grand scene of the signing of the Charter, and shown vividly the gloom and horror which overhung the excommunicated land; had he painted John's last despairing struggles against rebels and invaders, as he has given us the fiery end of Macbeth's life—we might have had another Macbeth, another Richard, who would by his terrible personality have welded the play together, and carried us along breathless through his scenes of successive victory and defeat.[3]

Rose's frustration is understandable. After *Richard III*'s confident, swaggering assertiveness, the brilliant clarity of its presentation, *King John* may indeed seem to suffer from a failure of nerve. Yet the diagnosis will not hold up. Rose, like many other critics, is surely wrong in assuming that Shakespeare would have felt fettered either by the old play, by "history," or by his audience's presumed tastes. He attributes too much authority to the reputation of TR (as *The Troublesome Raigne* is commonly known), forgets or did not know that Shakespeare had other sources for the life of John (which, however, he used only sparingly) and assumes, wrongly, that a monolithic view of John prevailed among Shakespeare's contemporaries.[4] In other words, Shakespeare surely had at least as much freedom with the John material as with that of the first tetralogy, and probably more. Indeed, as Rose reminds us, *King John* might easily have been another *Richard III* (though Rose in fact seems to take *Macbeth* as his real model). It may even seem remarkable that Shakespeare either neglected or refused this obvious opportunity, especially given the great popular success of *Richard III*. The fact is that in no other play does Shakespeare bind himself with such a dogged closeness to a source that is itself a play. That he *chose* such a course is clear;

therefore, the question must be why? What did he find in TR to answer to his needs of the moment?

The "moment," in retrospect, is the void between the two sets of historical tetralogies. The question is how to cross it, and the answer—in retrospect—turns out to be *King John.* Here, I think, is the trouble. In *Richard III* Shakespeare was beguiled by the sheer formal mastery that a strongly centralized king made possible. Through Richard he lights up the night of *Henry VI,* bringing the relief of form to the murky impulses and conflicts of those plays. But he gains the control by anesthetizing a desire for a deeper engagement of the audience—by fabricating a personality coherent only as an antitype of the providentialism it opposes. To use a term from *King John:* the relationship between play and audience, centered in Richard, is based upon a principle of mutual "commodity"—we feign engagement to keep from being truly engaged. Through Richard Shakespeare maintains a control that keeps us comfortably at a distance. What he finds he needs, the morning after the *Richard III* blowout, is a strongly centered play that, paradoxically, does not refuse to relinquish control. He needs to find or contrive a center where an authentic encounter between audience and play may be risked.

TR is the model Shakespeare clings to in order to cross the void without a relapse. Stoically, he accepts it as a grim substitute for the allure of *Richard III,* the temptation to resort to the hair of the dog that bit him. In holding to the old play Shakespeare thwarts his own manipulative tendencies, his natural impulse to overbear his limp material with exuberant reconstruction. In *Richard III* he had asserted "strong possession" by imposing a strongly theatrical personality. Now he deliberately splits the central power, not into contending halves like York and Henry VI, but into coordinate halves. In other words, he seizes upon TR's rather murky lack of a central figure as a positive opportunity to analyze the relationship between those powers that in Richard were overwhelmingly combined: the machiavellian and the antic, political power and dramatic power, power of will and power of consciousness, power of "land" and power of "presence."

In TR John's claim to heroism lies in his resistance to the Church, his weakness lies in his submission, and in the end he supposedly gains stature through his denunciations. Shakespeare neutralizes the antipapal material, leaving John without a polemical base from which to borrow his authority. Shakespeare also depolemicizes the issue of regal legitimacy, the question being not a legal one between "right" and "strong possession," but a dramatic one of what constitutes strong possession.[5] John's initial thunder to the French ambassador, asserting a shaping power that flows directly from his office, is quite new in the histories. But John lacks York's and Richard's special dramatic consciousness, their ability to stand apart and look upon experience playfully. John's is the power of the land; yet he has no consciousness to inform that power, to quicken and transform it into a power that we in the theater can share. Consequently when he goes to prove his claim, his "strong possession" dissipates like smoke. Unable to convey it, like an actor cut off from the part and from the audience, he has nothing but will to exert, exerts it with double vehemence, and so underscores his helplessness.

The Bastard, on the other hand, possesses just that dramatic self-consciousness that John pointedly lacks. The expansion of the Bastard's character is Shakespeare's most marked departure from TR. The expansion is formalized in the first scene when the Bastard, though winning the legal dispute with his brother, is offered the chance to forgo it all, acknowledge his Plantagenet blood, and rise "Lord of thy presence and no land beside" (1. 1. 37). Thereafter, besides endowing him with the antic mediator's self-delighting wit and dramatic consciousness, Shakespeare carefully generalizes his function, detaching him from specific historical situations and muting or eliminating personal motivations.[6] And unlike his counterpart in TR, he is not obsessed with his namesake, Richard I—neither overly impressed nor distressed by his bastardy, nor envious of his lost inheritance. Rather, his bastardy frees him to be "lord of thy presence" only, "and no land beside." To rise as Plantagenet *means* to be derived from outside the "times" he satirizes—that is, from the mythical offstage figure of Coeur-de-lion—but derived powerlessly, blessedly unimplicated in the contents of history and all the more at home on the stage itself. For nearly three acts he maintains this role, enjoying and conveying something of Richard III's exuberant freedom, but with little of Richard's thrusting aggressiveness, and none of the shaping power of a dispossessed machiavellian plotter.

From this split of the power center all else follows. Shakespeare seizes upon TR's tedious episodic sequence and sculpts the material into a distinctively two-part structure responsive to our perceptions. In the first part (acts 1–3) the action moves from England to the arena of international political gamesmanship in Angiers. Here the Bastard stands forth as the improviser. He soliloquizes, satirizes, comments chorically upon the mercilessly formal public proceedings. He humanizes the play by eliciting our more private and critical responses to this action, and helps us to penetrate its highly polished exterior. The second part of the play (acts 4 and 5) returns to England. The tone is private, nervous, confused. Formally, or in the collapse of form, this part presents the chaotic interior of the glassy postures assumed in the first part. Our perceptions and perspective have been disturbingly shifted inward; we see John in private as a writhing hysteric, and like the Bastard, who has conducted us into this strange inner domain, we may lose our way. The Bastard is desperate to locate a center in a formless world. But the illusion and facile comforts of a sturdy center are just what this play refuses. The "indigest" that he strives valiantly to set some form upon is too profound.

In TR the "indigest" is inadvertent. But then TR takes its own polemical plot at face value and expects its audience to do so, too. Shakespeare, on the other hand, does everything to make us see plot as a kind of screen upon which shadows of real motivations, real issues, are projected. This is a matter of style. For although Shakespeare follows TR's sequence of incidents very closely, in fact he lifts only one line verbatim from the older play.[7] This careful transformation of the verbal texture serves to heighten the discontinuities between form and feeling and between public and private experience. In the first half of the play, the most extravagantly polished public style becomes increasingly helpless to shape or disguise the chaos—or the lust for chaos—that sits inside all the public postures like some vicious animal inside a cage, biding its inevitable release. Indeed, the most artful style can do nothing but bring on the moment of its release. Late in the day King Philip appeals to Cardinal Pandulph to "devise, ordain, impose / Some gentle order" upon the mess he has helped make (3. 1. 250–51). In other words, he begs the Cardinal to *perform* a way out of the cynically solemn oath of alliance he has just grandly sworn with John (and by which he had forsworn his earlier oath to Arthur and Constance). Pandulph's superbly impenetrable casuistry easily does the trick—but the point is, it is a stylistic trick before it is a philosophical one. And it is precisely the powder-dry sophistication of his argument (253–97) that licenses the savagery of the war that follows Philip's new oath-breaking. But then, by this late point in the long Angiers day, it has become clear that the most formal pretensions of language are not so much a covering as a version of the bloodlust they strain to express. "France," pants John,

> I am burned up with inflaming wrath,
> A rage whose heat hath this condition,
> That nothing can allay, nothing but blood,
> The blood, and dearest-valued blood, of France.
> (3. 1. 340–43)

And Blanch, new-made bride, fresh from her sacrificial political wedding, solemnized by heartfelt vows and the best Petrarchan conceits, can only gasp to her new husband: "Upon thy wedding-day? / Against the blood that thou hast marriѐd?" (300–301).

> The sun's o'ercast with blood. Fair day, adieu!
> Which is the side that I must go withal?
> I am with both. Each army hath a hand,
> And in their rage, I having hold of both,
> They whirl asunder and dismember me.
> (326–30)

No one but Blanch laments or even notices her dismemberment. Her little fate is swallowed by the large and indiscriminating war lust that smokes behind the formal confrontations at Angiers. John had warned the Ambassador that his "strong possession" would be voiced by his cannon. Indeed, his voice *is* his cannonshot. There is no language by which to assert and gain "strong possession" except that of cannon. John comes literally to speak destruction. Whose does not really matter, it is the self-assertive act that matters. To possess is to destroy.

Not surprisingly, the language of possession and destruction is that of rape. The object of the rape is not important since what one possesses through sexual self-assertion is ultimately oneself; but Renaissance psychology understood very well what a waste of spirit, how self-defeating, such a pursuit of selfhood is. The rival kings' language of cannonshot and rape expresses a lust, but it does not express or distinguish the kings themselves. Take John's appeal to the Citizen of Angiers, where the city is cast as a maiden threatened by the savage French, and John as her protector. The French, he says,

> Have hither marched to your endamagement.
> The cannons have *their bowels* full of wrath,
> And ready mounted are *they* to spit forth
> *Their iron indignation* 'gainst your walls.
> All preparation for a bloody seige
> And merciless proceeding *by these French*
> Comforts *your city's eyes, your winking gates,*
> And but for our approach *those sleeping stones,*
> That *as a waist* doth girdle you about,
> By the compulsion of *their ordinance*
> By this time from their fixèd *beds of lime*
> Had been *dishabited,* and wide havoc made
> For *bloody power* to rush upon *your peace.*
> (2. 1. 209–21, my italics)[8]

The slippery personification continues with the "city's threat'ned cheeks," "a shaking fever in your walls," and "calm words folded up in smoke, / To make a faithless error in your ears." John's speech makes Angiers a maiden, but one already jumbled and dismembered. Is the violence here John's, or an accident of the conventional style he employs? The rhetorical strategy is to threaten while offering safety, but how "playfully" is it used? Where does the libidinal desire for destruction lodge—in the speaker or in the social code he speaks in? The effect is of menace loosed, unrooted in personality. Philip's more sanctimonious speech is less sinister only because it is less playful, its libidinal appetite expressed through a simpler mechanism of displacement:

> And then our arms, like to a muzzled bear,
> Save in aspect, hath all offense sealed up.
> Our cannons' malice vainly shall be spent
> Against th' invulnerable clouds of heaven,
> And with a blessèd and unvexed retire,
> With unhacked swords and helmets all unbruised,
> We will bear home that lusty blood again
> Which here we came to spout against your town,
> And leave your children, wives, and you, in peace.
> (2. 1. 249–57)

Despite the difference in style, what we hear beneath the highly polished rhetoric—and hear it doubled—is a persistent grating lust for violence and blood. But no consciousness bridges the lust and the language: it is not John's will, nor Philip's, that is expressed, but something far more general and impersonal that possesses *them* as they manipulate the verbal conventions of sex and war. When language is a version of cannonshot—and both words and shot are regularly said to be discharged from "mouths" in this scene—it fails to distinguish the speaker. And indeed, aloofly overlooking his suitors, the Citizen finds nothing to choose between the two rival claimants to "strong possession":

> Blood hath bought blood, and blows have answered blows,
> Strength matched with strength, and power confronted power.
> Both are alike, and both alike we like.
>
> (2. 1. 329–31)

The setting intensifies the dream-dissociations of the action.[9] The Angiers day drones on and on beneath the Angiers sun. "Angiers" is really a formal space, like the stage itself, and the struggle to possess this space is fraught with menacing ambiguities and reversals. On one hand the surreal clarity of the Angiers action serves to heighten the contrasts, bringing forth shadowed intentions vividly. On the other hand, the studied formality of opposition, the intense artificiality, produces a hypnotic effect. Both the heightening and the hypnosis are effects potential in any drama, but here our attention is channeled in these conflicting directions by two onstage mediators. The Bastard has maintained a drumbeat of satire varying from outright scorn for Austria to mocking admiration of the kings, including John:

> Ha, majesty! How high thy glory towers
> When the rich blood of kings is set on fire!
>
> (2. 1. 350–51)

Opposite the Bastard stands the Citizen of Angiers,[10] equally detached, certainly neutral, seemingly passive in his stance, and respectful of the proceedings. The Bastard pulls us back from the debate, urging us to observe the style of kings. But the Citizen is soberly attentive, absorbed in the issues, peering into the debate for its intrinsic significance. He mirrors that part of our attention hypnotized by the conflict; the Bastard mirrors our critical faculties. Both are detached, but one is anonymous, respectful of the conventions of public rhetoric, the other, though loyal to his king, a maverick and cynic.

Given that balance—rather comfortable to us as theatergoers—consider the effect when one of our onstage surrogates turns on the other. The Citizen has refused to distinguish between the kings; stymied, smoking with frustration, they can only think of returning to combat. We laugh in our detachment: the kings are trapped in the absurd frame of the onstage fiction they have created. Then the Bastard steps forward:

> By heaven, these scroyles of Angiers flout you, kings,
> And stand securely on their battlements
> As in a theatre, whence they gape and point
> At your industrious scenes and acts of death.
>
> (2. 1. 373–76)

Suddenly the Citizen-judge looks naked, his solemn robes collapsed about his ankles. Heads turn toward him darkly, with new awareness. Why (continues the Bastard) should the kings not join forces to "brawl down" the "flinty ribs of this contemptuous city"—and then afterwards fight it out for mastery? He spells out the kings' aggression, releases it from its conventional trappings and aims it at the city, the maidenly city, directly. Indeed, what *do* they really care whom they rape and dismember? In the Bastard's words they hear their underlying wills legitimized as "something of the policy," the invitation to violent release as a game: "I'd play incessantly upon these jades, / Even till unfencèd desolation / Leave them as naked as the vulgar air" (385–87). The kings are like children, delighted: they will "lay this Angiers even with the ground, / Then after fight who shall be king of it" (399–400).

At the bottom of "policy" lies this vortex of self-consuming energy. This is the historical will, possessing those who would possess it. It makes puppets of heroes, helpless boys of strongest men; but here, the Bastard half-inadvertently exposes a demented cackling child inside a war machine. And yet, the moment of exposure itself is exhilarating, as is any moment when the theater suddenly discovers itself. The Citizen has been flushed out of his spurious idealism; the wrath of the royal actors, trapped in their vicious cycle of "industrious scenes and acts of death," spills over to threaten the detached observer; the field of play is abruptly widened. The Bastard beams: he sees the battle to come, the more anarchic the better, as a fresh resolution of diplomatic hypocrisies.

But in his aggression upon the Citizen, the Bastard also attacks *us* in our security and detachment, our passive credulity, our sedated attention to the glossy surface of the formal action of Angiers. Now, within the onstage fiction, the Citizen responds to this aggression by a kind of diplomatic violence of his own: in place of attack, he proposes a cynical wedding match, which is cynically accepted.[11] But how can we, as offstage audience, respond to this new kind of violence by the Bastard? Only, I think, by growing sharper, less passive in our attention; only by refusing to credit the stage image, the fiction of kings contending over issues of honor and legitimacy. We respond through a quickened perceptiveness, a coming-alive in the theater. We break our attention away from the hypnotic formal surface; returned, we thrust, we penetrate, forcing what lies inarticulate behind the smooth-faced rhetorical surface to show itself; to speak to us. Through the awakened sharpness of our attention we demand to know what is going on *inside*.

In other words, we repudiate the Citizen's share in us, and with his neutrality goes our comfortably balanced perspectives of credulity and detachment. We become now openly dependent on the Bastard, just when he himself is thrown off-balance and into consternation by the giddy dismembering events that follow. In his famous soliloquy ("Mad world! Mad kings! Mad composition!" 2. 1. 561 ff), taking a breather, groping for balance, the Bastard finds a name for the spirit of Angiers; lovingly, gratefully he mouths the word that, because it is discovered *outside* the general parlance, temporarily keeps him free and poised as a shaper and satirist. "Commodity" is a solid word for a swiftly widening whirlwind, and the Bastard invokes it magically. But its inadequacy is forgone. The soliloquy, at midday, movingly demonstrates his deepened character, just because he knows he is losing his easy independence, even as he grabs for a cynical role by which to assert it. By the end of the day—after the wedding, after Constance's implacable hysteria of betrayal, after Pandulph's ruthless sophistry and Philip's second pious treachery, after the whole atrocious day at last dissolves into its orgy of blood-letting—"A wicked day, and not a holy day! / What hath this day deserved?" (3. 1. 83–84)—in the end, the Bastard is pulled into the centripetal center of chaos. "Now, by my life, this day grows wondrous hot. / Some airy devil hovers in the sky / And pours down mischief" (3. 2. 1–3). We have had the last of the antic satirist, securely centered in his own strong "presence." We are on our own.

By every public standard we have been offered, John's victory, the result of a speed and force that even his enemies acknowledge with awe (3. 4. 11–14), establishes his strong possession. But precisely in the flush of triumph Shakespeare conducts our gaze right through it. The Bastard is dispatched to England to ransack monasteries. In TR this mission becomes the burden of the scene, and indeed we follow him into a long comic action where he uproots a nun and a monk from each other's closets. In Shakespeare, the focus (which is to say our gaze) settles on John; the antipapist business is so much public image-mongering, carried on remote from the center of feeling. Shakespeare, indeed, finds the focus in response to our critical attention. The sudden revelation of John comes as if a rock had been sharply cracked open by the pressure of our gaze. It is our first revenge upon the smooth hypnotic surface of Angiers. Quite suddenly, all the public issues with which the play seemed so concerned up to now have become superficial, as if conducted all this while by a dummy-king, the real king only now coming into view in his secretive seduction of Hubert. John wants Arthur dead; the boy is a political threat. What comes through in the seduction, however, is not machiavellian policy, but something in excess of political needs, discontinuous with public plotting. John employs a sidewise lover's language. Crafty-shy of speaking, he presses his desires upon Hubert with a heavy-sighing wordy wordlessness. As a machiavellian he tries to convey and conceal his intentions simultaneously. But there is something else at work not nearly so well controlled—a leaking of personality. John seems on the edge of hysteria, full of nervous energy, first overextending himself, then seeking to cancel intimacy even as he utters it—to circumscribe the self, hold it back from discovery. What causes this strange behavior? The pressure of our attention feeds John's nervousness and elicits both this lurid exposure and the reflex attempt to cover it up. The emotional energy spent here exceeds its original motivation; motivation must be found to contain the energy. It is therefore improvised in the form of a seduction to murder a harmless child.[12]

The play's second part opens out from that scene. John returns to England, publically strong, but the real action is interior; we are aware of being in touch with the increasingly chaotic personality in the center of that public edifice. The sense of collapse extends outward from John to the play itself, as if time, held so archly at bay in Part 1, were taking its revenge upon the false formalities of the Angiers action. In another sense we are the aggressors, taking our revenge in Part 2 for the intolerable mode of drama in Part 1. There we endured as public theater-goers, our perspective arrested through five long public scenes (with breaks provided by the Bastard's monologues). The action in Part 2 is distributed over ten restless and irregular scenes: the settings shift rapidly, the rhetorical level fluctuates wildly, the business becomes increasingly frantic and futile.[13] Rather than sit as spectators to a public show, we wander within the public domain, which we discover rotting from the inside out. We overhear private confessions and desperate strategies; hear reports of incursions upon the ramparts; witness distracted efforts to publish an official image of vigor to the world. When the Bastard returns to the play in 4. 2 it is already in shambles and he feels himself a stranger within a collapsing body politic. "Commodity" is too robust an explanation for the kind of feverish self-destruction he encounters now, and he almost yields to despair. Yet he agrees to be John's public relations man, to represent him to peers and to enemy invaders as "strong."

But before he returns, the crucial scene of the play occurs. Young Arthur persuades Hubert, his one friend in the world, not to torture and murder him (4. 1). This is the play's central scene because it is the most private, the most naked one. Shakespeare has utterly depoliticized it. Arthur is a boy with no interest in the crown, rather than a young man posing a real threat as in TR, and he dissuades Hubert, not through logical argument, but strictly by an appeal to his sense of horror and pity.[14] In other words, the intimacy is a further stage in the emotional penetration begun in the seduction scene. There John's political motives seemed only distantly related to the seduction. But here those motives are wholly dissociated. The full emphasis falls upon the sheer gratuitous attempt to blind the boy with red-hot irons; even the intent to follow up with murder fades from view.

All the play's generalized violence condenses here into the all-too-particular form of a virtual rape. Arthur piteously pleads his love of Hubert; the fierce hot irons are repeatedly invoked against the boyish innocence and vulnerability, the delicacy, of Arthur's eyes. Here the reified images from Angiers—the cannons' "iron indignation" and the "winking eyes" of the maidenly city's gates—have become excruciatingly literal. And Arthur struggles in the only way available to him, by talking as much and as fast as he can, to waken Hubert's pity. The point is that Hubert is unable to do the deed not because Arthur's arguments carry weight as arguments, but precisely because they force him to see the deed as simply too heinous, too physical, too real. And Hubert's recoil is our own. The apparatus of fire, poker, chair, and Hubert's repeated thrustings, only to be thwarted by the sight and sound of Arthur, all make the scene, though bordering on melodrama, pathetic and potent. And if not played sentimentally—that is, histrionically—and if Arthur's speech is uttered not decoratively, but as a life- and eye-saving strategy, then the scene in the theater will have us squirming. We might remember how *Richard III* maneuvers to distance us from the pathetic murder of the boys by framing it in a twice-removed and mannered monologue by a minor character. *Richard III* refuses to offer or risk such an intimacy. Here, in *King John,* we find ourselves looking on at the most nakedly private encounter of the play, and unless our presence here is justified by our sympathy, we will be here either as voyeurs or as mockers. Both we and the play (its actors) are on the line here, joined in a complex moment. This is the rape, the outrage that underlies the diplomatic diffusions and reifications of the earlier scenes. Our revenge on those scenes has been to elicit this view of the interior. The violence is located because we have come to understand it, and partly because it *is* located it can, for the one time in the play, be refused.

The refusal is the rub. I said earlier that the patches of passion in *King John,* and preeminently in this scene, found no rooting in the play's general ground, and in turn were unable to nourish such a ground. We are likely then to be embarrassed by these self-declaring shows of feeling. But such embarrassment may accurately reflect the internal chaos we have uncovered. For Hubert's humane refusal of violence not only seems to count for nothing in the play—Arthur goes on to kill himself in a pathetic attempt to run away—but in his attempt to integrate his action into the weave of John's dodges and deceits Hubert only contributes to the tangle. What is more, the impulse vanishes in the confusion—it bears no consequence, even in terms of a sweetening or deepening of Hubert's character. At most we are aware of something lost, as the Bastard is in seeing Hubert lift the body of Arthur: "How easy dost thou take all England up!" (4. 3. 142). Arthur has never remotely been "all England," but nothing else fits the Bastard's strong but obscure pain of loss. From uncertain sources (indeed, from us, if he could only know) an incursion has been made into this "England"; from the breach lifeblood, vitality, flood out like chaos.[15]

"History" in *Henry VI* is a tide of time swallowing even the most assertive of characters, those who would shape it in their own image. In *Richard III* Richard himself controls this time: he is Mercury speeding the king's execution order upon Clarence, and he is the cripple bearing the countermand tardily. Sequence is that of *his* plot, the materialization of his wishes. He energetically imposes his temporal ordering upon the wider world of the city and the realm, and thence upon that of his audience. But then his decline is manifested as a dissociation of time from himself. Henry Tudor, the fixed future, approaches like a clock striking (4. 1) and the play begins running to its conclusions impatiently, without waiting for Richard to resolve things. The sense of headlong impatience, of mechanical plot taking over, is the image of *our* impatience; the play reflects us. Time, dissociated from Richard, becomes "history" since without Richard there is nothing else for it to be. And "history" turns out to be the triumph of the very providential structure of time whose debunking Richard has thrived on.

King John refuses the providential structure of time, the prefabricated system whose negation might serve as the play's dramatic structure. Shakespeare allows his public material to collapse in order to probe in its rubble for a means of transformation from the inside out. He seeks an internal rhythm of time, rooted in sentience, that might offer some authentic dramatic resistance. Following the privacy of the torture scene we feel waves of disintegration breaking outward into the public domain of the play. The "lily-gilding" scene (4. 2)—the longest, busiest, most superbly wrought—comes at once: here, as Honigmann observes, "practically the whole span of John's reign [is] crammed into one scene and made to appear simultaneous, for the dramatic advantage of heaping up John's troubles and omens of misfortune."[16] Everything here happens in frantic excess. John is crowned for a second time, to strengthen his "possession," though as his fretful peers point out in gilded-lily speeches, the act only makes any claim to authority seem arbitrary. Hubert enters twice and is dispatched twice; there are two reports of rumors and disquiet over the news of Arthur's death; that news is both reported and rescinded; there is news of Lewis's invasion and of the deaths of both Constance and John's mother. Through all this John's moods and reactions vacillate wildly as he seeks out a "policy" through which to recenter himself. But it is plain that policy is self-defeating now; the harder he tries, the more swiftly he undermines himself.

When he hears that "the copy of your speed is learned" by Lewis, and that his mother is dead, John cries out:

> Withhold thy speed, dreadful occasion!
> O make a league with me, till I have pleased
> My discontented peers.
>
> (4. 2. 125–27)

Time is no longer his to command; indeed, having been squandered in the Angiers action, it now turns on him savagely. "Five moons were seen to-night" (182)—all is out of order; above all, *sequence* is undone. There is no stately mechanical tolling of the clock of Providential reprisal as in *Richard III*. Rather, it is as if some central dispatching system had broken down and John finds himself in the middle of a ludicrous pile-up of rush-hour traffic. The scene is a frenzied action of comings-and-goings, only John on stage throughout. And it is, strangely enough, his best scene. It fulfills the earlier hints of a morbidly interesting character beneath the crush of conventional heroic posturing. In his seduction of Hubert he gave off a strong whiff of excessive nervous energy, as of a character rotting away, without sufficient motive for the spending-off: the order to blind the boy before killing him was an arbitrary attempt to give form to this motiveless energy of decomposition. Likewise, in the lily-gilding scene John is charismatic as a comic victim because under the absurdly uneven odds he simply breaks apart, fails to cohere, to show himself as anything other than a bundle of commodity-driven reactions to the assaults of "dreadful occasion." While he disintegrates in his frenzied dodges, twists, and turns, his rapid succession of postures and voices, his attempts at machiavellian manipulation, accommodation, assertions of "policy," he glows with a terrific nervous energy. An hysterical antic, he runs through his actorly arsenal of effects at top speed, discarding them with each new assault, finding none to sustain him, none with which to resist the implacable tide.

The scene gives splendid form to a cascade of disintegration similar to that in the *Henry VI* plays, but with more compressed and rousing energy. We must feel that John reveals and exhausts himself completely; that he has physically performed his way through every effect at his disposal without finding an answering form, a center of self-knowing sentience to resist the wild undoing of form. Thus, the suddenness of his decline and death in act 5 really follows with wonderful logic from this scene. Shakespeare is often criticized for failing to motivate the poisoning, whereas in TR it is elaborately staged and explained in the context of the anti-Rome material. But in Shakespeare the point is surely the leaking of vitality itself. An organism fails to find the means, in its actions, to recreate itself: it wastes away. Fever has been in John's blood from the beginning; he has not been able to arrest or shape its course through the play of consciousness. Clearly the fever is time itself, located, for the first time in the histories, literally as an internal organic process.

After this scene, if anywhere, Shakespeare might have intervened with an answering form, like the resurgent providential structure in *Richard III*. He does not; the very plot and movement decline into a giddy "indigest" before a form is set on it in the end. The emphasis meanwhile falls on the sense of a loss too dire for a credible recovery. The collapse of specious form—specious presence—in Angiers yields above all negative form and negative presence. By this I mean that we experience centerlessness in Part 2, as does the Bastard, giddy and amazed, when he tries to locate the sense of loss in Arthur's corpse:

I am amazed, methinks, and lose my way
Among the thorns and dangers of this world.
How easy dost thou take all England up!
From forth this morsel of dead royalty
The life, the right and truth of all this realm
Is fled to heaven, and England now is left
To tug and scamble and to part by th' teeth
The unowed interest of proud swelling state.

(4. 3.140–47)

All of the second part of the play is marked by what is not there: the Bastard's antic wit, Arthur, all the women. This last omission is a curious feature. The two mothers die, Blanch simply vanishes. To be sure, the play is quite barren of women or of the feminine from the first—self-denying Blanch is just the obverse of the overbearing mothers—but even these traces are washed away by the time Part 2 emerges from Part 1. Constance's last tirade has been a curse on every male around for cowardice, brutality, treachery, and (by implication) the obscene expenditure of manhood. Lewis, his bride "dismembered" by the war, bleakly sums up the exhaustion following the expense of spirit in this waste of shame:

There's nothing in this world can make me joy.
Life is as tedious as a twice-told tale,
Vexing the dull ear of a drowsy man,
And bitter shame hath spoiled the sweet world's taste,
That it yields nought but shame and bitterness.

(3. 4. 107–11)

The rape of Arthur would have been a natural extension of this mood: easier to do it than not to (and there *is* no good machiavellian reason) until Hubert's pity is aroused.

But neither Arthur nor the women are central to the play. The betrayal, dismemberment, and rape are better realized than are the victims themselves. Arthur speaks a uniquely moving language in the torture scene, and yet in the play at large it is allowed to count for very little. Like Blanch, Arthur is self-ciphering—he wishes, early on, that he were "low laid in my grave. / I am not worth this coil that's made for me" (2. 1. 164–65)—and of course he fulfills that wish soon enough. Like Blanch he suggests, but with a meekness, a ghostliness that flirts with the ludicrous, his own alternative to the "bias" of a giddy centerless world, that all-changing commodity.

What *is* sacrificed in Arthur is an opportunity to value something ineffable, someone uniquely *not* self-serving, self-interested; an opportunity to commit oneself with no guarantee or even likelihood of a profitable return. Through such a hazardous commitment, the willingness to exchange oneself with an object not in itself obviously valuable, comes the possibility of a quickening. Hubert provides the paradigm, coming alive through his compassionate valuing of Arthur, even in the sacrifice of his "interests." But in the chaos of the play the real sacrifice is just this exchange itself, this quickening, this possibility of renewal. Hubert's act, though inadequate, declares the need and desire for a sacrifice that *is* adequate. Later, when the Bastard tries to transform Arthur's body into the symbolic center of an enlarged idea of "England," the effort itself, however expressive, dulls the Bastard's character. He loses the advantage of antic-equipoise, skeptical detachment, without gaining a clear or functional new character. He loses lordship of his "presence" without taking up potent residence as lord of the "land." Thereafter he can really only play, without much sense of commitment, the vague official voice of an officially reconstituted realm.

But between his "brave" of Lewis in 5. 2 and his submission to Prince Henry in the end, the Bastard is thrust forward in a quirky little scene where Shakespeare seems to focus precisely on the moment of self-diffusion. The scene (5.6) is preternaturally still, catching the Bastard as if by surprise in a private moment laden with the possibility of revelation. It all recalls the "dark glass" that A. P. Rossiter sees as the history plays generally: "The mystery beneath the surface of the magic mirror with its shows of kings is chill and deeply saddening."[17] Hubert has found the Bastard wandering "in the black brow of night," "half my power . . . taken by the tide." In groping recognition he is asked who he is and replies, "Who thou wilt"—and only then rather bitterly proceeds to claim his known, public identity. The scene is marked in this play by the plainness of its language and the pained reluctance of its approach to the public world. It catches the momentary sense of a nameless loss and a revulsion from the mechanisms of Providence and Order that are to be endorsed the next morning. Told by Hubert that "the lords are all come back" and that someone called "Prince Henry" has materialized, the Bastard's only acknowledgement is oblique. "Withhold thine indignation, mighty heaven, / And tempt us not to bear above our power!" (37–38). Something else preoccupies him, almost wonderfully, as if he had been on the edge of a vision:

> I'll tell thee, Hubert, half my power this night,
> Passing these flats, are taken by the tide.
> These Lincoln Washes have devourèd them.
> Myself, well mounted, hardly have escaped.
>
> (5. 6. 39–42)

For a moment he stares, as if to pierce the dark and arrive there at the meaning of these intimations. He must stare at us, without seeing us but perhaps feeling the intense return of our attention. He is feeling his own nakedness reflected by the stage and is darkly urged toward the relinquishing of himself to an unseen presence. He had assumed the stage in act 1 as its resident satirist, confiding in and guiding us with effortless éclat. But he had lost his detachment, become immersed (as *Lord Jim*'s Stein would say) in the dream of reality, the fiction of the play. And now in the heart of that fiction he stands on the edge of the void, sensing a theatrical intimacy far beyond that which binds a satirist to his audience. But he turns back. He has no choice—there is nothing left in him with which to make the leap in the void—and in this play there is no time to follow up these obscure promptings. "Away before," he bids Hubert, "conduct me to the king."

This ends the bright hopes—ours and perhaps Shakespeare's—roused by the character of the Bastard. New-made, nonhistorical, he was Shakespeare's most carefully poised and lovingly articulated mediator-figure yet—a parodist without heavy armor against involvement, a vigorous shaper of the historical matter, without the lust to possess it. He is the chance—the desire—to transform this mean and sodden stuff, and he fails. It overwhelms him. And so he must fail, given the conditions of his genesis. Shakespeare brutally flays his material in this play, and neither John as a character nor the story-stuff of *The Troublesome Raigne* can sustain the abuse, absorb it, and return it recreated. The Bastard can neither maintain John himself, nor join the assault by seizing John's power. For he is not ambitious for power, only for life and life-allowing form. He *is* the antic element split off from the machiavellian love of power, and it is only the machiavel who is able to sustain a plot long and complex enough to admit the possibility of gratifying form. The Bastard can crack open a deadly structure, as he does with his "wild counsel" in Angiers, or he can impose a temporary form upon incoherent materials, as he does in the end, but he cannot possess the center of the play and positively reform it.

I assume that after *Richard III* Shakespeare turned aside, for a short while, from his histories, to concentrate on other, less starkly ironic forms: sonnets and narrative poems, *Romeo and Juliet, Love's Labor's Lost,* maybe *A Midsummer Night's Dream,* and possibly other early comedies.[18] In this period he gains the craft, the knowledge, the supple ways and marvelous intuitions that make for generative drama, occasions of transformative theatrical power. His desire to transform his intransigent historical materials reasserts itself. It also reawakens his revulsion, and so in turn underscores the need to find a way to deliver over this besotted material, truly, as generative theater. Surely the "way" is not to recapitulate *Richard III:* no longer can he be content to exuberantly expose the passive violence of the historical will, to mock it down through parody. Parody, of course, is a vital *part* of the way: *King John* is, first of all, a parody of TR. But the Bastard, in the ambiguity of his status, expresses the ambiguities of feeling and form that Shakespeare does not seem eager to suppress—a strong theatrical force where Shakespeare distrusts such force, a loyal partisan where Shakespeare distrusts such feelings: a strong character, but incomplete, and in the late acts uncentered, floundering—above all, expressing the downright need for vulnerability and sacrifice.

Shakespeare knows by now that if he is to elicit new life from the materials of history he must engage a dramatic mode radically different from the manipulative, self-protective mode of the history plays up to this moment. *King John* is therefore a "holding action," the necessary middle of a process, incomplete and destined to be wasted in the process. The need it expresses cannot be summed up in the choral pieties of the last scene. It is not a need for national integrity, much less the need that an ideal ("right") prevail over a reality ("strong possession") as the basis for such integrity. Rather, the play expresses the need for transforming the meaning of "strong possession" from its narrow political significance to an embracing theatrical significance. The question, in other words, is how to "possess" the theatrical occasion and all of us that make it up, "strongly." The political idea of "strong possession" depends upon the stifling of circulation, the dissociation of blood from consciousness, in which case the blood remains brute and ruling, running in ever-tightening circles toward self-exhaustion, while consciousness remains decorative, or at best merely satirical. We have witnessed this pattern of dissociation repeatedly in the *Henry VI* plays and have seen the cul-de-sac it comes to in *Richard III.* But the theatrical idea of "strong possession" depends on the integration of the vital elements. Consciousness quickens blood, blood embodies consciousness, the circulation widens to include the audience in the enlarged and lively field of play.

King John is unable to make this transformation, but the play makes it possible and clearly foreshadows it. The tone of the ending registers quite a delicate awareness of the audience. In the last scene the Bastard arrives grim and breathless with the news of his forces lost in the Lincoln Washes and Lewis raging at his heels. He finds John dying, Pandulph "within at rest," having already arranged a peace with Lewis, and all the doubly forsworn rebel peers, their lilies thrice gilded, rallied around the young Prince Henry (the child-figure resurrected from Arthur, according to Honigmann) who, we are told, is "born / To set a form upon that indigest / Which [John] hath left so shapeless and so rude" (5. 7. 25–27). Miraculous legitimacy: a form of sorts is indeed "set" upon the indigest, rather than growing out of it. The Bastard kneels, leads the company in an oath of fealty to the new king, and closes out the whole with the choric speech often cited as the showcase of Shakespeare's patriotic poetry:

> This England never did, nor never shall,
> Lie at the proud foot of a conqueror
> But when it first did help to wound itself. . . .
>
> (112–14)

Considering how mercilessly this play has dealt with the public postures this ending so blandly assumes, it is remarkably persuasive. Shakespeare knew how over-eager we are to participate in a ritual of resolution, a show of healing harmony. A play, especially one so bleakly angry, is an exhausting experience. Even in the comedies that offer recreative enlargements of experience, festive resolutions grown authentically out of the woods of the play, Shakespeare chooses to remind us in the end of the costs of such resolution. Always he appeals to our memory of the play's experience, as against a too-easy desire to participate in an ending. This in the comedies; how much more necessary in *King John?*

Bitter as the play is, its ending is only gently sardonic. As with the endings of the "problem comedies"—*The Merchant of Venice, Measure for Measure, All's Well That Ends Well*—*King John*'s allows us to believe in it if we must. Audiences and readers have done so for centuries, it seems. The point is that Shakespeare does not force an attitude. Already I think he is looking ahead, having given us a kind of voucher for another kind of play, one derived from the insights and debris of *King John*. The ending is an incomplete imaginative act, its feeling suspended, its form perfunctory, its language worked up for the occasion. Yet we come to it by way of a penetrating theatrical experience, one that has enlarged the play with our own empathetic presence. Therefore, in the incompleteness of the end, we can discern access to a new kind of acting, one that taps regenerative energies through a bold eagerness to spend, risk, waste the constituted self.

8
Sacrificial Energy in *Richard II*

The king improvises for his life, for "strong possession," but it is a deadly art. He is, in Shakespeare, the actors' actor, coming alive at the leading edge of the company's life, just where it dissolves into the void of our reception. What Michael Goldman calls the actor's strangeness, or terrificness, has to do with his ability to bridge that void, to present himself to us as of two worlds at once, *that* and *this, theirs* and *ours*. The king especially is strange and exhilarating, the most representative figure of his fictive world, yet its most treacherous. To be at home in the theater is to be a stranger in the fiction, a faker of the role of king, and to be found out. We perceive him coming toward us, stepping forth from among his fellows and inevitably drawing their attention to his falseness. When Richard II falls to the ground to tell sad stories of the death of kings—all murdered, he says, conceding no other way of being unkinged—his followers stand baffled not only by his suicidal withdrawal, but doubtless by their own rising hatred, too. For this king, whom they cannot understand, is pulling the center from their life. From that point forward, his own murder is inevitable; the only question is whether he can manifest himself among us, across the void to which he has committed himself, and over which there is no return.

The first Richard—the crooked one—asserts his strangeness from the beginning. It consists of his improvisational powers, his antic-ness, not of his machiavellian power to plot. The antic makes the machiavel credible to us. But when the machiavellian impulse overtakes the antic, when the play's world becomes valuable to him and he binds himself to it, he loses his antic strangeness. The world overcomes him, he sinks back into it, merely exhausted. He has not come across. In *King John* the Bastard stands apart for two acts, our antic mediator of the historical action. But then he thrusts his strangeness at us to counteract the sedative effects of the Angiers action; he wakes us, but loses himself in the thrust. John, meanwhile, his cover of "strong possession" blown by the very effort of securing it, wildly improvises his role as king. He flails, becomes a caricature of the bad actor, blindly clutching for the role, his body wracked with contortions of strangeness, of strong possession indeed. The theatrical tradition attests to the ambiguity of the death scene—it was one of the attractions of the role in the eighteenth and nineteenth centuries—gratifying but grotesque. King John is murdered not because he outraged the church but because he outraged the role. He gilded the lily, had himself twice crowned, and so advertised his strangeness. Yet he does not know himself, nor come across whole to us. The murder half redeems him, gives him his death scene, strongly weak, and leaves him forever unfocused between worlds—as freakish as the play of his name.

To assert actorly strangeness is to lose it. But there is no choice. The actor lives only in acting. How to improvise upon this condition is the only real question. In the king the polarities of the actor's bondage and freedom are intensified, and nowhere so radically as in *Richard II*. Richard III and the Bastard assert their antisocial selves and lose them. John acquires his, negatively, out of the rubble of the public action, but he does not command it. Richard II also acquires his strange selfhood, also out of the rubble of conventional reality. But he causes the collapse that reveals him, he draws his dramatic energy from the outrage committed against his fictive world. John clutches, revealing the chaos of himself inadvertently; Richard coolly (perhaps too coolly) orchestrates the conditions of his estrangement, hazarding all on a successful passage of the void. He would convert his death into a work of art, a tragic artifact.

The thrust toward self-revelation is the basic action of the play, repeated and refined till all its intrinsic ambiguities are uttered. In this movement *Richard II* clarifies *King John's* groping urge to manifest its inner life. The formality of the royal theater in the opening act resembles the spurious formality of the Angiers action that helplessly betrayed its basic self-destructiveness. But in *John* the impulse to self-destruction was generalized, centered in no one. In *Richard II* the splendid style of ritual theater is the image of Richard himself. When he throws down his warder, aborting the organized violence of the lists, he draws that violence to himself. It is an act comparable to the Bastard's fingering the anonymous Citizen, except that here Richard plays both the antic and the victim. The act identifies him as generator of the action. To be sure, his motive is shrouded; doubtless he acts self-protectively since presumably the joust, if continued, would weaken him politically; but the immediate effect of his spectacular show of authority is to turn all lights directly upon the king.

Stage center, Richard virtually forces everyone to admire the way he performs the role of king. He calls attention to his performance by deviating conspicuously from the ideal model (his grandfather, Edward III). He boasts extravagant powers, absurd autonomy; plays capriciously with the "breath of kings" till Gaunt tells him what is obvious, that the king's word, in itself, is impotent. Gratuitously Richard calls into question the grounds of his own authority, wakes the sleeping infant of peace (which he had said he wanted undisturbed) into a general suspicion and anger against himself. His actions go beyond obtuseness, beyond arrogance. To harrass Gaunt, his mainstay, and dispossess Bolingbroke, who like his father is willing to abide by forms he does not like until the forms themselves are smashed, is downright suicidal.[1]

The first two acts, then, present us with this strong sense of volitional collapse. Wilbur Sanders invokes D. H. Lawrence's dictum that for every murderer there is a "murderee" to explain the force of Richard's desire for self-destruction.[2] But we are not dealing with psychological aberration here, nor simply a desire to be victimized, or to seek refuge in a land of Grief from the responsibilities of reality; these motivations are schooled and contained by a more general and relentless logic of action. What happens to Richard personally also happens to the play. The movement from the first two acts to the last three (which repeats a similar movement in *King John,* now better understood, better dramatized) constitutes an emergence from an unconscious to a conscious process of self-destruction. This emergence is acted out through Richard's own fall into time and hence into consciousness of mortality. It is also acted out through the stylistic shift of the play from what A. P. Rossiter calls the "heavily overwritten Elizabethan High-Renaissance manner" of the first two acts, into the far suppler, more sensitive and probing—and more engaging—mode of the last three.[3] Richard's and the play's emergence into self-consciousness are parts of the same general action, mirroring functions of each other. In the first part of the play Richard is the Uncreated King, alive chiefly in terms of conventions, historical and verbal, that constitute his world. Willful destruction of these conventions forces him into self-creating activity. In turn, the birth of his "personal" self in act 3—which is to say, the beginning of his true mortality—is answered by the emergence of an increasingly realistic political world, constituted by the characters who inhabit it rather than by dramatic fiat according to a superior model.

King John lost the ordering of the present time and was mercilessly crushed by a chaos of time. But Richard willfully offends time, openly provoking time's revenge. "For how art thou a king / But by fair sequence and succession?" pleads York, deploring Richard's rape of Bolingbroke's inheritance and hereditary identity. "Let not to-morrow then ensue to-day; / Be not thyself" (2. 1. 197–98). Richard manifestly assaults himself by assaulting others—that is, in his vain, silly, brutal, wasteful, and destructive actions we feel a tenacious will working to come free of all predefining constraints. The interruption of the joust was essentially a declaration against fair sequence and succession—Richard declaring the end of the natural processes of time, and appropriating time itself as an artifact of his will. The response to this outrage is, ironically, the evidence of his success. While it served fair sequence, the power of the king's breath was granted: Mowbray and Bolingbroke would risk their lives in its recognition, Gaunt would pointedly uphold it (1. 2). But once fair sequence is smashed, Richard is mocked for assuming the breath of kings. Once asserted, the power is implicitly denied (as Gaunt denies Richard's power to undo caprice, to *add* years to a fatally damaged life). The energy of denial swiftly gains momentum: Bolingbroke, Mowbray, Gaunt, and York, and through them "a thousand well-disposed hearts" all are forced to address themselves to Richard's growing strangeness, their suspicions of an imposter rising. In the gathering wrath of the denying lies the evidence of Richard's power.

But it is a dramatic, not a magical power. Not only has he no power to coerce events through "prayer," as Kenneth Burke says, but his every attempt elicits an answering force.[4] In the arrogance of his self-assertion he generates the wrath of a mirroring plot. In this plot he stars as the murdered king who "wasted time / And now doth time waste me" (5. 5. 49). Ironically the plot grows into something stronger than he, strangely autonomous; but meanwhile the actor and the plot reflect each other intimately. In a single unbroken sequence (1. 4–2. 1), Bolingbroke's departure is described, Gaunt's death noted, Bolingbroke's dispossession decreed, and the rebellion reported as underway, with Bolingbroke already returning to England with massive support. This recoil of time is the result of Richard's attack on time. He is right: there is no "normal" time; the king does have the power to make it declare itself. Furthermore, in provoking time's revenge, Richard does in just two acts what Richard III and John take entire plays to do.

From the darkness of self-obscuring power, Richard emerges powerless, which is to say that he exchanges ceremonial power within the constituted world of the play for dramatic power over its ultimate shape. He gives voice to silence, form to obscurity. He enters into the symbolic identity as Son of the Sun King, Phaeton, doomed performer of his father's natural work. He steps forth toward us to illuminate his own catastrophe: "Here, cousin, seize the crown. / Here, cousin . . ." (4. 1. 181–82). This is drama, heavily stylized but true because it has the power to make itself true, to assign roles compelling enough to absorb prior paler realities. Whatever Bolingbroke's intention might have been in coming back from banishment—and he is notoriously vague on that point, presumably even to himself—henceforth his return can only be read in the light of Richard's drama. He came to seize the crown. It is his fate.

Peter Ure aptly describes the effect of the transition between acts 2 and 3:

> Power slides from the absent and silent Richard with the speed of an avalanche: this is not a play about how power is gained by *expertise,* nor even about how cunning overcomes stupidity—Richard is simply not there, either to provide the one, or counter the other . . . [When he re-enters in 3. 2] he is a man whom the audience knows, after this series of bloodless victories and defeats, to be a king without power ready to receive the bad news that he is so.[5]

Richard's absence is not fortuitous or inadvertent; it forms the structural analogue of the death of his conventional persona. Public time has been smashed and public identities betrayed. While Bolingbroke and his followers ripen toward their unknown new futures, feeling each other out with a dangerously uncertain new language—"All my treasury / Is yet but unfelt thanks . . ." and "Your presence makes us rich, most noble lord"[6] (2. 3. 60–63)—Richard returns to the scene of the crime with a new language of his own, in a nerve-quickened state of freedom and horror: freedom from the bog of a power that had "stopped [his ear] with other, flattering sounds" (2. 1. 17), horror at what he has done and lost. He feels raw and new and newly able to feel, but not at all sure how or what he feels. If he does not reenter knowing how powerless he is, he talks as if he did. His "readiness" to receive bad news of the slide of his power is a shift in registration—as if in the freshened air he detected our knowledge of his powerlessness. In his new stage-presence his ears are unstopped, he seems to be listening for sounds from beyond his fictive enclosure, responding to our sense of his absurdity. He is playing to us (even entertaining us, perhaps, with his giddy new gestures) and moving swiftly beyond the perceptions of his coterie. No wonder he makes them nervous ("Mock not my senseless conjuration, lords" [3. 2. 23]). He has become strange, and they scarcely know how to address him to effect: "Comfort, my liege. Why looks your Grace so pale?" "Comfort, my liege. Remember who you are" (75, 82).

He does not know who he is, and the fear gives his voice a new resonance. "From the moment when he greets the English earth," observes Lois Potter, "it is he alone who embodies the spirit of Mowbray's lament for his native tongue, Bolingbroke's 'English ground, farewell,' and Gaunt's famous purple passage."[7] Yet Richard's new voice is engaging not because of the sentiments he utters, but because he is groping backward for them. These sentiments do not come naturally to him, he is fighting for a form to express them even as he moves beyond them. So he "embodies" the spirit of those other voices perversely, or rather dramatically. Like the others, Bolingbroke's farewell is grounded in a well-known convention: "sweet soil, adieu, / My mother, and my nurse, that bears me yet!" (1. 3. 305–6). But Richard *uses* this convention with glaring self-consciousness, reconfiguring the conceit, even staging his own words:

As a long-parted mother with her child
Plays fondly with her tears and smiles in meeting,
So weeping, smiling, greet I thee, my earth,
And do thee favors with my royal hands.

(3. 2. 8–11)

His reverence for Gaunt's England is grotesquely strained (*he* is the "mother" now); yet it does not follow that he displays mere foolish hypocrisy (which Potter takes as the alternative to "sincerity"). Richard plays, but feelingly. He responds in play to a sense of dispossession; in doing so he disengages himself from the themes and personae of the historical fiction and establishes a bond with us. Through the stagey rhythm of outrageous postures offered up, shattered by news from the world outside, then offered anew, Richard comes alive. The postures—in whatever degree sincere or self-indulgent—are experiments, meant to be used up in performance: not hypocrisy, but improvisations. He acts, in other words, in the only way he can; and through him we feel something of the capacity to feel the earth alive, and England a garden after all. We feel the potential integrity of the fictive world he has betrayed. Because he is losing it—because he *can* lose it—he makes it live.

But this is a very perilous strategy. The manic behavior—the absurd bravado, sudden despair, the affectation, wily pathos, rhetorical craziness—attests to Richard's nakedness, but it also strains our patience. As he gains confidence in the new conditions of his performing—especially in the Flint Castle and divestiture scenes (3. 3 and 4. 1)—his roles grow more poised, bolder, more grandiose, and more persuasive. But in the homecoming scene (3. 2) he is still improvising upon sensations of loss that just barely anticipate confirmation by his messengers. So he pitches himself to us blindly, across a very real void, sensing our presence but not, after all, knowing it or able to identify it. Nor has he the luxury of the fiction of direct address, the too-easy gesture of confidence. To "soliloquize" us directly would be to beg for our special protection, to neutralize the risk he takes, and so the sentient self we discern as he leans into that void.

So the king's doubleness most exquisitely displays itself in Richard, most a king and least. In his every kingly utterance glows the falseness, the artifice and strain that makes him least king because most strange. Indeed, he does stink of mortality.

Yet as he is exposed to murder, he looks more like a king than ever, and in losing the world exerts a stronger control upon it.

> Yet looks he like a king. Behold, his eye,
> As bright as is the eagle's, lightens forth
> Controlling majesty, Alack, alack, for woe,
> That any harm should stain so fair a show!
>
> (3. 3. 68–71)

He imposes the aesthetic images of himself upon the world, the rhythms of his lapsing life upon the implacable tides of time. In the wings waits Bolingbroke, "grim necessity."[8] Vaguely created, strategically ill-defined, he is the future itself, content to be upstaged and bide the all-too-inevitable passing of Richard's show, convinced it is nothing but empty words and shadows. He is just rising to his power, sure of his own reality, full of candied courtesy toward those whose tribute will certainly be forthcoming. But Richard, meanwhile, indisputably steals the show as it transpires, forces it into his own mannered image, and does so precisely by his willingness to waste himself. The obscure thrust toward self-revelation in act 1 grows now into a reckless willingness to shed protective coverings; his very language becomes spendthrift, and especially most commanding in his most stagey moments of descent and dispossession:

> What must the king do now? Must he submit?
> The king shall do it. Must he be deposed?
> The king shall be contented. Must he lose
> The name of king? A God's name, let it go!
>
> (3. 3. 143–45)

> Down, down I come, like glist'ring Phaeton,
> Wanting the manage of unruly jades.
> In the base court? Base court, where kings grow base,
> To come at traitors' calls and do them grace!
>
> (3. 3. 178–81)

> Ay, no; no, ay; for I must nothing be;
> Therefore no no, for I resign to thee.
>
> (4. 1. 201–2)

These are awesome moments because the language is openly "dramatic." Somewhat surprisingly, the wit bites. It is privileged, to be sure, by the accents of regal pathos—this is *king-*

killing—but the pathos is not, as earlier, only self-indulgent, because now its credibility is purchased from us: to live for us, the king must truly die. In these heightened moments we form a bond with Richard made up of our shared pleasure in his special language, but the pleasure derives from our shared awareness of its cost. Performing, he gives himself up to us, thereby emerging into momentary clarity as a sentient being and acquiring something of the potency as cynosure that he had vainly asserted earlier. Doubtless in our uneasy complicity in his sacrifice we endow him with such potency. We make him a god, a Phaeton or an Orpheus, even as we consume him. Indeed, what we witness in Richard's dismemberment ("Now mark me how I will undo myself" [4. 1. 203]) is the spectacle of the Orphic poet—he of the magical power of speech, of the privileged tongue—destroying himself into his art.

Leaping ahead, we may say that the "art" into which Richard destroys himself is the great reconfigured context of his tragedy: England, herself, her tragic future, the betrayed and bloodied mother earth, the cannibalized garden. He gives Bolingbroke his own reality, his strength, his future, and so *his* muted tragedy, too. And both Henry IV and Henry V look back with sadness and helplessness at the sacrificing of Richard. Yet the image of Richard as tragic prophet, however compelling it becomes, does not accord with the dramatic figure in these scenes. The "art" he seeks is something less than epic tragedy; he does not see himself as the spirit of the future so much as the central figure in an endless retelling of the past.

If we try to specify a point where doubts about the quality of Richard's sacrifice begin to creep in, we will never be able to agree. Throughout acts 3 and 4, we as spectators are implicated in the action more subtly than we have ever been before. We may even yearn for the simplicity of our experience with *Richard III.* There we were teased with a sense of personality, but it only showed itself in violent exterior action. The question of whether that outward image was sufficient to express the inward experience never really arose. In *Richard II,* by contrast, almost all the violence is internalized: the impressive ritualism all goes to present us with a personal and symbolic tragedy. Of course, we may not credit the symbolical show any further than Bolingbroke does: Richard's grief may not exist, it may be *all* show, it may be trivial—mere self-pity. Yet Richard does not perform for Bolingbroke, he performs for us (and indeed dramatizes Bolingbroke for us). As a histrionic character he appeals to us (of course indirectly) to sanction his show of grief; he bids for our trust and our credulity. So we are indeed implicated, if we have been at all responsive to the spendthrift passion in his voice from act 3 on, at all compelled by the drama of his self-sacrifice. The question is, how far are we willing to be implicated, how far persuaded, how far willing to fortify him with our sympathy and belief? How much of the inwardness of his experience do we want to allow because we long for it as a mirror of our own? Perhaps we find ourselves attracted by Richard's lushness, and then recoil. Dry Bolingbroke seems so content with his opacity—no nervous need there to bare some inner truth of self to his fellows or to us. What he seems, he is. But Richard shrieks for self-revelation. The glass betrays him by showing no signs of grief. Do we—should we—provide a better glass?

The uneasiness we are bound to feel mirrors a tough dramatic reality. Richard embodies the king in his double role most purely, mediating between two worlds with his life. As he streams Phaetonlike from *that* world into *this,* he sets up his own resistance to the crossing and we become increasingly aware of his strategies for hanging onto his role in *that* world. We grow aware of a character who—whatever his intimations of mortality—acts in instinctively canny defense of his life, who is capable of adopting a *style* of self-sacrifice, who resists the uprooting from the mother-soil of his fictive world. The drive toward self-revelation turns out to be complex and full of unforeseen frictions, and our reception of Richard naturally reflects those difficulties. In 3. 2 he plays all the range from omnipotence to sweet despair in his absolute impotence. He constructs an artifact of mortality, orchestrating not only his fellows' voices, controlling the impact of their dread messages, but also the enemy, whom we hear of only by report because Richard anticipates their advances, capitulates, and so continually maintains his insularity. Even death is confined to an allegorized role in his private morality play of the death of kings. 3. 2, then, is a kind of dress rehearsal for a real act of divestiture; he substitutes an aesthetic of death and loss in defense against the real thing.

The "real thing" is the actual confrontation with Bolingbroke himself at Flint Castle (3. 3) and during the actual deposition (4.

1). Yet even here tragic sacrifice is shortcircuited by Richard's control of the occasions. In these scenes he makes his best art by dramatizing himself as Bolingbroke's actual victim; but conveniently for Bolingbroke, Richard all the more persuasively maintains (temporary) control of the play's disintegrative rhythms by assigning Bolingbroke his role as usurper, successor, conqueror:

RICHARD
For do we must what force will have us do.
Set on towards London. Cousin, is it so?

BOLINGBROKE
Yea, my good lord.

RICHARD
Then I must not say no.
(3. 3. 207–9)

. . . .

RICHARD
. . . Here, cousin, seize the crown.
Here, cousin . . . .
(4. 1. 181–82)

Richard never really uses Bolingbroke himself in this process so much as an image of him that Bolingbroke silently accepts (and becomes). Bolingbroke's massed power remains always offstage, unmaterialized.[9] He functions safely under the control of Richard's tyrannical imagination, feigning an autonomous strength that is really passive: fodder for Richard's fantasy. Strangely enough, only Richard really acts in this play; Bolingbroke only need wait for him to come down.

But unlike Richard III, Richard II acts to generate the world, to give it a substance that "more witnesseth than fancy's images." In giving strength and coherence to the mirror world, in giving Bolingbroke his strength and England her tragic future, Richard consigns himself to a kind of display-case identity and significance. And yet he fights this, too. The double-edged quality of his rhetoric is painful—he crystallizes his life every time he speaks, then speaks to shatter the crystal. His effort to lose himself is like striking poses in a house of mirrors. When at last he calls for and shatters the real mirror, crying "my sorrow hath destroyed my face," Bolingbroke's dry rejoinder, "The shadow of your sorrow hath destroyed / The shadow of your face" (4. 1. 291–93), is no less a truth for being a narrow one. We begin to see the "Orphic poet" as a role, set off by those quotation marks that declare it a self-protective posture of self-sacrifice.

Here we come to the cul-de-sac of the sacrificial drama Shakespeare had refined from its impulses in *King John.* Richard has "gone into" the great inverse mirror of the plot; he spends himself to show himself; in the expenditure—the spilling out in performance—is the projection of an inwardness, the unmistakable exposure of a suffering and sentient personality. Yet it cannot come free from that existence in the mirror of the plot, it cannot reach us autonomously. The point comes when, after all the unprecedented intimacy, we find ourselves unsure about the authenticity of Richard's pain, therefore embarrassed by the "external manners of laments" (296). He may claim that "my grief lies all within," and we may be strongly moved to credit him. Still, unmanifested by the larger mirror of the plot, the answering presence of Bolingbroke, the grief must remain hypothetical and hence unresolved. When Richard declares his sacrifice finished, himself "Nothing," the artifact of his tragedy completed, there is still the question: what now? For he is still very much alive on the stage after the ceremony. Indeed, his own vigor belies his claim of nothingness. It comes through in the bitter joke by which he half-acknowledges the limits of his power to turn the world into his tragic monument: the true king's last request is to be allowed to leave the false king's sight. The false king grants the request by having him sent to the Tower, hence his death. Is this Richard's will, Bolingbroke's, or neither's? It has the form of tragic necessity, but we cannot know the depth of Richard's true grief, the extent of his devastation. He simply does not have the language to express a grief that is not a perfect reflection of the occasion.

With Richard's exit in act 4, the play—so far as he is concerned—reaches bottom. He has been concluded, arrested in the glass case that is the projection of our own ambivalence: kill him, save him. He has grandly commanded the stage throughout the deposition scene, raising the sacrificial drama to a high art, powerfully eliciting our participation without resolving its stresses and contradictions. When Richard leaves, followed by Bolingbroke and his retinue, the brief sad exchange among

Carlisle, the Abbot, and Aumerle reminds us of how the context of Richard's drama—the biding historical necessity—has been silently enlarging itself in the background. All the king's supporters have been cropped or marked for cropping before the deposition, so that the scene of Richard's cropping occurs in a splendid isolation that is shaped by the cool new politicians. While Richard's drama transpires, these new politicians seem to us to be subject to its authority (though they still act as if they had the upper hand). But as soon as Richard leaves, the authority of his drama fades. And if *we* let it go—as, in our embarrassment of this would-be Orpheus we might well be inclined to do—then it is in danger of fading altogether: to decline into the picturesque passion of York's description of Richard's entrance into London ("Where rude misgoverned hands from windows' tops / Threw dust and rubbish on King Richard's head," 5. 2. 5–6), or the pretty farewell to his wife, or his futile attempts at imaginative enlargement in Pomfret Castle. The fact is, if we abandon our faith in the *size* of Richard's inward inexpressible grief, we become parties to the killing-off of a small and rather pathetic creature. Once again the need for an adequate sacrifice would be frustrated. And yet the grounds for faith have been swallowed by Richard's own performing style.

Critics have never been able to agree whether that style (the special music of the play, its splendid rhetorical texture) is properly Richard's or Shakespeare's—that is, "Shakespeare's medium . . . which he uses to show—and by means of images to show as lustrously as possible—what is going on in Richard's mind and heart."[10] This begs the question of Richard's inwardness, but that really is the point: king and plot (or "world") are locked together to create the medium. Indeed the relationship between the two may seem too carefully rigged. Richard controls the world; he calls it into being through the center-stage performance of his dispossession. But to perform he needs the privilege of center-stage and a "world" tuned to reflect his style. His coming-down must be validated by Bolingbroke's going-up, as in the awkwardly apt ceremony of the two buckets. So long as Richard's voice conveys inward complexity—something real to lose—then the bucket-structure is suspended in the charged reality of the fiction. But the special relationship between king and world is always in danger of betraying the designer's hand.

In some plays, notably the comedies, the revelation of the designer is a deliberate part of our experience. In *A Midsummer Night's Dream,* the "king of shadows," Oberon, manipulating lovers' wills beyond their own imaginative capacities, is a surrogate for the larger King of Shadows in whose fuller design we are all glad to participate.[11] *Dream,* however, makes no particular investment in the autonomous reality of its characters; indeed, quite the contrary, we are encouraged to see them as "shadows." But in *Richard II* we are surely encouraged to think of Richard as forging his own identity through special dramatic powers, shaping himself tragically against the obscure tides of time and "grim Necessity" (5. 1. 21). And through act 4 we are made to feel a personal will at work, at first in his self-destructive behavior, and then increasingly through his voice, which is his chief instrument for controlling his destruction while maintaining our faith in his inwardness.

And yet, for all the power of that voice, a king of shadows echoes out of his poetry, sanctioning his language by providing and shaping the ceremonious occasions it requires. Richard does not really thrive through naked lyrical assertion nor through the magical enchantments of Orphic address (the invocation of divine power on his behalf). He thrives—acquires theatrical authority—because his language is inversely mirrored in the plot structure; because divine assistance is pointedly not forthcoming. In retrospect, we can see that Richard nowhere even teases us to think that he has earned his privileged mode of utterance, or that he generates it from some profundity of being, some original reality of his own. He just "has it," we must conclude, because he is that ineffable thing, the king. At some point, depending upon the depth of our investment in his performance, we perceive that he expresses his Orphic gift by "divine" grace after all, just as he himself claims to in act 3. But the source is not heaven, but Shakespeare, king of shadows, furtively inspiring his favorite, endowing him with magical speech and a perfectly responsive plot through which to act out his perfect self-sacrifice. Ironically, the effect of this favoritism is to numb the sense of Richard's interiority, hence the authenticity of his sacrifice. Since he exists *in* a reflexive relationship with the plot, it is not "in" him to step outside it. For that would be to suffer a negation more absolute than the sweetly indulgent "nothing" he laments—a "nothing" without the language to lament his vanishing, a "nothing" that Shakespeare will not really confront until *Lear* and *Macbeth.* To the extent that Richard can indeed be the playwright of himself, employing a tragic language that creates the world through the passion of self-sacrifice, then a new dimension of dramatic power, beyond parody, is opened. But Shakespeare cannot help finding out the limits of that sort of power, and in the end his attitude toward it goes unresolved; it hovers between awe at what seems authentic verbal potency and sardonic revulsion from artistic deception, the privileged conditions of its utterance.

Our dilemma reflects that of the play. First we are enlisted by the outreaching power of Richard's performance, then frustrated as that power begins to seal him off in postures of perpetuity. But the play itself does not choose a posture, either of tragic catharsis or of withering irony. In the last act of *A Midsummer Night's Dream* Shakespeare meditates upon the art of the woods by fabricating a miniature recapitulation: whereas the "four nights" of the dream had filled a space between betrothal and nuptial, the parodic miniature of "Pyramus and Thisby" fills the smaller space between nuptial and consummation. Within that space—as we are told by the dialectic between Theseus and Hippolyta that opens the scene—the explicit subject is the nature of the art that had been taken for granted in the body of the play. In the last act of *Richard II* a similar movement occurs. Shakespeare represents the play's general ambivalence in a carefully stylized miniature. Nothing is resolved; rather, we get a cool meditation upon the play's artistic dilemma, and then a paradigmatic resolution. The dilemma is that the dramatist's presence, his need for control, has paralyzed the play in midpassage. It is too late now to solve the problem in this play, but Richard's final two scenes, though they change nothing, provide a model for the dramatist's self-removal from future plays.

In the farewell scene (5. 1) Shakespeare replays Richard's vacillating styles and sharply reenlists our ambivalence. First Richard presents himself in the all-too-familiar display-case idiom, bidding his wife pass the "tedious nights" of future winters by telling the "lamentable tale of me." Self-pity milks authority from the vision; unable to imagine a future not starring himself, he shrinks *on stage* to a small defeated figure, scarcely the stuff of heroic sacrifice. But when Northumberland enters, Richard suddenly strikes out with penetrating passion, focusing a vision of the future more comprehensive and realistic than the one he had just urged on his wife:

> Northumberland, thou ladder wherewithal
> The mounting Bolingbroke ascends my throne,
> The time shall not be many hours of age
> More than it is, ere foul sin gathering head
> Shall break into corruption. Thou shalt think,
> Though he divide the realm and give thee half,
> It is too little, helping him to all.
> And he shall think that thou, which knowest the way
> To plant unrightful kings, wilt know again,
> Being ne'er so little urged another way,
> To pluck him headlong from the usurped throne.
> (5. 1. 55–65)

Precisely because he is *not* memorializing himself, Richard shrewdly foresees the impact of his sacrifice upon the future. He himself is absent from this vision, and that absence gives him one of those flashing moments of dramatic power that *do* make him memorable: "Northumberland, thou ladder wherewithal / The mounting Bolingbroke ascends my throne." It is a power like that in the deposition scene, which creates personae: henceforth Northumberland's character and fate are fixed. And for the moment at least, we are content to call that power Richard's rather than Shakespeare's, if only because it evokes the best moments of his struggle through acts 3 and 4.

But having flared like the sun, Richard at once reverts to lyrical self-absorption in the lingering farewell to his wife. Nothing new comes out of the scene; the vacillating styles are simply juxtaposed with exceptional and surely deliberate clarity.

In Pomfret Castle (5. 5) Richard attempts one last time to be his own mirror, to elicit his own inwardness and give it dramatic credibility. But the method he uses—"Yet I'll hammer it out"— suggests the futility of the attempt. He will hammer out a vision that has been denied by his own glittering brightness, the brightness of public performance that is the mode he is condemned to ("Yet looks he like a king," "glist'ring Phaeton," etc.). Now in private he will create a world from his own thought, then step aside, absent himself in order to look upon that world, and thereby escape the prison that Pomfret embodies in concrete. What he will hammer out, in other words, is an *imitation* of tragic self-forgetfulness. For his search for a nonperforming language, a language by which he might transfer his own life to the brood of his mother-brain and father-soul, can only come out as a self-mocking performance. The soliloquy is a frozen display of the habits of a self-enclosing mind, and the result of his exertions is a painful parody of sacrificial artistry, a failed attempt to escape his own self-constricting presence by playing dead to his own thoughts. He ends up more tightly imprisoned than ever.

His verbal hammer is the simile:

> I have been studying how I may compare
> This prison where I live unto the world. . . .
>
> (5. 5. 1–2)

Simile is Richard's true rhetorical mode. But earlier expressions ("Down, down I come like glist'ring Phaeton"), however mannered, have theatrical passion, the sanction of something-to-lose. Here Richard is trying explicitly to create—to convert himself from king to poet as one last defense against "nothing"—but the only strategies he commands are those of the stymied art that insists upon hanging onto its privileges.[12] Simile is the likening of two things without the loss of either's original identity: unless they are fused by passion, the likening becomes a protected game, no risk entailed, no recreation. That is the whole sense of Richard's soliloquy—a fundamental inability to relinquish control of his images. He thinks about his own thoughts:

> Thoughts tending to ambition, they do plot
> Unlikely wonders—how these vain weak nails
> May tear a passage through the flinty ribs
> Of this hard world, my ragged prison walls;
> And, for they cannot, die in their own pride.
>
> (5. 5. 18–22)

The conceit enacts futility itself. In effect, what he says is that thoughts which remain only thoughts—"conceits," self-contained nuggets of expression—remain only thoughts indeed, without power or substance in the world: which is to say, without power in the drama, power to reach and claim our credulity, faith, and consenting imaginations.

Early in the play, Gaunt's deathbed speech presents an implicit criticism of the king's rhetorical style. Like Clarence's dream narration in *Richard III,* which serves a similar function, it draws its strength from our awareness of its futility *within* the fictive world; it appeals to us directly through a privileged convention:

> Methinks I am a prophet new inspired
> And thus, expiring, do foretell of him. . . .
>
> (2. 1. 31–32)

The "sceptered isle" aria thrills not by virtue of its content nor by its rhetorical strategy, but because it expresses a stifling soul passionately seeking to spend its breath as deed—to become material and consequential in the world of men. Gaunt seeks the quintessential dramatic power—to impress an image of "England" and so of Richard's failure into the play by way of our consciousness, so that henceforth the world we help constitute through our perceptions, a world shaped in part by Gaunt's powerful image, is the world Richard must actually struggle in. Gaunt, then, appeals beyond Richard to us. The prophetic truth of his performance is to be apprehended not as a metaphysic "hammered out" but as an utterance heard in the process of expiration: the using up of breath. Unheard, ripped from its life-and-death context, Gaunt's truth becomes (as it is for Richard) a "frozen admonition."

Of course, Gaunt also appeals to the nugget collector in us, his eulogy to England having become one of our most cherished artifacts. Quoted retrospectively, Gaunt's speech becomes a series of conceits precisely like those that Richard in Pomfret addresses only to himself. But living drama does not abide conceits, it dissolves them into action. It uses them up in a generative process that occurs not just between father-soul and mother-brain but between breath and language, mouth and ear, stage and audience. To make his utterance heard Richard must truly *expire* in speech. But in Pomfret he hangs onto his conceits, unable to reach through the prison of language and across the void to us. To be sure, we may be moved by the pathos of the futility and avoid going altogether cold in a moralizing retreat from sympathy, but still there is no way to pretend we are participating in a compelling tragedy.

Yet our concern is not simply undercut with cold irony, as it is, say, in the end of *2 Henry VI.* Shakespeare presents the scene with great care, precisely registering its dilemmas, finely pacing our impatience. Having arrived at the empty center of his contemplations, Richard suddenly hears some music. First he allegorizes it, starts minting new conceits of time; then he strikes out at it as an unsuitable effect for his solipsistic drama. But then he hears it freshly, as humanly produced: it is, after all, a "gift of love" from some anonymous person *outside* his little cell. He grows tired of the all-hating world—that is, of his own stymied role in it: it goes on, after all, and so must he. The groom brings him news of Bolingbroke's conquest even of his horse; Richard flashes in anger at the image of himself as an ass "Spurred, galled, and tired by jauncing Bolingbroke" (94). His passion reaches through the prison walls to bring on the "world's" response in the form of Exton. "Patience is stale, and I am weary of it" (103)—the murderers come in as if this were their cue, as of course it is. The swelling relief, the externalization of frustrated grief, must follow "nothing." Richard reasserts his control of the one role he can play powerfully, that of his death ("Farewell King!"). And he does it well; he does not mar the performance now by self-consciousness or self-pity or an eye for how the tale will be told. He sees himself not as a tragic figure to be preserved in memory, but as "blood":

> Exton, thy fierce hand
> Hath with the king's blood stained the king's own land.
> (109–110)

Yet, satisfying as this conclusion is, Richard's outburst does not proceed inevitably from his character or from the implications of the fiction. (One need only compare *Macbeth* or *Coriolanus*.) Not that the action is untrue either to character or to fiction, but that, like Richard's Orphic gifts, it is gratuitous. As much as anything it reflects our desire, and Shakespeare's need, for Richard to act his death in a large way.

The entire last movement of the play unfolds rather like a dream sequence, the springs of the action deeply ambiguous. In the farewell scene the queen tries in vain to stir Richard from a virtual trance of self-pity. And his isolation in Pomfret and then his sudden breakthrough in the end are both dreamlike situations. Exton is the materialization of dramatic necessity rendered as our wish. Once the job is done he is banished out of remorse and perhaps artistic embarrassment. No one in the future really blames him for the killing, for in truth he scarcely exists except as an agent of a coalition of wills: Bolingbroke's Shakespeare's, and ours.[13] In other words, the scene's felt fictive life has grown meager; what is alive in it is the shadowy conflict of wishes and needs, Richard's, but also—and perhaps indistinguishably—ours and the dramatist's. Furthermore, with the slackening of internal dramatic authority, we become aware of a new influence bearing upon the ghostly scene, also from outside: history itself, the past as destiny. Why must Richard die? Because "history" (as well as "Exton") says he must. But what says he must die heroically? His character? Shakespeare's fiat? *Our* desire?

Shakespeare does not indulge these ambiguities nor strain for effects. Having reached a cul-de-sac with Richard himself, he now seeks to dramatize the problems that thwart the tragic self-declaring impulse of the play. The overt ambiguities of the ending project the play's fundamental irresolution, which makes it finally impossible to say whether Richard reveals an inner emptiness or the play itself can simply go no further in its self-consuming momentum. This blurring of the source of experience makes for a richly indeterminate play—the best of tragic histories or historic tragedies. Nevertheless, the indeterminacy rests upon a mechanism of deception. The ending is characteristically Shakespearean in its recourse to parody as a way of exposing the mechanism and, in effect, destroying its efficacy. The parody is not a facile mockery of the king-as-poet, but a means of getting free of crippling anxieties and artistic traps that he reflects. Shakespeare parodies himself; he uses rather than denies his own artistic temptations and pretensions, his own capacity for self-deceit and self-indulgent lyricism, self-powering Orphic address. Parody becomes a way of using up a drama's ghosts, calling them forth from the shadows and making them name themselves. And what Shakespeare parodies in the Pomfret scene is his own underlying affinity with Richard: his own attempt to control the field of the play's sensations—and through them, our reactions—by defusing that control through Richard's personal style. Richard's style is to ceremonialize all rival energies, either by banishment or by preemptive theatrics. But the play as a whole cooperates with this style, sharing his fear and disdain of unruly energies, excluding from the stage all prose and prose-speaking low-lifes—those whitebeards, draymen, and oyster-wenches who reportedly swell the cause of Bolingbroke (1. 4. 24–32; 3. 2. 112–20). No other history play shows such anxiety.[14] In no other, so far, has the dramatist identified so deeply with the central figure, maneuvering simultaneously to fulfill and to protect him. For what Richard attempts in the Pomfret scene—both to control and to escape his solitude by peopling it with the brood of his solipsistic imagination—Shakespeare has been doing in the play as a whole, through a furtive and gratifying identification with his protagonist. And yet, against the impulse for aesthetic tyranny runs the contrary impulse for self-sacrifice, which may in the end be the strongest impulse in the play. The parody becomes Shakespeare's way of waking from, and casting off, a ghostly infatuation.

The ghost called up from *Richard II*'s shadows is a deep unwillingness to abandon control; it is a refusal to submit Richard, and hence the historical world he inhabits, to the full destructive force of the dramatic process. The disintegrative energies released in Richard are delivered to us through a carefully managed structure of restraints; they are allowed to blaze only within a secured formal garden quietude. Nevertheless, as Leonard Barkan shows, the form of the play, moving toward semicomic and externalized kinds of violence in the last two acts, also expresses frustration with its own formal restraints.[15] And indeed the ambivalences run deep; the very elaboration of controls suggests the power building up behind them. In the end, in the play's irresolutions, we may discern the old ever-elusive, still unregenerated, undigested historical will at work, though in a slightly new guise. We participate in Richard's dismantling, consume him, and so build up a powerful play. But the transaction is muted, not so much a flow of energy as a regulation of it. Richard acts, and so generates the strangeness that prefigures and is prerequisite to creation. But he also manages, and so fails to create. "Art" is his last defense against nothingness, his bulwark rather than (as in, say, *King Lear*) the experience itself. Ultimately it is "art" itself—disembodied, unlocated, dispersed, and hovering between character and poetic world—that stands between him and us, between us and the play.[16] It is "art" by which Shakespeare protects Richard from the full force of his own dramatic assault upon time, his own dramatic rage, and hence from *our* fully roused and liberated responses.

There, but shrouded still, is "history." *Richard II,* as Coleridge said, is the "history of a mind," and indeed it is deeply solipsistic in its imaginative character. But the corollary is that Shakespeare maneuvers to avoid direct confrontation with the grounds of that solipsistic energy. For the king of shadows to hang on to Richard's character as he does is to leave it ultimately untested against anything that is not its own reflection. By the same token, not to test the depths of Richard's character is to leave unexamined an automatic faith in the public nature, the ulterior reality, of "history" and in the adequacy of certain conventions of lyric language and emotive performance. As a result, "history" stalks unchallenged through the play. Like Perseus, Shakespeare faces his Medusa not directly but through a miniaturized reflection. He stages the confrontation in the theater of Richard's golden head. But until he can confront "history" in its genuine otherness, without yet turning into stone, the drive toward those depths of experience that echo from even the lightest of his plays will be stalled.

Part III
Playing Out the Play

9

Rebellion and Design in *Henry IV, Part One*

Looking back to *Richard II,* we can see how Shakespeare wrestled with the issues of imaginative freedom and control. The play revealed the playwright exerting control not, as earlier, through a conventional structure like Providence, but much more furtively and impressively through the disguise of a regal poet endowed with truly seductive gifts. By identifying with Richard, Shakespeare had found how to generate great dramatic force, but a force that looked suspiciously like vanity. He could compel our belief in Richard's unseen inwardness, but an "inwardness" that could have been a trick of theatrical mirrors. The play's ambivalence is surely Shakespeare's. What direction will he take now? Will he strive for a more seductive central figure? For less ambivalence, greater concentration, more far-reaching control? After *Richard II* he must have known himself to be on the verge of unprecedented powers. How strong might be his will to resist the temptation of artistic tyranny?

It is clear from the opening scenes of *1 Henry IV* that the temptation has been abjured. We are greeted by a compression of familiar effects, as if to draw us forward in anticipation of a major revelation; then there is an explosion, and suddenly a world appears, densely and diversely peopled, and already in full motion.[1] It is a truly spontaneous world, its life a matter of internal and native growth, its free-speaking citizens all intricately related, not by the invisible webs of a plotting playwright, but through the verisimilitude of contending strengths.[2] The play's form is not imposed, but emerges from the cross-hatching rhythms of instinctive opposition to imposed control. Rebellion is more than the subject of the play, more even than its central metaphor. Rebellion is its *style.*

The demise of Richard induces a struggle for power whose impulses are deeply theatrical. In this new dawn one feels as if a heavy restraint on speech, the author's own injunctive hand, were suddenly lifted. Something fearful has dissolved, and the result is exhilarating and dangerous both. Identities are problematical now, but the opportunities for creating them are vastly multiplied. The world bursts into excited tongues; rich creative speech jumps from virtually every character, often for no better or no lesser reason than that, abruptly freed to talk themselves into being, they will not be silenced. Falstaff incarnates his own "superfluous" speech; Hotspur would die in silence and so lives and kills in speech:

> He said he would not ransom Mortimer,
> Forbade my tongue to speak of Mortimer,
> But I will find him when he lies asleep,
> And in his ear I'll hollo "Mortimer."
>
> (1. 3. 219–22)

Even the minor characters seem to understand instinctively that in a world "turned upside down since Robin Ostler died," speech is, literally, life. Faced with this stimulated world, they respond by extemporizing vigorous performances in a language strong with individuality. This is clearly true of the play's great encounters—Hotspur with Henry or Glendower, Hal with Falstaff or Henry—but one has only to think of, say, the gritty jargon of the thieves and carriers (2. 1)—half-code, half-euphemism—to appreciate the range of dramatizing instinct in the play.

What astonishes is the readiness of the language to the occasions. Take Gadshill's mad harangue in the inn yard (2. 1). His subjects are brigandage, scurrilous companions, hanging; his excitement over the imminent "action," the robbery, takes the form of anticipatory action—that is, the speech itself as a performance resourceful enough to contain the excitement. Apart from the outright vigorous wit of his style, its striking features are the marshalled series of extravagant epithets and coinages and the incantatory rhythms and phrasings:

> . . . I am joined with no foot land-rakers, no long-staff sixpenny strikers, none of these mad mustachio pur-

> ple-hued maltworms; but with nobility and tranquility, burgomasters and great oneyers, such as can hold in, such as will strike sooner than speak, and speak sooner than drink, and drink sooner than pray; . . .
> (2. 1. 70–76)

This style links Gadshill to the major characters. Yet there is no compelling "reason" for the scene (it is usually cut in performance). Through the color, energy, and independence of their language, the minor characters simply make the world dense.

In *Richard II* this sort of impertinent low-life material was routinely suppressed, out of the play's commitment to Richard's centrality. In *1 Henry IV,* individual characters try to shape the world according to their fantasies, but the world is now too abundant to submit to any one figure's imaginative sway. Much of that abundance still occurs offstage—much, that is, of the serious political action, the "chronicle" material. But there is a cinematic quality to the swift succession of scenes. The "cutting" suggests a continuous flood of events. Foreground scenes seem to retrieve highlights of complex moments in passing; the background shifts too fast to be held and neatly lit up, nor is there a steady point of view from which "pertinent" scenes might be selected or framed.

This is the rebellion of style in *1 Henry IV*. Raw energy wonderfully assumes dramatic form, but it is the performance that often comes first, the pertinence only later. Especially in the comic scenes, *what* is being acted out is not clear *until* it is acted out. Nor is this sense of gratuitous playacting confined to the "expendable" parts, such as Gadshill's monologue. It characterizes Hal's entire relationship with Falstaff. No one thinks of the large tavern scenes as meaningless, and yet the meanings are not determined by plot, but rather emerge, like the plot itself, from the energy of "superfluous" performance. There really is no reason for Falstaff's presence in the play at all. He must justify himself as he goes.

Self-justification is a leading motive in the play's competitive world, giving a nervous edge to the most virile of performances. Henry sets the pace in his opening speech. The packed diction, the expansive periods, the regal centrality constitute an agressive attempt to seize control of the stage from the start, as if he knows in his bones that he who commands the language commands the stage that *is* the realm. He attempts to shape time ceremonially, to identify the beginning of the play with the true beginning of his reign. Yet his speech is resonant with his own disbelief, the strain of having to shoulder an impossible burden.

> So shaken as we are, so wan with care,
> Find we a time for frighted peace to pant
> And breathe short-winded accents of new broils
> To be commenced in stronds afar remote.
> No more the thirsty entrance of this soil
> Shall daub her lips with her own children's blood: . . .
> (1. 1. 1–6)

The *actor* of this speech is elusive, either disguised by crabbed syntax ("Find we a time . . .") or displaced by the vivid personifications of war. The speaker, in other words, is content to be diffused through his performance. But that performance, which celebrates the end of civil butchery, manages to evoke a sickening disorder in the very assertion of calmness: "No more the thirsty entrance of this soil / Shall daub her lips with her own children's blood"; "No more shall trenching war channel her fields"; "no more . . . no more. . . ."[3]

Henry takes away even as he gives. In the cataract of suggestive but incomplete images we can feel the onrushing of time he is claiming to have stilled. He creates a breathing space (the "time for frighted peace to pant") that separates the past ("no more") from the future ("new broils"), and in this isolated moment he asserts his power as king to start things anew: the journey to the holy lands. But the breathing space exists only in the act of the speech itself, and even that speech is heavy with despair of its own potency. As he speaks, offstage events mock his onstage efforts to legitimize his reign through ceremony. In fact, he has already made plans that must scuttle "our holy purpose to Jerusalem." By the end of the swift scene, everything originally presented in the opening speech seems to have been withdrawn. And beneath the smooth surface of compact rhetoric and military decisiveness we apprehend a reservoir of the unsaid or the unsayable. More has been done, more is being done, "more is to be said and to be done / Than out of anger can be uttered" (106–7).

We are left, then, with a sense of powerful disturbances grimly suppressed. After his strong opening claim on the stage, Henry relinquishes it—almost, we feel, with relief. He does not pause, like Richard, to marvel that the world defies his authority, but strides pragmatically off. Pretensions to ceremonial legitimacy are easily laid by; the winning of the stage itself can wait; obliqueness is as much his natural mode as directness was Richard's. His exit strikes us as that of a realist unbeguiled by theatrical illusions of power. Yet the exit sets the stage for an explosion. For that stage now seems highly vulnerable, unclaimed, undefended, undefined, a raw space.

The second scene capitalizes upon the instability left by the first. After Henry's time-pressured exit, the stage suddenly flowers into the luxury of a world with just enough time for everything to be said that needs or wants or even *is* to be said.[4] Yet far from dragging, this scene delivers all the energy that was suppressed in the first. Indeed, the scene rebels against nearly all prior conventions of historical drama and against all presumptions as to what is "pertinent" in a history. Falstaff at first might seem familiar as a *miles gloriosus* or bawdyhouse wit, but his dazzling verbal gifts and rich suggestiveness quickly take him beyond such prototypes. It is clear that he is a major figure and—though sheer invention—somehow central to this "history." In the end, of course, Hal steps forward in his soliloquy to impose an order upon the extravagance. He quiets the stage. But we are now aware of its compressed power, its capacity to erupt at any time into a new adventure of disorder. After this scene all bets are off as to what shape the monster will take next. Everything is, or could be, "pertinent"—and that is both the excitement and the menace of a rebellion that has thrown off the restraints of old form without yet having found its new one.[5]

When Henry returns to the stage in the third scene he has picked up its nervousness. He seems worried about his onstage authority, his ability to translate machiavellian vigor into dramatic potency. His anxieties betray, as usual, the awkward strain of self-division. He vows to be henceforward less "my condition" (his natural self) and more "myself" (his royal self), "Mighty, / And to be feared." These are not the words of a man at home upon the royal stage. He may act "mighty" and instill fear by force: he can suppress Worcester by dismissing him. But he cannot *express* the power of a king dramatically. He does not possess the stage.

When he turns his attention, then, to Hotspur, we are aware that the confrontation proceeds on two levels. The king is struggling to assert his authority in two interdependent domains, the machiavellian or political, and the antic or dramatic. He has summoned Hotspur to explain his apparent defiance in the business of the prisoners. Hotspur, though brusque, is deferential: "My liege, I did deny no prisoners." But as we follow, or try to follow, the quarrel at the level of apparent issues—the political level—we find them changing even as we begin to grasp them, shifting aside, so to speak, to reveal the deeper bases of hostility. Thus, Hotspur in his long "popinjay" speech charms away the issue of prisoners, and yet this issue is tied to something else, indistinct to us, which Henry—uncharmed—proceeds to bring forward: "Why, yet he doth deny his prisoners. . . ." Hotspur, apparently is still trying to bargain with the king, offering up the Scottish prisoners in exchange for the ransom of Mortimer. And suddenly the issue is "Mortimer"—Henry bitterly denouncing him as traitor, Hotspur, outraged, extolling him as epic hero. We feel the ground to have shifted, but there is no way for us to judge the meaning of these excited postures. Then abruptly the king decrees the argument ended; he forbids further mention of Mortimer, orders the prisoners to be sent "or you will hear of it," and leaves the stage. Instantly the issue becomes Henry's tyrannous behavior, especially his intolerable command to silence. In a whirling fury, Hotspur vows not only to "speak of Mortimer" but also to "lift the downtrod Mortimer / As high in the air as this unthankful king." Thus the idea of rebellion is first articulated, not as a plot or design centered upon specific political issues, but as Hotspur's impulsive reaction to the king's attempt to silence him.

The rebellion in fact originates in a clash of styles that feeds upon available issues like so much tinder. If we find the apparent issues of the quarrel hard to attend to, it is only partly because they are indistinct, mired in the sprawling background matter of the play. Partly they are hard to follow because we are being distracted all the while by the *other* level of combat, the antic struggle for the stage itself.

In Hotspur's first words, overtly deferential, we can hear the accent of a self-declaring native of the theater: "My liege, I did deny no prisoners." Henry must hear it, too—brusque, direct, impatient of the king's awkward protocols and jealousies. With native ease Hotspur steps into his role centerstage, drawing upon and exciting its awakened potential for disorder. Not that he does so deliberately. He is a theatrical animal, self-absorbed and self-fulfilling in his actions, but never self-conscious (as Henry always is). Eventually he will exhaust himself, stiffening into the postures of the chivalric hero; but until then he exerts a powerful charm from the magic circle of the stage.

Hotspur's "popinjay" speech (29–69) is any young actor's dream, crackling with easy anecdotal vigor. In the king's own presence, but reducing him to an onlooker or an admirer even (for Henry has confessed to admiration of this gallant puppy), Hotspur holds the stage for forty lines of superfluous playacting. The performance is superfluous both in that it fails to address the issue of defiance it purports to address and in that it literally "spills over" its occasion, taking too much time—from time-pressured Henry's point of view—just to be impertinent. What is worse, the performance *appears* to be persuasive: in its vitality it has the power to seem absolutely central to the most pertinent needs of the moment. Sir Walter Blunt is taken in, and so are we, our attention riveted. And because we are seduced by its earnestness, delighted by its vigor, the performance in fact *becomes* central in importance.

This is the point: our collaboration with Hotspur, our attention to the actor as he discovers his true role, significantly alters the nature of the staged event.[6] In a world imperiously pressured by its future, the antic-player creates time. He swells the present, extending it outward to us, now; dramatic time overtakes the fictional time. And so the performance makes Hotspur's style and presence the real and immediate issues; it gives the character his characteristic heat and before our eyes transforms the emerging political plot into a dramatic contest for our allegiance, credulity, and assent.

Henry has no recourse at this point except, futilely, to forbid speech and then simply to turn over the stage to his young rival. Hotspur's whole style is rebellion, an instinctive reaction against form or restraint of any kind. Henry, for all his "savvy," has no way of containing such "superfluous" energies and can only attempt to suppress them—and so provoke them into organized opposition. For the time being, Worcester and Northumberland have the play's rhythms on their side. Picking carefully between Hotspur's superman fantasies and their own more mundane instincts for self-protection, they begin the delicate task of imposing a form upon his wildness. They work to reclaim him, as it were, from the antic stage, and bring him gently, but usefully, back into the frame of the political action.

They do this by making Mortimer's claim, retrospectively, the form and pretext for an organized assault upon the crown.

Thus the end of this scene also subdues vitality to design, shaping from Hotspur's antic energies the political plot of the play. But the political plot, through the very process of its emergence, has become explosively dramatic. The stage is flexed for a new outburst.

The world is *1 Henry IV* is imbued with the great "as if" of drama, making for drama's disturbing doubleness of feeling. In performing is life: therefore Hal lingers with Falstaff, therefore Henry engages Hotspur in a life-and-death rivalry, not over issues but over style. But the performing inevitably seems a substitute for life as well. Repeatedly we are made to feel as if original "true" energies had once, in some mythically prior time, been violently deflected into play speech. And in the urgency of their styles the characters themselves seem responsive to this condition, always pressing their speech to become more real than whatever it is that prompts it. What makes the acting-out so fascinating is—for all its intense gratification—its deep sense of futility, as though emotionally hearkening back to a center, a "point" that is no longer there.

This anxiety about the "point" of performance disturbs the political scenes. But the Eastcheap scenes play it out more openly. In Hal's first speech, he chides Falstaff for having "forgotten to demand that truly which thou wouldest truly know"—a provocative reply to a request for the time of day. What Falstaff may have forgotten and what he would truly know are never specified. Instead they are "dramatized" in the richly layered series of verbal performances, thrust and counterthrust, in which both characters engage with the finesse of a practiced comic team. Who either of these witty people "truly" is, apart from his membership in the team, is a slippery question. When are they masquerading, and when are they playing out "real" selves in dramatic form? When are they fabricating personas and when does the invention, however extravagant, "denote me truly," as Hamlet puts it?

The idea of a "true" self, behind or beneath the acting self, may be chimerical. Both flaunting and denying his own manifest bulk—"'Sblood, I'll not bear my own flesh so far afoot again" (as if somehow "I" were not quite the same thing as "my own flesh")—Falstaff is forever pointing both at and away from the assumed center of his huge performing power. He is one model of the live actor; the more palpably present he is on the stage, the more he seems to body forth something that is absent—a *source* of presence—and therefore, to point away from what *is* toward what may be. Audiences in the theater and in the study have always found enormous humanity in Falstaff, and yet there is no "secret" or undisclosed character there. Any formulation of a "true" underlying self is bound to be a reduction of the character, a denial of the very mode of prodigiousness in which he is perfected. Falstaff withholds nothing, is forever spilling his guts; his lies are certainly like the father that begets them, "gross as a mountain, open, palpable." Even his soliloquies are provocative extensions of his barroom postures, not disclosures of secret motivating factors. And yet it is undeniably part of the character that he induces belief in a "self" that beckons from a center, without ever openly revealing itself.

The purer the antic mode, the sharper the strange double vision it induces. At one moment it looks like mere frivolity—"Hostess, clap to the doors . . . What, shall we be merry?" We are sure that the hostess's doors will soon give way to a heavier, more real time. But then again the antic mode, being unpressured by the need to pattern time pragmatically, seems always to tremble on the skin of the surprisingly true, always about to yield up a vital mystery. Falstaff's bufoonery seems to mask the astonishing wisdom of ageless immediacy. After all, he is the *bacchic* fool. And because his is, or seems to be, a safe world (Hal may put down the buffoon, but never the god)—a world free from the external pressures of time—it freely allows the subterranean life to be uttered. By contrast, King Henry's world, with its suppression of language and feeling, and with its commitment to a life beyond this immediate stage-life, seems hollow, haunted by what cannot be present. Yet the very fullness of Falstaff's domain causes problems, too. The outright vigor of its inventiveness, its bouyancy, wit, and rhythm, draws us inward, toward the presumed fountainhead of its exuberant energy. At the same time, the acting itself throws up a kind of screen to thwart our access to that which we "would truly know."

In the first two acts, Falstaff seems able to recycle life into play indefinitely. Everything that comes his way from "outside" is grist for in-house performance. But of course a sense of direction does emerge; the playing itself seems to be driving toward revelation, if only through the process of festive abandonment. Caught up in the play, the players find themselves performing more "truly" than they ever could by intention. Waiting for Falstaff in the Boarshead, Hal perpetrates a "jest" on the hapless drawer, Francis. In this jest Hal gives form to the complex pressures of his situation, his alienation from the presumed center of his life as heir apparent. Thus he expresses a need to command, judge, punish, as well as a need to justify his own half-guilty freedom from "masters." And so he urges Francis to rebel against his bondage and bullies him for being unable to do so. But I think Hal also responds to a more basic need (more basic in the sense that it goes to the heart of his obscure preference for Falstaff's company over his father's), namely to "drive away the time till Falstaff come." When Poins asks him the "issue" of the jest, Hal answers in the nervously explosive style of a man whose wit is all that keeps him from being swamped by a desperate sense of his own idleness. He uses a quasi-theatrical metaphor, as if he were literally full of, and must give vent to, countless personalities: "I am now of all humors that have showed themselves humors since the old days of goodman Adam. . . ." In other words, I act because I must not stop acting. He can "explain" himself only by finding new forms to accommodate his profligate energies. Thus he goes on to parody Hotspur, thence to "Call in ribs! Call in tallow!" to play opposite him as "Dame Mortimer" (2. 4. 105).

Falstaff—held offstage until the perfect moment—enters at the climax of Hal's strained solo exertions. We can feel the stage come alive; Hal's own exuberance gathers up our own and explodes with relief. No longer laboring at his antic self, he can now afford to relax and unleash all his instincts for invention, abusiveness, moral outrage. With Falstaff—in the "men in buckram" comedy, and subsequently in the twofold performance of the Prodigal Prince—Hal becomes an intensely absorbed performer. The result is a comedy so superbly structured that the actors exist only in their personas. Is Falstaff "pretending?" Is Hal "serious?" Centuries of quarreling have not resolved these impertinent questions. The more committed the playing—the more carelessly it risks both its performers and its material—the more ambiguously "real" it becomes. Such playing has the power to use up Hal's detachment, his alienation, his need for purpose, his need to impose a design.

The playing is immediately satisfying to him, therefore to us. Yet it also conveys a reality beyond itself. When Hal plays his father, and Falstaff his son, how many selves, how many voices are there present? Wit begets wonder. In its momentum the playing leads inexorably toward the ghosts at the heart of this world.

At the end of the playing we and Hal both are ready for the real meeting with his father. Like Hal, we have been drawn toward the receding center of an absorbingly fertile world, its flesh continuously redeemed by its imagination, but we have come to rest nowhere. We are drawn by pleasure, increasingly beset by anxiety.

The play centers upon Hal's meeting with his father in 3.2. At the simplest level, the scene is crucial to the public plot, that plane of historical action, largely derived from Holinshed, concerned with putting down rebellion and insuring lineal succession to the throne. For these ends it is necessary that the prince emerge from his wildness, reconcile with the king, and go on to prove himself the true heir by defeating his rival at Shrewsbury. The atonement of father and son provides the morale, the power of spiritual unity that translates into superior battlefield strength.

But apart from the demands of the public plot, what pulls father and son together in the middle of *1 Henry IV?* What are the internal forces? Perhaps, after all, there are none. There is no history to the relationship, not even much of a desire to imagine or insist upon one, as in *Hamlet.* No mother is ever mentioned (except once, as a generic joke). Hal was "born" at the end of *Richard II* as a problem for his father: the salient fact about him was his not being there to help legitimize the coronation. And now again his absence translates, publically at least, as the king's doubtful authority. For Hal's part, his father seems to exist chiefly as a transmitter of the crown. He expects to inherit it as his right and desert, but never appears to think of deriving it personally from Henry. In other words, the distance between father and son may signify nothing more than the temperamental coldness and mutual distrust of political rivals bound together by a powerful formality. There may be no personal relationship at all—nothing between them but this negative space that must be bridged only so far as the public plot and political interests require.

And yet we are certainly led to expect something more satisfying from the encounter than a pragmatic political pact—something, that is, more responsive to the true range of experience in the play. For of course the scene *is* central in more powerful ways than a cold review of the characters' motives suggests. Our expectations are roused by an artful pattern of allusions, beginning with Henry's remorseful glance at Hal's absence in the opening scene and climaxing in the great "rehearsal" at the Boarshead in 2. 4. We are never told why Hal keeps his distance, but are constantly reminded of the awkward fact that he does so. In fact, the whole play turns upon the separation of father and son. Hal's absence, after all, not only makes way for Hotspur's charismatic presence, hence the rebellion; it is also the dramatic excuse for the very existence of Falstaff as embodiment of the alternative world. Structurally, in other words, the play loads the gap between father and son, and therefore their encounter, with a terrific burden of meaning.

"Where there is a reconciliation, there must first have been a sundering."[7] Stephen Dedalus's logic seems apt. And where the reconciliation is made to seem crucial, we may imagine a sundering of commensurate importance. Yet on the origins and therefore the meaning of the separation Shakespeare maintains one of his great fruitful silences. We "ask and ask," as Matthew Arnold puts it; "Thou smilst and art still." Surely, we insist, the separation cannot mean *nothing*—too much rides on it. Surely the drive toward atonement implies some psychic violence, some blighted or repressed affection, some remorse or pain of dislocation—some source, in other words, of the dramatic urgency. We pour our questions, expectations, and explanations into the gap between father and son. They are received without comment and without altering the mysterious fact, the plain existential fact, of the vacancy itself.

The play does not repudiate the idea of a "natural bond" but simply presents it as a cipher. The filial relationship has no prior meaning except that of king to heir. In the Boarshead rehearsal Hal tries intensely to imagine a relationship, but it all turns upon the intermediary role of Falstaff. What the relationship truly is in itself—what Hal or Henry or we will "truly know"—must wait to be created in the actual encounter onstage.

But that encounter turns out to be ambiguous. It presents us, in fact, with at least two valid but conflicting ways of understanding the scene.

The scene works centripetally, drawing us from the outside in toward the elusive center. In their first speeches Hal and Henry cling to the "Holinshed" framework while warily circling the deeper unspoken issues that would absorb them. After a characteristically convoluted opening (a mixture of guilt, reproach, self-pity), Henry sharply charges Hal with "rude society" and a betrayal of the "greatness of thy blood." Having anticipated this much in his rehearsal, Hal responds with a smoothness that if anything sounds too well rehearsed itself: neither denying nor explaining, but in a general way accepting some of the blame and reasonably suggesting that his reputation for wildness would have been exaggerated by "smiling pick-thanks and base newsmongers."[8] It is a well-balanced reply, respectful of his father's anger without inflating its importance by an undue defensiveness. It says enough, and no more—and so leaves the next move up to Henry, either to proceed at this same level to specific allegations, or to make the political pact at once. So far both men have stayed away from anything very personal.

Clearly Henry is not interested in Hal's peccadilloes, and the smoothness of Hal's first response encourages the king to move in closer toward the real issues. "Yet let me wonder, Harry, / At thy affections," he begins. The "let me" is a typically indirect command to silence, for he goes on to "wonder" for the next 100 lines (with only a single line-and-a-half interruption from Hal). Hal's silent part in this performance is crucial: he must be passive without seeming indifferent, attentive without seeming secretly busy with his own thoughts. He must be tactful without being condescending, allowing his crafty, self-deceiving and self-torturing father to trust him even as he reproaches him. And so the king is (as John Russell Brown puts it) "drawn backward and inward, to an imaginary reliving of his past, as if he seeks to convince himself that Richard's behavior is the reason why he usurped the 'sunlight majesty' of the nation he now rules."[9] As this long and powerful speech unfolds, it becomes clear that what the king wants and needs is not to pardon, or even to understand his son, but to recreate him as a better—that is, a more legitimate and successful—version of himself. In the glorification of his own youth we hear both an attempt at self-extenuation for his sense of failure now and an appeal to Hal to be that youth, but clarified and unchallenged, and so redeem what he, the king, has become. No wonder that Hal's role in this is to remain empty, unspecified, malleable to his father's fantasy.

And yet, returning from his long, half-cunning and half-mesmerized reminiscence, Henry finds that it is not Hal but Hotspur he has invoked. "And even as I was then is Percy now" (l. 96). The true son is "my nearest and dearest enemy," while the image of the king's sunlit dream of youth mounts usurpation with the same "worthy interest to the state" as Henry himself had in supplanting Richard. Thus the king invokes a shining past upon a field of failure, confusion, and unspecified loss. He sounds clear and resolute, of course, but that is ever his style—a tough and vigorous shell around an inchoate interior. He extols Hotspur's heroic style:

> Thrice hath this Hotspur, Mars in swathling clothes,
> This infant warrior, in his enterprises
> Discomfited great Douglas; . . .
>
> (3. 2. 112–14)

This is precisely the style he rebuked Hotspur for using earlier in defense of Mortimer ("Thou dost belie him, Percy!"). But now he makes it plain that for Hal to be "more myself" means for him to preempt Hotspur in just this mode. Filial identity, it seems, is to be determined by the best claim on the succession, which goes to the most Hotspurian of the claimants.

But however firm and singleminded he seems in demanding a Hotspurian son, Henry himself might be told that "thou hast forgotten to demand that truly which thou wouldest truly know." His sense of self-displacement and his strenuous efforts to subdue it that dog him to his miserable end in the Jerusalem Chamber in Part 2 are enacted in this appeal to Hal, too. "Had I so lavish of my presence been," he sneers, he had been left in "reputeless banishment, / A fellow of no mark nor likelihood." But of course he has rationed himself not only to the "vulgar company," but apparently to his son as well. And now, in the interests of atonement, he urges upon Hal just those self-hoarding, self-manipulating policies that have caused the need for the atonement in the first place.[10] On the face of it he is asking for a strictly formal relationship; he is asking Hal to play the role of Hotspurian son. But the face is strained with confusion. If it is too much to say that he "truly" is pleading for the intimacy he has always withheld and discouraged, his speech is nevertheless troubled with obscure longings and regrets, never expressly voiced but evident in the distortions of his performance: its excessive length, its rationalizations, evasions, and contradictions, the very effortfulness of its apparent control. When after forty lines of self-absorbed revery, the king turns again to address his son, he himself seems surprised by the tumult of feelings his own performance has elicited beyond the bounds of its initial, political conditions:

> Not an eye
> But is aweary of thy common sight,
> Save mine, which hath desired to see thee more;
> Which now doth that I would not have it do—
> Make blind itself with foolish tenderness.
>
> (3. 2. 87–91)

Henry cannot be wholly sincere (one can almost hear Falstaff's lugubrious parody). Yet these lines come up so unexpectedly that they bespeak real longings underneath. By contrast, Hal's response is masklike:

> I shall hereafter, my thrice-gracious lord,
> Be more myself.
>
> (92–93)

Is this merely formulaic, or quietly heartfelt? We cannot be sure: it gives nothing away. Henry himself shows no sign of having heard, for now that the floodgates have opened he has much to say before he has finished flushing out his passion. And now we can appreciate the deftness of Hal's response. Empty, minimal, it simply allows his father to go on talking, and hence to be drawn once more "backward and inward" into his fantasy.

His strange outpouring arrests our attention and fills the stage. Clearly something more is being revealed here than Henry either intends or understands. And our awareness that Hal, too, must realize this intensifies the experience of a supersaturated moment. Such a moment might spill over in any number of ways; *anything* could happen. What is being dramatized is the whole mystery of the separation of father and son. When Henry ends, his bitter passion rising to an outright charge of treason, then settling with a snarl—"how much thou are degenerate" (l. 128)—the hush that follows unmistakably pinpoints the crux of the scene, and indeed the crux of the play itself.

In terms of dramatic power, Hal gains much from his patience. Unlike Hotspur, who cannot keep quiet, he understands the uses of silence to set off speech. In the Boarshead earlier, Falstaff's extrication from the men-in-buckram trap was the more marvelous for its being so long delayed by the battle of insults preceding it. Hal has played just such a role with his father, allowing him to say the worst without interruption, seemingly at unanswerable length, before he attempts a defense. Now as he rises, the "all this" that he gravely promises to redeem "on Percy's head" bears the burden of all we have heard tormenting the king, both explicitly and implicitly. In performance it is scarcely possible not to feel the power of Hal's response, its dead seriousness, its fierce concentration, its galvanically rising energy of purpose. His soliloquy in act 1 was made suspect by its callow coolness. The vow here recapitulates the plan of the soliloquy—emerging in glory, redeeming time—but it is not so much a confirmation of the earlier speech as a fleshed and fully felt version of it. Hal himself, like his father, clearly is moved by the occasion, regardless of how perfectly he had anticipated it. *Being there* is new. He cannot have foreknown, after all, the complex power of his father's voice and presence, any more than Henry could have foreknown the gratifying persuasiveness of his son's deft gifts, first of silence, then of eloquence. These things they could not have known without risking each other's presence. Now the live encounter reaches its climax in Hal's declaration. The speech gathers up personal, domestic, and dynastic history, as well as the play's major themes and connections, and packs them into a single simple yet powerful logic: I am your true not counterfeit son, therefore the prince and heir apparent; I will prove it by vanquishing Hotspur; we will thereby put down rebellion and establish succession beyond all question.

HAL
And I will die a hundred thousand deaths
Ere break the smallest parcel of this vow.

HENRY
A hundred thousand rebels die in this!
(158–160)

The prince, as John Russell Brown sees it, stands before the king at the end of this speech "transformed." Others will see it later, but the king and the audience have seen it while it was happening. And Hal's dramatic credibility now will be vital to his claims of legitimacy later on.

Wonderfully composed as this scene is, it remains somehow disturbing. In performance it can certainly seem a fully satisfying drama of atonement at the filial and therefore the dynastic level. But as soon as we step back, reconsider the larger context, and as soon as the action picks up again, we may well have second thoughts. Does it really do what it had seemed to promise—disclose and somehow answer to the crucial void between the father and son? Does the reconciliation grow out of a deeply sounded sundering? To answer no to these questions is not to abjure our sense of the scene's satisfying fullness. Rather, it is to raise the deeper question of the scene's—and the play's—persistent ambiguity: its capacity to excite multiple, and irreconciliable, responses in us.

Subtle differences in performance can crystallize major differences in perspective. Often in performance Hal's reply takes off from the end of Henry's with little or no pause, as if the two speeches were really one interlocking set. There is something to this. The speeches balance each other so well, Hal's so firmly reverses the emotion and momentum of Henry's, that we become aware of an orchestrated relationship. A union is dramatized, father-and-son. And no doubt our aesthetic pleasure in this harmony is enhanced by an awareness of their own. Perhaps Henry is moved just as we are by his son's sheer skill, and both of them are excited, in part, by the nimbleness with which they have skirted emotional dangers. But to see the two performances as essentially one, coordinated by tacit agreement, should not obscure the fact that a choice has been made. And the moment of choice will be clear if we postulate a hush between Henry's tirade and Hal's response. At this moment, which I have described as supersaturated, a number of possible futures present themselves. Conceivably, had the silence been extended, the moment might have deepened into something like the dream form of *2 Henry IV*, where the implications of this troubled relationship, its fears, deep distrusts, guilty desires, surface disconcertingly. At this moment, in other words, we have the possibility of an unexpected revelation of the play's defended center—of an access through its relentlessly bouyant and opaque style.

What Hal does by jumping in with his perfect timing and perfect speech is to veto those possibilities—he chooses one future and suppresses the others. Rather than succumbing to the silence, he mounts a drama upon it, inventing with brilliant resourcefulness out of the volatile materials at hand. In effect he levers the power of the moment—the bitter passion of his father's rebuke still shuddering in the air—into a play of the future. His first words, a line of firm simple monosyllables, enact the shift of tenses:

> Do not think so. You shall not find it so.
>
> (129)

He reshapes Henry's sharply personal attack into this generalized forward thrust, the "it" going carefully unspecified. He does not deny the charges, the past, but merely asserts what the future will be.

> And God forgive them that have so much swayed
> Your majesty's good thoughts away from me.
>
> (130–31)

No denial, but an emphasis upon what Henry thinks. Hal is forming a future out of Henry's thoughts, recreating his father's guilty past into a shining image: "wasting the former times" by a powerfully cathartic style.

> I will redeem all this on Percy's head . . .
>
> (132)

"All this" means, finally, the world according to Henry IV: the past gathered up and spent in a single image, a single combat.

> A hundred thousand rebels die in *this!*
>
> (160, my italics)

We are caught up, Henry is caught up. It is what he wants—at least part of what he wants, or what he thinks he wants. And in any case it is clearly what they both need to be able to command the future. But the very perfection of Hal's heroic drama closes off the possibility of intimacy, either canceling or deferring the resolution of their private business. No matter how "sincere" they are, they are settling for a simulacrum of a personal atonement.

The play's rebellious energies have driven it toward its own center. Yet the central scene leaves us with a deeply ambiguous sense of what has been discovered there. The scene seems both full and hollow, both perfect and inadequate. Nothing better could have occurred, yet something vital has failed to occur. All the elements of historical experience—personal, filial, dynastic—have been accommodated as efficiently as possible, within the imperious limits of time. But time itself—or is it the characters' submission to time?—forces them to settle for a hearty fabrication of what they "would truly know."

Father and son go forth from this scene as if their relationship were fully resolved. And from this "as if" the play takes its momentum and direction, moving toward the great Shrewsbury scenes where Hal confirms his oath. But how does the ambiguity of the reconciliation bear upon the heroic plot that grows out of it? How does our awareness of the "as if" in that plot affect the meaning of its culmination?

It is impossible to separate these questions from the more general question of Hal's nature as an "actor," with all the doubleness the term implies. For all its live complexity, the interview scene is circumscribed by Hal's own secret plot. From this point of view the reconciliation is one of a series of staged events through which he will assume his regal and "true" identity. This does not mean that he detachedly manipulates the scene or his father. His dramatic genius lies in his coolly playing the prodigal son, allowing his father's vitality to vent itself spontaneously and to give the scene its compelling edge, while still controlling the ultimate shape it will assume. It is a subtle and risky kind of manipulation in which he makes himelf part of what is being manipulated, and it shows promising kingcraft as well as stagecraft. Certainly it shows a maturer sense than did his soliloquy of how his present life as an actor relates to his destiny as king. Nevertheless, there are clear limits to the risks he is willing to take as an actor growing into his destiny. To guarantee the fruition of a particular future, he has to rob the dramatic moment of its existential urgency. There can be no real possibility of its turning out tragically.

Of course, what he steals from the present he vows to make good on, gloriously, in the future. In the eschatological myth of redemption implied in his soliloquy, the old machiavellian impulse, so familiar from the earlier plays, resurfaces in its most complex form so far. Obviously Hal is no Richard III, nor is the historical vision of this play nearly so constricted as that of the early ones.[11] Hal's role is to bring all the rambunctious vitality of *1 Henry IV*—its vastly broadened vision of historical experience—into coherent and gratified form. His role, presumably, is to comprehend that vitality. This all implies a wise as well as skillful actor, his performing instincts capable of replenishing the ground from which he rises into glory. Yet just here Hal inspires as much doubt as confidence. Rather than transcend the play's besetting ambiguity—its twin sense of purposeful surface and thwarted interior—his acting style actually heightens it.

For Henry, language always half-reveals and half-conceals his character; we always seem to be catching him in the act of covering himself. By contrast, Hal in his heroic declarations can seem to say "all," to hold nothing back, because in fact he withholds so much:

> For my part, I may speak it to my shame,
> I have a truant been to chivalry;
> And so I hear he doth account me too.
> Yet this before my father's majesty. . . .
>
> (5. 1. 93–96)

The style is "pure" and unconflicted, rolling on with unimpeded confidence because it is so impersonal. His "I" is forthright rather than furtive like his father's because it is so purely a verbal fiction. The persona is not a lie, however, but an improvisation, nimbly fashioned for the occasion from the flood of materials on hand at the moment—the political crisis, his father, the king's past, his own past, his rival, his future, himself. He has the playwright's capacity to stand back from the very experience in which he takes part and to regard it all, including himself, as passing matter, his to shape.

The result, however impressive, is utter clarity on the one hand, utter vagueness on the other. Do the personas imply a single creative will? Certainly over the course of the two plays we gather a strong sense of continuous subtextual character. It is, as Daniel Seltzer observes, one of Shakespeare's major achievements, the creation of a figure "who contains—as do all the important creations of good playwrights—an inwardly oriented *raison d'etre,*" and whom we perceive as actually growing *in* dramatic time. "The character is that of a man in flux, and we should attach more importance to that sense of changing, of continual process, than is implied in our more or less common academic understanding that this is a prince 'educating' himelf."[12] Agreed. But I think it is not until Part 2 that we begin to feel a character dragging against the flow of time and struggling to come into focus. Nowhere in Part 1, except perhaps momentarily in some of the Falstaff scenes, do we feel unmistakably that Hal "himself" glints through the surface of the dense and supple verbal action. In one sense, his performing style disturbs because it is just too good. He performs perfectly in whatever context he inhabits; immerses himself so completely in the dramatic situation that we lose the distinction between actor and character.

Paradoxically, this ability to "lose" himself in the moment creates the impression of some fundamental detachment from the occasion. We never see him sweat or seem to sacrifice one thing in order to embrace another. Each of the twin Shrewsbury eulogies is effortlessly appropriate to its distinctive object—chivalry for Hotspur, mockery for Falstaff. Hal himself is the bridge between them, and yet "he" is little more at that moment than a ritual inheritor. He has no voice of his own, certainly evinces nothing like his father's struggle into a style of yoked contradications. He responds to all occasions attentively, but with unnerving efficiency; except in the Boarshead, as when he is manically "driv[ing] away the time till Falstaff come," he squanders nothing. Thus from one angle he appears to fill the moment vividly, while from another he seems to be pushing forward some energetic pantomime of a "true" self withheld. Vigorous as his acting always is, his commitment to the dramatic present has none of that massive time-stopping self-abandonment that we find preeminently in the great tragic figures, and to some extent in Richard II. Hal has no wish to stop time, to enlarge the present moment by pouring himself into it. He is always busy levering the present toward the future, maintaining a sort of running negotiation with the demands of time. In itself the present has no enduring hold on him, nor is it overwhelmingly real. But as it does not profoundly exist for him, he does not profoundly exist within it.

Still, to belabor the disturbing effects of Hal's acting will rightly seem a heavy-handed response to what is more immediately an invigorating performance. And after all, the performance seems to work. The myth generated between father and son is precisely what is played out so impeccably at Shrewsbury: son rescues father, is acknowledged the true son by father, then turns to face and vanquish the pretender, true Harry against false. This play (in contrast to Part 2) will not require from Hal any deeper or more personal attestation of inward character than what shows forth in the battle. In its wonderful synthesis of action and design, vitality and spontaneous form, *1 Henry IV* is decidedly a springtime play: hopeful of the future and prodigal of its past, the source of its forward-thrusting power. Hal can get by with being inventive in many moods—witty, bouyant, solemn, pious, outraged—and finds no reason for doubting the adequacy of this skill to any situation an heir apparent is likely to come up against.

And yet, just this sunny harmony of hero and play does cast a shadow, muted as it is. Hal, assuming his destiny robustly, by his own gifts as an actor in this world of rebellious energies, begins to vanish into that consumer of characters, "history." He begins to vaporize into the legend that Vernon celebrates, in a speech of nine astonished similes, before an eclipsed and despairing Hotspur (4. 1. 96–109). Hal heads toward this future with such tranquil charm that we would surely troop along with him, cheering him on, were it not for the one large and indigestible fact of Falstaff, who has the power to throw everything into question. Falstaff renders everything conditional, revokes every terminal gesture. And we look to him, I believe, to redeem Hal from the hollow triumph of his own promise to square all accounts in the future. Falstaff keeps him alive in the play, holds off time, and so preserves the hope of creating rather than succumbing to history.

Hal's career can be charted in terms of his separation from Falstaff. Whether or not we find this movement satisfying, we surely grow aware of a major shift in the play's balance of powers. In shedding Falstaff, Hal gains one kind of power, forgoes another. Their polarization in the last two acts plays out in earnest—out of doors, so to speak—the tacit terms of their partnership in the first two acts. This process, as always in Shakespeare, will seem gratifying because it clarifies and offers to resolve ambiguity. Also it will sadden, for we witness the decomposition of a wonderfully complex relationship of mutual attractions and restraints, one of Shakespeare's most successful models of creative collaboration and perhaps the only authentic one in the histories.

We do not see Hal make his original choice of Falstaff, but the ritual quality of their opening exchange (1. 2) suggests that he must repeatedly reenact the choosing. However Hal may assess his own motives, we cannot miss the enthusiasm with which he responds to what is, after all, Falstaff's invitation to enter his domain. Merely to keep up with Falstaff requires a kind of abandonment to the delight and sway of language, a submission to its rhythms, an openness to its inadvertent suggestions. Hal in a role of authority may roundly chastise Falstaff, but never (until the end of Part 2) does he try to silence him. He may remove himself from his presence, he may act as if he had ceased to exist or were dead, but in this play he does not actively deny the verbal bond. They exist together *in* language as a living medium; it binds them together as members of each other, even as lovers of a sort. In its power to engage Hal in this collaboration—and in Hal's willingness to *be* engaged—Falstaff's superfluous mode, his very gratuitousness, grow compelling.

Hal plays for freedom, for multiplicity, for re-creation, for the delights and nourishments of a world beyond the power of history to conceive, or even to tolerate. Hal is there, in other words, for a lot of reasons that are not pragmatic in the sense of having a calculated usefulness in his plans for the future. In one sense, he is there to forestall or deny the future.

But Hal also plays, of course, for some very pragmatic reasons. The crudest is the one he formulates in his soliloquy, where he casts Falstaff as the sullen field from which he will rise to glory. But Falstaff is neither sullen nor passive; it is rather the vitality of the tavern life that will provide Hal the best grounds upon which to enact his heroic drama. That drama, after all, calls for a central character unburdened by Hamletlike doubts and the internal tumult of unsounded selves. Perhaps if Hamlet had a live Yorick to drain off antic energies he would not have to play that part, among others, himself. But Hal has his Yorick, and more. Falstaff is not only alive, but powerfully alive, and certainly no figment of Hal's fantasy. His very reality spares Hal the need of inventing him as the antic side of his own personality. In Eastcheap he can safely try out and liberate rebellious energies that would otherwise complicate the wished-for self of the heroic drama. The exertions of his "vile participation" allow him to be serene and personally unexpressive in his high style. In other words, Hal needs Falstaff so that he can eventually come free of him. This means that in Hal's eschatalogical myth of ascension to glory, it is Falstaff's role to be transcended. And the more compelling the clown, the greater the prince's glory.

In the early scenes, both sides of Hal's motivation—the delight in play, the rebuke of play—coexist in nervous suspension. He thrives on play but also on the expectation of its coming to an end. That is the theme of the partnership itself, enacted over and over again, the vital opposition repeatedly reformed under the pressures of the outside world. When the king's messenger arrives at the climax of the Boarshead festivities, Hal might have been thrown into confusion by his own conflicting instincts. Instead he is invigorated by the threat, and the vigor finds its natural form in a renewed intensity of play. What makes the collaboration genuinely creative is this ability to interpose, between the drumbeats of history, fantastic moments, like that of the "rehearsal," which overflow, and incorporate, and then newly body forth historical "realities."

Hal preserves the doublesness of his situation as long as possible, defying the lures of form, closure, completion. When ultimately he is forced to choose, and so dissolve the doubleness, it is not because history catches up with the playing, but because the playing catches up with history. The natural rhythms of Falstaff's world drive the comedy onto its own creative sources.

The result is the reconciliation scene, in which, as we have seen, Hal pitches the drama into the future tense, clamping the lid upon all possible outcomes except the heroic plot that he and Henry have agreed upon. Forced to choose, Hal chooses heartily: he does not even bother to deny his "vile participation" with Falstaff, but simply proceeds as if it had never happened (just as father and son march out of the scene, as I said earlier, as if they had resolved all personal matters between them). But Falstaff will not agree to "play dead" for the sake of this wishful scenario. He will not be corseted into the form of a "holiday" whose term is up. As Hal's machiavellian strain grows purer, Falstaff's role as spoiler of Hal's eschatological myth grows purer in response. From act 4 on, the play suffers a dissociation of formerly integrated elements. The heroic plot assumes a powerful automony, and Falstaff is forced to improvise guerilla-theater tactics for survival.

What is at stake, of course, is not simply Falstaff's survival as a character, but the credibility of his entire imaginative mode of playing as an answer to the assumptions of heroic—and ultimately historical—supremacy. What enduring claim does he make upon us? It will not do to remember only his triumphs in the great tavern scene. From that point on, as Edward Pechter puts it, "the play in effect conforms itself to Hal's version of experience, and for the first time seems decisively to define its own structure as a creature of Hal's and not Falstaff's imagination." Furthermore, Falstaff not only faces exclusion by the play's "natural" flow of events; he also faces a withdrawal of our sympathy as we are brought round to an "acceptance" of the heroic plot by "a number of strategies that make Falstaff seem a much less and Hal a more endearing figure."[13] Falstaff cannot hope to survive merely as a sentimental preference.

Let me trace the argument behind this formulation of the problem. From the end of the spacious tavern scene (2. 4), we experience a constriction of the imaginative life that Hal's festive partnership with Falstaff had so pleasurably encouraged. All along, of course, we have been prepared for an end to the festivity. The question is not whether the play would reach that end but whether it would manage to satisfy all the rebellious energies it has so urgently brought forth. This means, of course, not only Hotspur's rebellion, which exhausts itself, but Falstaff's as well. Can the play reach its appointed end only by suppressing Falstaff, or does he exhaust himself, too?

One answer is that in the last half of the play Falstaff indeed forfeits much of his claim upon our sympathies—that in the cold daylight of history we come to see the tavern charmer as a frankly unappealing figure: taking bribes from draft-dodgers, sending pitiful "rag-of-muffins" into the maw of war, scrabbling for safety, comfort and profit in a context where bravery, selflessness, and honor have become the commanding virtues. Furthermore, as Brian Vickers shows, Falstaff's language becomes more and more nakedly unscrupulous and self-serving.[14] As the heroic context reproves the festive ethic of perpetual play, we are brought to accept Falstaff's exclusion from the main action of the drama and to shift our allegiance firmly to the heroic plot itself. By the end of the Shrewsbury sequence—like Hal in his carefully affectionate eulogy—we have accustomed ourselves to the idea of a dead, or at least diminished Falstaff. Whether or not we are taken in by his counterfeit death, his expansive resurrection sends a surge of delight through any audience. It delights, that is, *because* it is illogical, paradoxical, wonderful. But for this reason it also carries a sense of vaudevillian irrelevancy—one last sportive fantasy interposed between inevitable stages in the linear, historical plot. Falstaff's rising forestalls, but by no means undoes, the fulfillment of Hal's eschatology.

My argument with this reading is that it tacitly reintroduces the idea of a manipulative Shakespeare, a "king of shadows" intervening to deck out Hal in rising glory while muddying up the one character who might credibly raise doubts about that glory. But *1 Henry IV* has operated from the beginning through the freely expressed and contending strengths of all its characters, and continues to do so through the latter half.

Falstaff's distinctive strength is, in C. L. Barber's phrase, his capacity for "humorous redefinition"—a seemingly endless ability to rename himself and the world, to recycle the threatening meanings of history through the extempore world of festivity, thence out to us to dissolve in our laughter. But from the "reconciliation" on, the play itself, aligning its structure and momentum with that of the heroic plot, appears to have gone to war against humor. Hal returns to the tavern (3. 3) and finds himself drawn into something like his erstwhile collaboration with Falstaff, but his new-minted seriousness overrides the lingering affection and pleasure. "I have come to procure thee, Jack, a charge of foot." At the end of the scene Falstaff wishes "this tavern were my drum," but the humor is weak, and the attempt at redefinition futile. The tavern fades, the play moves out of doors, and the stage becomes a field of battle.

Like all the play's conflcts, the struggle of the last two acts proceeds at two distinguishable levels: the politic or mimetic action, and the antic contention for the stage itself. In the first act we saw that Henry's soberly machiavellian instincts for drama were unavailing against the galvanic energies of Hotspur. Now, however, Henry has acquired dramatic authority as well as the military advantage of swiftly moving and loyal troops. Of course the two are connected; both in and out of

Shakespeare a king may inspire loyalty through regal charisma. But a king commands the stage itself only if that charisma extends to us. By act 5 Henry can justly dismiss Worcester's rambling list of grievances as "water colors" (5. 1. 80), but the fact is that Henry's own claims of legitimacy are, prima facie, no more convincing. He is credible as king because by this time in the play *we* have credited him, which we do because he now carries Hal's dramatic weight.

Falstaff wars, therefore, not just against the eschatology of the heroic plot with its linear structure, hierarchical assumptions, and narrow exclusiveness, but against its claim on our imagination. Act 4, scene 1, for instance, establishes the power of the heroic plot by showing the effects of the reconciliation upon the rebels. Northampton's "sickness," the king's swift advance, Hal's transformation, Glendower's collapse: the tide of news flows all one way, relentless. Nature herself seems to be marching in step with the heroic enterprise, Hal and his comrades coming on, in Vernon's eyes, as estridges and eagles, "As full of spirit as the month of May / And gorgeous as the sun at midsummer" (101–2). The strong emotional rhythms—Hotspur's desperate ups and downs against the images of rising regal potency—give the scene immediately gratifying form. The heroic plot becomes a self-sufficient narrative structure arching inexorably from the reconciliation to Shrewsbury: "Doomsday is near. Die all, die merrily."

Falstaff's answer to this scene follows. Of course 4. 2 gives us a "realistic" view of the war to balance the heroic, and Falstaff's "food for powder, food for powder. . . . Tush, man, mortal men, mortal men" satirizes the heroic perspective of battle as a struggle between mighty opposites. But more is afoot than satire or balance. Our hunger for culmination has been aroused, and Falstaff must reassert the claims of the antic mode of experience. Therefore he works to redefine the war—though now with somewhat bated humor—as a conflict not between mighty characters in an epic plot, but between that entire plot, full of all those characters, and Falstaff himself. Against the forward pressure of the changed "brave world" he asserts his rhetorical powers of invention, conjuring up a cast of outrageously pathetic "mortal men" who obviously have no place at all in an heroic view of history.

> . . . A mad fellow met me on the way, and told me I had unloaded all the gibbets and pressed the dead

> bodies. No eye hath seen such scarecrows. I'll not march through Coventry with them, that's flat. Nay, and the villains march wide betwixt the legs, as if they had gyves on, for indeed I had the most of them out of prison. There's not a shirt and a half in all my company, and the half-shirt is two napkins tacked together and thrown over the shoulders like a herald's coat without sleeves; . . .
>
> (34–46)

For all its grimy realism, the speech swells irresistably, generating details hyperbolically, forcing our attention upon Falstaff's own theatrical presence. He not only takes the new brave world as his theme; he bodies it forth, he invokes it with deadly exuberant particularity. You want war? he says to us. I'll give you war. You want to get serious? I'll give you more than you bargained for, and make you laugh to boot at what you know is not really funny, and your laughter will acknowledge the superior reality of my inventions. In other words, Falstaff counterpunches against the powerful autonomy of the heroic plot by dramatizing war as a product of the play itself, its native rebelliousness, rather than as a product of a narrowed epic convention. As such, "war" is seen as a risky venture between audience and performers, and not a controlled and shapely process leading to a predetermined end. Falstaff manages to delay the forward thrust of the plot by intruding his own unruly self into our consciousness, forcing us to hold competing images of experience in mind as the whole meaning of this "war."[15]

By act 5 the separated worlds—heroic and Falstaffiian—converge with violent dramatic results. Hal's offer to meet Hotspur in single combat (5. 1. 83–100) advances the heroic plot by honing the political struggle to a fine chivalric point. The decorum of the offer, its perfect lack of Hotspurian posturing, lends the moment a natural sense of propriety and immediate theatrical pleasure. But this sense of the duly ripened moment-of-choice personally threatens Falstaff. "Thou owest God a death," Hal soberly puns. "'Tis not due yet," Falstaff returns. Upon this flat counterpremise he inflates a rhetorical alternative to the linear squeeze-play of the heroic plot. "Can honor set to a leg? No. Or an arm? No . . ." The "no's" pile up, swelling by incantation and catechizing rhythms. This is the old Boarshead strategy ("Banish plump Jack and banish all the world"), adapted to a more naked threat. Again Falstaff makes himself an irresistable target through his wildly specious logic; but before we act to deflate him (thereby, like Hal earlier, playing Falstaff's game) we are led through laughter to glimpse another kind of speciousness: the myth of "honor" as a natural ethic rather than a cultural fiction. The performance lacks the old spontaneity, but it does its work and holds our attention long enough to reestablish the authority of the conditional mode and complicate our response to the heroic.

Falstaff makes his worst appearance during the battle (5. 3), mocking Sir Walter Blunt's king-costumed corpse ("There's honor for you!") and his own slaughtered draftees:

> . . . I have led my rag-of-muffins where they are peppered.
> There's not three of my hundred and fifty left alive,
> and they are for the town's end, to beg during life. . . .
> (35–38)

Sour as this is, Falstaff is simply refusing to submit to heroic categories of meaning. "Grinning honor" belongs to Blunt, but is meaningless for those who do not exist in the adventure story called history. In that story, after all, Falstaff and his spawn of rag-of-muffins are merely the sullen ground for the bright heroic figures. The only existence the "mortal men" have is the one that Falstaff invokes for them as an embarrassment to the heroic ethic. And the only existence *he* has is the one he maintains for himself by his stage presence. Between their death and obscurity and his life and endurance is nothing but the performance. Quite literally, that performance is "life; which if I can save, so; if not, honor comes unlooked for, and there's an end."

Not glory, not transfiguration, just an "end." To expose Hal's smiling plot as essentially humorless, its pleasures the machiavel's means toward an end, Falstaff maneuvers to grab the stage and hold it long enough to generate some extravagant but powerful alternatives:

Honor	Life
Air	Food
Pistol	Bottle
Blunt	Rag-of-muffins
History	Play
Death	Himself

Falstaff aligns not only war but all the values represented in this war with death: the values of order, design, completion, the impulse toward transcendence, the ideal of unity, the entire heroic myth of eschatology. What is more, death itself is mockery. Life alone is real—which is to say, this moment, this place, this continuing, overflowing absurdity. Of course the polarization is fraudulent. But in dramatizing outrageous alternatives of life and death—and before we recoil to dismantle his "logic"—Falstaff forces us to register our own gut allegiances.

The resurrection sequence (5. 4) recapitulates Falstaff's re-creative mode: the ultimate "putdown," the magical rising, the extrication and revitalization as he puns and riddles himself back into a commanding and central dramatic presence. There had been signs earlier of a waning enthusiasm, but now he rebounds with wonderful energy, shattering Hal's shapely design. Superfluousness incarnate, he cheerfully collapses hierarchies and distinctions, proliferating "counterfeits" until he dazzles us into belief in the democracy of all forms of play. There are no meanings but stage meanings; the play's assumption of a separate reality, of internal coherence, is a sham: all "boy's play," swords of lath, an actor feigning the dead Hotspur:

> . . . How if he should counterfeit too, and rise?
> By my faith, I am afraid he would prove the
> better counterfeit.[16]
>
> (5. 4. 121–23)

Then, suddenly, the vaudevillian punster shoves the blade into Hotspur's "thigh" (meaning, almost certainly, his groin) and our gasp reconstitutes the playworld. The sword is steel, the corpse is flesh, this world *is* real. How could we have forgotten? Hotspur has lived hotly in our imagination. In soliciting our humorous disdain for the "counterfeit" corpse, a mere caricature of "grinning honor," Falstaff has lured our attention from what we "truly know." In stabbing Hotspur he stabs contemptuously at us—at our short memories, our fickleness, our love of single meanings, our gullibility.

"Mark how a plain tale shall put you down," says Hal in the palmy Boarshead days. Falstaff's rising in 5. 4 is his answer. His "counterfeit" speech and then his castration of Hotspur amount to a tale plainer than the heroic story implied in Hal's twin eulogies. Falstaff's answer—always a version of "I knew ye"—is both more extravagant and more direct; to call the play "boy's play" is both true and an elaborate falsehood. He reasserts the great "as if" of dramatic truth itself, the vital conditionality of playing.

"This is the strangest tale that ever I heard," says John. "This is the strangest fellow, brother John," Hal concedes, and so must we. Falstaff will not be kept down, not even in our formulizing imagination. He continues to elude not just Hal but us, who had cornered him, or so we thought, as the Spirit of Play. He is the very Heisenberg Principle: catch him as mass, he has already eluded us as mobility; catch him as motion, the play's pure vitality, he'll be stealing our purse, our trust, our good name. He undermines the play and he makes the play. He *is* the strangest fellow still, the double man, the pun incarnate, two-in-one, the impossible confirmed by the twin testimonies of eyes and speech:

> Art thou alive,
> Or is it fantasy that plays upon our eyesight?
> I prithee speak. We will not trust our eyes
> Without our ears. Thou art not what thou seem'st.
> (5. 4. 132–35)

Like the thing of great constancy, however strange and admirable, Falstaff lives only in drama, and gives drama its cogency too. But the drama bodied forth by Falstaff is something more complex than the histories have shown us before. We see it, as we see Falstaff himself, freshly, with "parted eye," like the amazed lovers in *Dream*, or by a "natural perspective" as in the end of *Twelfth Night*. For a moment at least we may glimpse the astounding depth of life that feeds him, the play, and history, too.

Is there a "natural" tendency for an action to complete itself? Or do we simply project our desire for one upon the stuff of the play and call it natural?

Falstaff can rise up to thwart completion of the heroic story not because he is inexhaustible but because he plays across limits, to us and our time. He solicits our collaboration in forestalling culmination. When he grumbles, for instance, that "I'll not bear my own flesh so far afoot again" he gives us an open laugh; but he also conveys his knowing refusal to subside into the definition of his own body. This doubleness (if we are nimble enough to catch it) enriches our pleasure in his playing;

it also lights up our own mixed motives. For in addition to pleasing, Falstaff also attracts our desire to penetrate the secret center of his diffuse array of roles and meanings, to name him once and for all, and put him down. We too distrust idleness and want our time, even in play, to be well spent. We want form, we want meaning, and for these we need completion and resolution of the action. Falstaff illuminates the load of aggressiveness concealed in these "aesthetic" desires.

He can do this by standing firm against the terrific urge—ours and the playwright's—for an ending. Falstaff's demeanor in the last two acts—his ugliness, his ingenuity, his particular kinds of foolishness and intelligence—is a strategy for maintaining his distinctive importance: in a word, his body and the bodily values implicit in theater. For a contrast we might think of Richard III. In the end of his play Richard deserts us, leaving us no vital presence to be loyal to. Then we are freed to turn on him with moral indignation. Nothing substantial intervenes between our desire to judge and the historical monster Richard becomes.

Unlike Richard, Falstaff gives us an unfailing locus for our skeptical, defiant impulses. The body never fails, either in its presence or in its elusiveness. In his continuing vitality Falstaff defies our drift toward moral autocracy, our tendency to acquiesce in the convention of an End to Holiday. He reveals how deeply the play assumes that convention—how play and audience tacitly collude in a wishful ordering of experience into a "natural" culmination. In the process he exposes the aggressive impulse behind the very fashioning of "history"—the impulse to selectivity and silencing, the bias toward a hierarchical, self-justifying, single-focused view of reality. In short he brings to light the operative myth of *1 Henry IV,* that of history as a humanly fulfilling process—sunny, hopeful, whole, harmonious with the best and deepest truths of human nature.

But precisely because he holds so steady against such massive pressures of change, we come to see Falstaff differently. In the monologues of the last two acts he addresses us as an increasingly disturbing figure, speaking more and more directly out of the obscure heart of the play itself. His voice grows more abstract, less flexible; he becomes harsher, more dangerous, less personal, his allegiance going to something deeper than our good will. Through him the antic spirit emerges as more complex, a richer and darker phenomenon than we have known before. We perceive it as thriving on a darkness that presses around the lighted circle of the stage. Forestalling culmination, the triumphant antic spirit causes us to think on true endings all the more gravely.

Like Hal, frustrated and delighted, therefore amazed at this strange fellow, we do Falstaff the grace of the gilded lie. We give up our efforts to bring him down and end the story. But we do so knowing that there must be a real end, and authentic acknowledgement of the darkness in which "history" is played. What this means—since it is now abundantly clear that Falstaff cannot be brought within bounds—is that he must sooner or later be killed off. *We* must kill him off. The only real question is How? And to answer, "Not now, not yet," is to beg the question, to admit that there really is no right way. Perhaps that is the point. Hal's efforts to close the design by eliminating Falstaff are premature because they are wishful and evasive. Falstaff cannot be killed silently, passively, but only in full awareness of the costs and meaning of the act. In other words, Hal, we, and perhaps even the playwright, must suffer through a whole new process of self-knowledge. What must be learned is the meaning of completing an action: that there is no "natural" act, no "natural" design. Every act implies a cruelty. Every step into the future requires a death in the past.

By surviving, depriving us of the comfort of forward motion and finished stories, Falstaff renders the very idea of history problematical.[17] He also reveals its immense sadness. We perceive him dancing for his life upon a void; in the very density of his performing he shows us the emptiness he buffers us against. Once he stops dancing, there is only the plunge into the hollowness of history. But meanwhile, before our eyes, he turns the tragedy comic. He sets himself against the dramatist's own deep desire to arrest the flood of time that he has tapped by his own power. Thus Falstaff is rebellious even to the end, defying his own creator's will to set a form upon the indigest of history and mount a story upon the void. Always before, Shakespeare has stepped in to shape the end, and always it has meant relinquishing the autonomy of the characters whose antic energies have been his access to the true destructive nature of his material. York, Margaret, Richard III, the Bastard, Richard II all subside. None of them succeeds in holding Shakespeare's interest against the overwhelming need for form. Falstaff alone endures. Because Shakespeare finally cares so much for him he will not sacrifice him to his need. Because he cares so much, allowing his imagination to flow without stint into that figure, he has given Falstaff the power to wreck the "history," forcing the flood of time to redefine itself upon *him*.

And so Falstaff transforms the play's design—or rather, brings to light its true underlying design. True design is the shape that all the play's rebellious energies, freely played-out, assume. It is the materialization of the characters' collective activities. And in *1 Henry IV* the primary activity is the stimulated response to the sense of a missing center. Thus Hal's dissociation from his father is played and replayed obsessively in various keys, both with Falstaff and with Henry himself, until we begin to hear the echoes of a killing coldness at the heart. The melancholy sense of a Past emerges, all-important but known inevitably too late, realized only dynamically in the shapes that playing takes in the present. The "design" of *1 Henry IV* is the playing-out of responses to that sense of prior deprivation.

The muted tragedy of the play, brought forward by Falstaff's irrepressible comedy, is the inability of Henry and Hal to attend truly to the vacancy between them because of the need thrust upon them by their commitment to the future. Precisely because this vacancy remains unexplored there can be no ending, no final shape to their stories. Hence Part 2.

10

Henry IV, Part Two "Unfathered heirs and loathly births of nature"

> Open your ears, for which of you will stop
> The vent of hearing when loud Rumor speaks?

So Rumor opens *2 Henry IV*, implying that the audience ("my household"), even in consenting to hear the play, thereby consents as well to aid him in his business of spreading "continual slanders," "false reports." Like Richard III in his opening monologue, he engages the audience on the premise that the play itself is an act of deception, and as in *Richard III* this premise eventually fulfills itself upon its maker. What we are party to is a process of confusions—false promises, forfeited claims, betrayals, and "strained passions"—for which Rumor asserts responsibility: ". . . who but only I, / Make fearful musters and prepared defense / . . . And no such matter?" And indeed he sets the play in motion precisely as a mischievous playwright: "The posts come tiring on, / And not a man of them brings other news / Than they have learned of me." But the very train of frustration and false promise begun by Rumor thrusts forward Henry V at the end of the play "to mock the expectation of the world, / To frustrate prophecies and to raze out / Rotten opinion. . ." (5. 2. 126–28). The frustrator frustrated, the mocker mocked,[1]—the false playwright routed. The "dream" from which Henry, repelling Falstaff, so chastely wakes in the final scene is not just his profligate youth, but also this entire play full of fearful musters and mocked expectations: in other words, *2 Henry IV* itself. Hal's awakening is the ultimate mockery, the delivery of the "true" play from the deceptive stuff of dreams. To be Henry V means to assume the role of the true playwright, he through whom play-language becomes *real*.

Such at any rate is the play's posture at the end. The new king hears out the Chief Justice, appoints him priestly guarantor of the royal word (5. 2. 119), and forbids Falstaff his characteristic mode of speech, the "fool-born jest." But only the most resolutely moralistic readers and playgoers would find this posture altogether credible. Our own responses to the complex events of this play, though initially engaged by Rumor, are not likely to be so neatly comprehended as he is, nor so happily narrowed at the end to the scope of Hal's admiring subjects. Hal gravely commands the tongues that Rumor had capriciously loosened. But the process by which he actually comes to assume that role is notoriously troublesome: strained, unfocused, indirect to the point of evasiveness. Compared with the forthright exuberance of Part 1—with which it everywhere invites comparison—Part 2 seems deliberately effortful, even self-destructive. For it is not only the characters' expectations that are mocked, but repeatedly our own as well. As Sigurd Burckhardt puts it, "2 *Henry IV* is littered with the rejections of dramatic opportunities, or rather of dramatic obligations, incurred partly by the structure of the play itself, partly by what we will (and are carefully reminded to) expect from 1 *Henry IV*, and partly by what we expect from the established legend."[2] So if Part 2 postures or "plays" the emergence of the true playwright, then what we have is a parody of the playwright's most immediate dramatic interests. The very displacements from our expectations, in other words, serve to enforce our attention upon the play's anxious concern with its own creative processes.

The central action of 1 *Henry IV* concerns Hal's emergence as "true" king—not, however, as glory-craving vanquisher of Hotspur, or even as image-mongering politician, but as king suitable both to the fictive world of his realm and to the complex dramatic experience he must bring into focus and carry across to *us* as the play. The dissociations between his asserted role and the field of dramatic material that should be symbolized in that role are muted, left chiefly implicit. But Falstaff stands as the play's refusal to be subdued to Hal's trim design. He exposes the prince's bias toward a facile formalism. a capacity for self-deceit, and a desire (for all his manipulation) to be the passive recipient of the crown—to wake up from a play, or dream, and find himself king. Falstaff's presence at the end of the play thus announces: you have not yet emerged as "sun" from the "mists"; what you thought you controlled controls you. Play out the play; you have yet to *take* the crown and be the playwright of your own play.

Thus the genius of one play, Falstaff, creates the need for a new one, in which the shadows that dog the triumphs of the first become the substance of the second.[3] The crucial silence of Part 1 on the distinction between Hal's emergence as prince and his ascension as king (the distinction between *son* and *sun*) is displaced into an entire play. Part 2 repeats the central action of Part 1, the making of a king, and finds the original successes that had seemed so "natural" too easily come by, indeed fabricated. As "counter-song" (or "under-song") *2 Henry IV* parodies not only the scenes and situations of *1 Henry IV*—the rebellion, the "trapping" of Falstaff, the encounter of father and son—but also the very source of the play's vitality, the ease with which vigorous self-conscious speech is spent into, and consumed by, gratifying forms of action. In Part 1 Hotspur's verbal manner is sufficient to generate, sustain, and exhaust a complete course of action; in Part 2 the rebels, bereft of his antic heat, strenuously mouth causes and cautions, "translat[ing] . . . insurrection to religion," but between them and their objective their language grows rigid, their cause stifles, and they fall to Prince John by a verbal trick. In Part 1 Hal's "detached" verbal mode drives his masterplot: for all its reductiveness the show of effectual action is nowhere balked. But in Part 2 Hal is twice shown reproving his own idleness and half-hearted preference for "small beer" while his father and the realm sicken; on the second occasion he speeds from the Boarshead as he had in Part 1, in the high resolute style that had served him so well then. But it comes to nothing now. Not for two acts does he reappear, and then only after the "tempest of commotion" has settled and his father, as he thinks, is dead.[4]

2 Henry IV is a play about thwarted effort. The seemingly organic unity in Part 1 of fertile speech and kinetic design has suffered a breakdown. We find on one hand a series of stillborn actions—a "design" of painfully frustrated intentions—and on the other a proliferation of verbal goblins like those "unfathered heirs and loathly births of nature" (4. 4. 122) that are said to mark the king's decline. Rumor, indeed, figures forth this dissociation. Gratuitously personified, he literally balks the "natural" continuity of speech and act by interposing "smooth comforts false, worse than true wrongs." He deploys his agents: "And not a man of them brings other news / Than they have learned of me." The news "should" issue into action: "What news, Lord Bardolph?" cries Northumberland, awaiting word of Hotspur's fate at Shrewsbury. "Every minute now / Should be the father of some strategem" (1. 1. 7–8). But "the times are wild" and the minutes breed only repeated occasions of language gone amuck: Northumberland's "strained passion" after the wildly unreliable reports from Shrewsbury; the archbishop's tendentious "translation" of himself "out of the speech of peace that bears such grace, / Into the harsh and boisterous tongue of war" (4. 1. 48); the king's apocalyptic deathbed vision (4. 5).

To some extent even Falstaff, gone slack in dissociation from Hal, grows fat in speech, running to garrulous monologues. Though he is still capable of amazing feats of bouyancy, a note of strain creeps unmistakably into his performances now, as he sweats out his verbal inflations. Whereas the archbishop turns "insurrection to religion," Falstaff will turn "diseases to commodity." And like the language of effortful transformation itself, stand-ins and surrogates seem to multiply. Until the rejection scene Hal and Falstaff meet only once, in the Boarshead, in a sad recapitulation of the counterpart scene of the earlier play. Otherwise they meet through surrogates—the page, Falstaff's letter, Poins, the Chief Justice. In general, the proliferated cast of comic characters extends the ways in which language seems everywhere banked into forms of perverse independence: Pistol's demented theatrics, Mistress Quickly's malapropisms, Shallow's dribbling repetitions, and so on. Some of this is hilarious; some of it is comic in the Bergsonian sense of mechanical habits upset by organic processes; some of it is distinctly grotesque and oddly moving, like Doll Tearsheet's nervous fits of obscure rage:

> He a captain! . . . God's light, these villains will
> make the word as odious as the word "occupy," which
> was an excellent good word before it was ill sorted.
> Therefore captains had need look to't.
>
> (2. 4. 131–36)

In the aggregate, however, these mannerisms make us aware

of the crucial changes dramatic speech has undergone since Part 1. Verbal self-consciousness has become a kind of Frankenstein's monster, obscurely potent, like Tearsheet's "captain" or the word "swagger," which so frightens Mistress Quickly (2. 4. 67–100). Now far from talking themselves into being, the characters seem to regard their own language in a hardened corporeal form. Like Falstaff's interposition between himself and the Chief Justice of the "disease of not listening, the malady of not marking" (1. 2. 115–16), a hyperbolic sensitivity to the *presence* of language continually intercedes between the characters and their intentions, thus preempting the expected course of action and so thrusting forward those "loathly births" themselves, those perversely palpable creatures of speech, as the real "action" of Part 2.

2 Henry IV is a parody of *1 Henry IV*, but we should not therefore assume a merely parasitical relationship. Shakespearean parody is a slippery and potent technique, tending to work in both directions. This is especially true if the parody acquires some distinctive, robust life of its own, as Shakespeare's always does. Even if we imagine him setting out in Part 2 intending only to shadow his triumph in Part 1, we know he could never hold his new play to a mere parodic pattern. It is far likelier, in any case, that he undertook Part 2 because of unfinished business in Part 1. In one sense the nature of that business is obvious: Falstaff must be silenced, Hal must be crowned. In a deeper sense Shakespeare has yet to bring the unfinished business, swelling the play with its mysterious "other grief," to light.

Part 2 repeats, mocks, and "wastes" Part 1, recasting it in a terminal mode. The aesthetic objective is not simply to destroy, but, as happens so often in Shakespeare, to uncover the sources of his own creations: a pursuit particularly appropriate to the historical sequence. The process of self-destruction in Part 2 is vigorous enough—though in its own mode. More important, the parodic process turns up a surprisingly original kind of life in the new material.

Any good production should show how the play moves beyond its predecessor into its own tough, distinctive reality. In the Stratford, Ontario, production of 1979, for example, Martha Henry's appearance as Doll Tearsheet brought an audible gasp from the audience. What we saw was great sensual beauty gone grotesquely to disease, its legacy not only sores and semibaldness but a fierce derangement that was funny, ghastly, dangerous, and deeply unsettling. The audience I am sure had never expected to be moved by this slummy creature with the tag name, let alone moved by a bizarre mixture of the fearful, the attractive, and the repellent. The comic pathos of her crying, quarreling, and nuzzling with the aging Falstaff was built upon that initial shock; the comedy could temporarily mask, but never really transcend this revelation of the uncanny within the conventional stage-type. The point is that Doll came across as vivid, compelling, and unique—beyond precedent. She may indeed have grown out of *1 Henry IV*, the natural product of a closer second look at the Boarshed milieu. But once materialized, Doll in no way depends for her dramatic life upon the mother play. If anything, she helps make it seem, in retrospect, surprisingly lightweight, somewhat naive, like vanished youth.

Sensitive production can bring forth the play's own difficult vision of life and therefore its complex structure. The "tiredness," the preoccupation with disease and stifled springs of action, come through not as the static imitation of a more robust original, but as a peculiar kind of vigor—artificially induced and desperately sustained, but vigor nonetheless. Scene after scene, image after image, presents us with the spectacle of dramatic power subsiding toward stillness. The power may take the form of boisterous farce, Pistolian dementia, inflated oration, and a dozen other kinds of "fearful musters and prepared defense." But until the end of the play, we are not given to understand the stillness itself as anything other than chill and empty death. Repeatedly we are arrested, drawn into the dramatic life of the play, only to find ourselves distinguishing, as if with ever-fresh recognition, the ubiquitous death's-head behind the playing. With almost manic inventiveness, the play generates variations on this experience. Allusions to disease, literal and figurative, pervade every level of action, but are orchestrated with great deftness. Through modulated phases the play takes us from a thickly felt sense of its fictive life to a stark awareness of its heavy cost.

Falstaff most of all embodies this process. It is commonplace to observe his "change of mode." But we are not simply presented with a diminished Falstaff—or a Falstaff of diminished antic energy. We are made painfully to experience the changing of this supposedly changeless creature. For despite his preoccupation now with morbidity and deliquescence, despite his turning into a Bergsonian comic figure, looking to survive in a world everywhere lapsing toward death, Falstaff manages after all to stay afloat, for most of the play, through versions of his old ebullient form. He now excites a wilder mixture of responses from us—including, sometimes simultaneously, both sympathy and revulsion. But he is coming apart, losing his once uncanny control of his humorous effects and losing his vital knowingness. As he softens, he also vaporizes. His former capacity for recycling worldly realities through energetic play, redeeming the world from death by the comedy of his own indestructability, wears down before our eyes. He subsides into the relentlessly realistic context of the playworld. But his presence there lards it, thickens its reality with his own.

The compelling density of the play's presentational life, set against the persistent reminders of the futility of action and perversity of structure, makes this a dramatic experience more perplexing and "modern" than anything that has gone before. In its power to disconcert us, simultaneously seducing us by realism and upsetting us by form, *2 Henry IV* anticipates the so-called problem plays, *Hamlet, Measure for Measure,* and *Troilus and Cressida.* It is most like *Measure for Measure* in that our expectations are continually thwarted, but at the same time nourished. Hal's promise to make "all this" good in the end never drops utterly out of mind. And yet, as James L. Calderwood suggests, we may begin to lose our faith that such a pattern of disorder and frustration as the play presents can ever be truly "redeemed." But that is exactly what Hal presumes to do when he steps forth at last to mock expectations that have already been mocked so many times over. By inverting the play's entire pattern of frustrations, banishing Rumor as playwright, he presumes nothing less than the freeing of language from its caked forms, its loathly births of nature, that it may destroy itself through lively utterance. This is a noble action, worthy of the real playwright: true father of fair heirs.

And it is a task that Hal might rightly shrink from undertaking and that we might rightly doubt his capacity to master, just because, by the end of the play, there is so much more to be redeemed than he and the audience and probably even Shakespeare could ever have imagined when the promise was made. By way of the parodic "wasting" of old form, the unfolding of 2

Henry IV has revealed a surprising new depth of experience that now becomes part of the load which Hal must bear. In other words, *our* experience of this difficult play becomes part of the field that Hal, as playwright-king, must address himself to as "redeemer."

No wonder that he does, in fact, shrink from assuming this role (in contrast to his confident self-assertion in the last play). For of course he does not stand passively by, watching the play breed its monsters and death's-heads without cause. He actively holds back from that moment of choice that in Part 1 came to him so easily, at so little cost. In his very reluctance to assume his destined role, the strange intransigence of *2 Henry IV* is played out: its dreamlike sense of being everywhere out of phase, everywhere hurt by an unarticulated "other grief," all the while intent on "fearful musters and prepared defense." The gathering sickness, the desperate fear of the passing of time, the built-up resistance to any sort of gratifying action—all this is focused in the issue of Hal's succession to his role as deliverer. For if he is playwright-to-be, he is also his own "despised dream," to be delivered into wakefulness. There is no such thing as unmoved mover, manipulating king of shadows. Mocking the mocker, false playwright Rumor, means for Hal, far more truly than for Richard II, turning himself inside-out and sacrificing himself to his play.

In one sense Part 2 is the "other grief" that Part 1 is swollen with—its dream life. By the dramatic logic of Hal's own scenario, only a moment lapses between the endings of the two plays. It is the moment in which Hal makes the simple transition from sunlit prince to princely sun. What postpones the succession by thus protracting the playing is Falstaff's resurrection. Indeed, looking back from Part 2's final scene, Hal safely transformed to Henry V and Falstaff at last expunged, we may say that the resurrection had pried open the moment of transition, requiring that in the act of his transformation Hal undergo a strangely clotted "dream" journey through the suppressed implications of that "natural" process. Thus in Part 2, with its repetitions, distortions, and mockeries of Part 1, Hal confronts the stifled specters of his determined self-idealization and of the play he has devised in order to realize himself in that role. The real "logic" here is that which is repeatedly brought home in Shakespeare: art is a sacrificial activity, and no action, howsoever disguised as passive acceptance of the Given, is undertaken without costing the actor something of himself.

Avoiding both battlefield and court, Hal is conspicuously evasive of the play's overt action. In the only two appearances he does make before meeting his father, he is illuminated in curiously effortful, self-abasing postures, while much preoccupied with thoughts of his father's death.

> Well, thus we play the fools with the time, and the
> spirits of the wise sit in the clouds and mock us. . . .
> (2. 2. 131–32)

> By heaven, Poins, I feel me much to blame,
> So idly to profane the precious time.
> (2. 4. 337–38)

In Part 1 the "reconciliation" scene, however fraught with unresolved filial issues, did nevertheless forward the play's public business. Here, however, the meeting occurs only after the diversionary public action of the play has been exhausted. And so Hal's odd reluctance, and even dread, finally force the encounter, when it does inevitably occur, into a radical expression of the play's real action. What Hal would evade by, in effect, "playing dead," he kindles into a full-blown, vividly materialized scene.

Therefore, though Part 2 as a whole can be said to dramatize the ghosts of Part 1, the climax certainly occurs in that long-delayed confrontation of father and son. Despite its obvious and ironic correspondence to the "reconciliation" scene in Part 1, its true counterpart in that play is the scene of ritual rescue-and-recognition at Shrewsbury (5. 4). There Hal's ostentatious rescue of his father from Douglas neatly plays out the "rescue fantasy" familiar to modern psychoanalysis—the process whereby parricidal wishes are self-defensively inverted.[5] But whereas Part 1 allows the realization of these energies in action (as well as in quickening play with Falstaff) it is just this fulfillment that Part 2 denies with its dreamlike and cynical self-knowledge. No credible cause presents itself, and no credible Pretender (unless it is Prince John, the all-too-fit hero this chilled time around). And even Falstaff's powers of self-creative play have waned (and in any case Hal largely keeps away from him as well). Thus, opportunities for just the kinds of "acting-out" that fire Part 1 are everywhere suppressed in

Part 2; "action" moves, as it were, underground: like Hamlet, Hal's passivity becomes his only defense against the father-killing drives (and fears of self-nullification) that swarm within the "fated" and impersonal role awaiting him as Successor.[6]

So the confrontation, which is a life-and-death struggle undertaken verbally, must itself substitute for the efficacious action of the "rescue fantasy" of Part 1, forcing the emotional components—hostility, guilt, yearning, fear—into monstrous verbal forms. But also, just as the Shrewsbury scene symbolically enacts Hal's drama of the true son's emergence, so the sick-bed confrontation symbolically enacts the actual moment of succession—that nightmarishly protracted moment in which the son replaces (or becomes) the father. The scene, in other words, plays out the "other grief" of the play—discovers it and delivers it into drama.

Only dream logic, it seems, can account for the depths of hostility and fear that have opened between father and son since their "reconciliation" in Part 1. The breach has materialized out of no new business except for Hal's absence, which is to say that it rises out of the repressed past and thwarted selves that shadow the compromises reached in the interview and at Shrewsbury in Part 1. Through the very restraints of controlled language and purpose, this "other" now dangerously asserts itself in the careful haste with which Hal seizes the crown and in the torrential vision of ruin it undams in the king. Language itself, so responsive an instrument in Part 1, seems a minefield now. In Henry's language the familiar mixture of self-knowledge and deceit, guilt and stifled desire, is grotesquely magnified, as when he wakes to find his crown—and Hal—missing:

How quickly nature falls into revolt
When gold becomes her object!
For this the foolish overcareful fathers
Have broke their sleep with thoughts, their brains with care,
Their bones with industry.
For this they have engrossed and pilèd up
The cankered heaps of strange-achievèd gold;
For this they have been thoughtful to invest
Their sons with arts and martial exercises.
When, like the bee, tolling from every flower
The virtuous sweets,

Our thighs packed with wax, our mouths with honey,
We bring it to the hive, and, like the bees,
Are murdered for our pains.

(4. 5. 65–78)[7]

In his crafty rhetorical conventions, in his bitter self-pity, Henry seeks to focus and *use* an uprising of anarchic passion that threatens to overwhelm him; hence the terrible concentration of his own dissociations upon his son. Of course, the outburst is self-indicting. Hal, after all, has only retired with the crown to the next room, thinking his father dead, "Washing with kindly tears his gentle cheeks" (l. 83). Nevertheless, in his paranoiac rage Henry strikes past appearances to a deeper truth. The king's son would murder him—indeed *is* actively murdering him: "This part of his conjoins with my disease / And helps to end me" (ll. 63–64).

By "murder" we understand that he means self-destruction, identifying Hal with the "headstrong riot . . . rage and hot blood . . . lavish manners" (4. 4. 62–64) that he himself has always, notoriously, suppressed, and so now finds everywhere threatening. For instance, after the declaration that "we will *our youth lead on to higher fields* / And draw no swords but what are sanctified" (4. 4. 3–4; italics mine), the second sense of the passage, the yearning to redeem his own wasted age, is shortly brought to the fore: "Most subject is the fattest soil to weeds, / And he, *the noble image of my youth,* / Is overspread with them" (4. 4. 54–56). So long as he can imagine Hal in his own wishful image, as his "youth . . . santified," Henry is able to contemplate death and succession with some equanimity (as for instance in dispensing patriarchal advice to Clarence on how to cope with the touchy new king in 4. 27–48). In a self-denying role as ritual Successor Hal would redeem Henry's own self-denial and justify his career of endlessly *acting* the king he can never truly be until retrospectively legitimized, or "sanctified," by his son (4. 5. 197–201). But the Hal who refuses to come forward in that ritual role, but rather "dines in London" among "dead carrion" (4. 4. 80)—this is, suddenly, another "son" altogether, whose succession means no redemption after all. It means, rather, that "my grief / Stretches itself beyond the hour of death" (4. 4. 56–57): the future as continual parricide. Clearly the king fears Hal as the vengeful uprising of his own repressed and violated self, his internal "riot" that strikes grinning at midnight and on the announcement of "good news" and salutations from the battlefield.

But Hal-sanctified and Hal-riotous are simply conventional images assumed by the king's wishes and fears. His fear of being murdered, for instance, expresses his concern for the decorum of his son's succession. He is outraged not by Hal's personal *desire* for the crown, but by his premature forcing of the inevitable—his timing:

> Thou hast stolen that which after some few hours
> Were thine without offense, . . .
>
> (4. 5. 101–2)
>
> Thou hidest a thousand daggers in thy thoughts,
>
> . . . .
>
> To stab at half an hour of my life.
> What! Canst thou not forbear me half an hour?
>
> (4. 5. 106–9)

Guilty and wasted, the old king wants to be saved by a nobler ceremony than he himself has ever found possible. All too well this Henry Bolinbroke could understand a muddled, self-serving, strategically half-conscious act of usurpation, a simple linear displacement: the argument, as Richard II had put it, of "grim necessity." But he yearns to be absolved from such a system of causality—to be not merely displaced but reunderstood, comprehended by a consciousness superior to his own. This becomes clear in the steep dislocations of his speech—for instance, the self-pitying plea to be loved and absolved that sounds through his terrible denunciation:

> Thy life did manifest thou lovedst me not,
> And thou wilt have me die assured of it.
>
> . . . .
>
> Let all the tears that should bedew my hearse
> Be drops of balm to sanctify thy head.
> Only compound me with forgotten dust;
> Give that which gave thee life unto the worms. . . .
>
> (4. 5. 104–16)

It is Hal, of course, in whom this superior dramatic consciousness would be realized. But Hal not only fears succession as a kind of murder, too; he also shrinks from the office as a kind of self-destruction. In Part 1 it seemed he could exercise consciousness over the dramatic material and still somehow be the Hal who comes most vividly to life in his taut contentions with Falstaff. Now it is clear that to be playwright means to exercise consciousness in the drama, not over it; that to deliver the drama "Hal" must be sacrificed—and with none of the furtive gratifications that Richard II's self-sacrifice entailed. Of course Hal is to be reborn as Henry V—an epic hero, father of his brothers, moralizing mirror of all Christian kings; but as a sentient self, occasional and shadowy indeed. No wonder then that he resists assuming this office, first by his evasions of court and battlefield (despite declared intentions) and then, the encounter inevitable, by devising a ritual play by which to preempt the question of consciousness altogether.

Unbidden, after having so conspicuously avoided his father for so long, Hal appears only after the king has fallen sick and asleep. Precipitously he discovers that the feared and looked-for moment is upon him. Although he had supposedly come as one son among many, to pay respects to his father, the true purpose of his coming—to inherit the crown—is thrust upon him after fewer than ten lines of filial compassion for the ruined old man:

> . . . By his gates of breath
> There lies a downy feather which stirs not.
> Did he suspire, that light and weightless down
> Perforce must move. . . .
>
> (4. 5. 30–33)

This urging of proof by downy feather, like the entire compacted speech itself, is altogether too effortful, too carefully channeled into its rhetorical conventions ("O polished perturbation! Golden care!") not to betray the urgency of thinly disguised haste behind it. And in itself, the rigid concentration of Hal's entire attention in the crown conceit implies the effort of control. Quickly he reckons accounts: "Thy due from me / Is tears and heavy sorrows of the blood . . . / My due from thee is this imperial crown" (ll. 36–40). He emphasizes lineality—"This from thee / Will I to mine leave, as 'tis left to me" (ll. 45–46)—and departs, to be found doing his weeping in the antechamber. The entire scene occupies twenty-six lines.

The point is not that Hal is pitiless, murderous, or greedy for the "golden rigol." When Henry subsequently charges that "thy wish was father, Harry, to that thought," he means the thought of his death. But the whole scene of the theft is the form Hal's wishes take—the death and succession as a fait accompli, a necessary process miraculously having taken place by itself. Hal's ritual play, were it successful, would have enabled him to murder his father unconsciously, to act *in* a design he had no part in devising. But the little play is not allowed to stand. Just as *2 Henry IV* forces a reinterpretation of *1 Henry IV*, all superficial action thwarted in order to expose what that action would conceal, so Hal is hailed back to Henry's sickbed and made to accept the full role of playwright: to murder his father volitionally, and hence his own independent self as well.

"I never thought to hear you speak again," says Hal (4. 5. 91). By speaking, the king destroys Hal's play into a wider, more painful, less artificial one. The first point to be made about Henry's extraordinary outburst of recrimination is that he will not be denied it—will not die peacefully and silently in Hal's wishful drama, nor allow Warwick's assurance of Hal's grief to diminish the force of his great culminating performance. In his projection of the world raving into universal riot through Hal's parricide-wish, Henry *will* give vent to his paranoia. The second point is that Henry is playing—that his performance, in the very gratuitousness of its passion, constitutes a plea for an answering performance that will dissolve his own, and so redeem his harrowing guilt by an act of love he cannot himself imagine:

> What! Canst thou not forbear me half an hour?
> Then get thee gone and dig my grave thyself,
> And bid the merry bells ring to thine ear
> That thou art crownèd, not that I am dead.
> Let all the tears that should bedew my hearse
> Be drops of balm to sanctify thy head.
> Only compound me with forgotten dust;
> Give that which gave thee life unto the worms.
> Pluck down my officers, break my decrees,
> For now a time is come to mock at form.
> Harry the Fifth is crowned. Up, vanity!
> Down, royal state! All you sage counsellors, hence!
> (4. 5. 109–20)

Hal's response is that of the instinctive dramatist. He backs off, relinquishing self-assertion, in order to gain command of this wider, riskier play that Henry has forced upon him. As in the corresponding scene of Part 1, he is cannily able to divine and oblige his father's wish; he lets him rave, act out his guilty vision and his plea for love and forgiveness; lets him exhaust his performance before thinly answering:

> O, pardon me, my liege! But for my tears,
> The moist impediments unto my speech,
> I had forestalled this dear and deep rebuke
> Ere you with grief had spoke and I had heard
> The course of it so far.
>
> (138–42)

Nothing in Hal's reply to the indictment is prima facie convincing except the earnestness of its avowals, and yet it is, as Dover Wilson says, "completely satisfying to his father."[8] As an answering performance Hal's "pleading so wisely in excuse" satisfies Henry's need merely by not violating the credibility of their mutually created drama.

At the simplest level then, father and son have tacitly agreed on an efficacious stylization of their troubled relationship—a kind of symbolic drama of breach-and-restoration that eases Henry's passage to "Jerusalem" and Hal's to the crown, while it both liberates and controls potentially terrifying psychic energies. But the little drama is too obviously useful to be deeply convincing in its resolution. What both Hal and Henry feared most has not come to pass: it is as if the whole course of *King Lear* threatened from the beach between father and son, only to be abruptly foreclosed, the possibility denied, the *convention* of reconciliation reasserted.

Nevertheless, Hal is not allowed to escape responsibility for the drama as a means of staging his father's death. He struggles, indeed, to escape that responsibility, by denying self-consciousness. He claims to have put on the crown "to try with it, as with an enemy / That had before my face murdered my father, / The quarrel of a true inheritor" (ll. 166–68). This image—or rather, this scene that Hal now conjures up—is a means of displacing his own motive. As in his solo bedside performance he projects his most dangerous impulses onto the crown,[9] and thereby controls and, in a measure, evades them. But the deeper dramatic rhythms press through. Hal cannot blindly act out parricidal urges through a displacement, but must himself be the playwright of that action, of that very effort to escape. Henry had grieved, "This part of his conjoins with my disease / And helps to end me." And when Hal sheepishly confesses, "I never thought to hear you speak again," Henry shrewdly replies, "Thy wish was father, Harry, to that thought." As wish-effecting "father," deviser of this "part," Hal has, even while seeking to escape it, anticipated the true nature of his role as successor—that is, as the playwright-king ordained to order the future in ways the old father cannot conceive. To be sure, Hal badly bungles the job and turns out something of a "loathly birth" in the process. But even that stillborn drama is turned to account. Henry insists upon Hal's responsibility for the scene of the theft, even if his sense of the marvelous must assume conventional form: "God put it in thy mind to take it hence, / That thou mightst win the more thy father's love, / Pleading so wisely in excuse of it!" (ll. 178–80). Which is to say that Hal, as character, thieved the crown in a purposefully inept play that Hal, as playwright, would destroy into a more comprehensive one; whereby what was "parricide" in the first becomes, in the second, the absorption of the father by the son. This transaction occurs on the spot. Hal assumes his office by exercising it, by making speech out of the dumb, unconscious acts of the past. Thus he quotes himself, as a character in history:

> I spake unto this crown as having sense,
> And thus upbraided it: "The care on thee depending
> Hath fed upon the body of my father.
> Therefore, thou best of gold art worst of gold.
> Other, less fine in carat, is more precious,
> Preserving life in medicine potable,
> But thou, most fine, most honored, most renowned,
> Hast eat thy bearer up."
>
> (157–64)

The playwright subsumes himself as character, making out of the past the speech that is the present performance, the one by which the "reconciliation" of father and son is enacted. This is a paradigm of the act of the history plays. Hal alters the helpless past to appropriate it for the present. He destroys history, dissolving it into drama in an act of absorbing consciousness, in order to make it live, unfinished after all, and hence—so Henry dumbly hopes—redeemable.

Hal's gift as playwright-king lies in letting his subjects

speak—in organizing "history" into theatrical occasions whereby they can act themselves out through him. In his debut as Henry V he fittingly demonstrates the gift, challenging the Chief Justice to explain "how might a prince of my great hopes forget / So great indignities you laid upon me" (5. 2. 67–68). The Justice's lengthy defense not only affirms his rectitude, it also—not incidentally—locates the power of a true king in the rectitude of his representatives. The true king acts through his agents, or "images," but he alone has the power to authenticate those very agents: "I then did use the person of your father. / The image of his power lay then in me" (5. 2. 73–74). Therefore, by upholding the Justice Hal can do what he implicitly promised his father: redeem his despairing dispersal into facsimiles, mere robes and roles, and "sanctify" him retrospectively.

The new king listens, just as he had listened to his father, allowing the (after all)—superfluous speech to complete itself. Only then does Hal forgive the Justice, as if the speech itself had worked his change of heart. In the Justice's speech he allows the memory of the past to "be washed in Lethe, and forgotten" (l. 72). Of course this demonstration of royal grace is one of Hal's gilded lies. But it is also what makes dramatic life possible, and failing to understand that, Hal might have foregone the beneficently deceitful ceremony and forgiven the Justice preemptively. To do so would have been to assert tyrannical and graceless authority, to deny the value of speech as itself a creative activity. Hal is the first of the kings who knows to let his subjects *be* by acting themselves out through him—so that they may *be* communally and see themselves festally in their corporate body, one in multiplicity. In that sense, as a "mirror" of free and creative speech, Hal redeems the lost time, the debasement and futility of dramatic language so grimly enacted by the earlier histories.

To some extent the cost of this success is Hal's reduction to a ritual role. Falstaff gone, there is no one to challenge him or the easy grace with which he stages the efficacious illusions of freedom. He will henceforth preside symbolically over a realm full of diverse and energetic speakers, while personally remaining masked, unclarified, unrealized. Yet it would be easy to overstate this proposition—as easy, perhaps, as to overstate its opposite number, that the ending is wholly the "show" of a cynical machiavellian prince in full control of its effects. The ending of the play seems as delicate and subtly complex in its orchestration of effects—and hence in its invitation to our responses—as we might expect in this climax, not only to *Henry IV*, but to the whole long troubled sequence of histories.

Were Hal's act of succession complete, then the drama would succeed to myth: a world so perfectly created as to have consumed all signs of the creative act itself. In that case the pain of genesis would be all absorbed, the yearning self fully dispersed into its work. The dramatic impulse itself would be fully gratified by its form, and the playing would be over. But it is never over. Instead, old king and new at once begin plotting "to busy giddy minds / With foreign quarrels" (4. 5. 213–14). In other words, the succession perfected does not purify dramatic character of its human content, however much it might narrow Hal's. To the extent that he can destroy himself—his past—into the present, as in the final scene he claims to have done, Hal has found the "right" way to succeed (to murder) his father. To the extent that he resists his own sacrifice into the playmaking role, he suffers the pain of the parricide. But in the crafted calm of his speech to the Chief Justice, naming him in effect his new father; in the gravity of his address to his brothers, grieving for the old father; and in the icy violence of his judgment upon Falstaff, Hal shows the strain with which he labors to put himself beyond the pain of parricide—to busy his own mind and waste his own memory by construing the reconciliation with his father as a perfection of their identities.

> My father is gone wild into his grave,
> For in his tomb lie my affections,
> And with his spirit sadly I survive, . . .
>
> (5. 2. 123–25)

Both the coldness and the "grim necessity" of the rejection of Falstaff remind us with what ruthless vengeance *2 Henry IV* plays out its self-destruction. The studied reduction of Hal in the play to his role as Successor, of Henry to sacrificial father, and of Falstaff to the Martinmas fool, arriving at the moment of his sacrifice ready for the slaughter, are mutely tragic forms of self-violence.[10] The pain in all of this, the impurities of the masks and motives, the resistance of the dramatic matter itself to the drive toward termination and absolution, constitute our own gathering recognition of the face of history. As Edward Berry reminds us, the ending of the play produces no simple, single effect, nor is there any reason to expect it to be pleasant, the genre being history and not comedy: "The triumphs permitted by history are always equivocal and too perplexing for joy."[11]

But I do not think the genre of history governs the mixture of effects in the end. I think that they constitute Shakespeare's rediscovery of what "history" is. Over and over we have witnessed this process of feeling out the nature of increasingly complex, indeed almost overwhelmingly complex material, one of whose signal characteristics is its tendency to disintegrate, or to crystalize, under dramatic pressure. The discovery of "history" seems as much a matter of artistic restraint, a standing-back from judgment, as of active craftsmanship. In the quietness of that restraint Shakespeare finds the form through which we grow as much aware of what is lost in final moments as of what is gained.

The Stratford production saved the final part of Hal's address to his brothers in 5. 2 for the end of the play, making it his coronation speech. Thus it came after the rejection scene and was delivered from the balcony to the world at large—meaning to us. The impulse behind this rearrangement was clear enough. In the play as it stands we are left feeling chilled if not stunned by the rejection, and hardly rewarmed by Prince John's brisk summing-up and glib forecast of new adventures coming up overseas. Not much of a real ending, in other words. Stratford, in elevating, isolating, and illuminating the new king in his rich crimson robes, certainly mirrored our desire for a transcendent conclusion. But it also falsified Shakespeare by giving in to that desire.

Shakespeare's endings have always made major demands upon their audiences, but in *2 Henry IV* our role appears to have been focused with greater intensity than ever before. The part we played in Part 1, though highly active, was never so well specified as here. Rumor, of course, begins the process, speaking in the guise of the playwright of "false reports," and enlisting us as coconspirators and rumor-mongers. He addresses us as an audience as falsely coherent as he is himself, with his many conflicting tongues: each of us encapsulated in our verbal cells, sanctioning the "false reports," each of us hearing only what we can or will hear, which is to say, suffering from the "disease of not listening, the malady of not marking." This caricature of the audience is Rumor's projection, of course. But it is also at least half-accurate. We do come to a play as an inchoate, atomized, speciously unified body. Whatever expectations we may have of being translated into something nobler, Rumor begins by translating our fragmentation into a mirror-image of the diseased society assembled upon the stage, itself fragmented for lack of a truly unifying tongue. Both bodies, onstage and off, "expect" the play to heal and unify them.

We are indeed Hal's wider audience for his coronation speech. But we are also the "world" whom he addresses in his real last speech—that in which he repudiates Falstaff. When he halts the coronation train to face his old senex-father-playmate-lover, we are aware that the old threat and promise of "I do, I will" has finally come to term, and with it the doubleness inherent in that haunting formulation. Now Hal's credibility is to be doubly tested, for he must "make good" his promise both to the members of his inner fictive realm, those onstage celebrating his ascension, and to the much more knowing members of the dramatic audience, us. "I will" means I banish Falstaff from my company as king; "I do" means I banish him from the stage altogether. To do the one, Hal risks his standing with his wider audience—and not many of them down through the years have been wholehearted supporters of his action. But he clearly must accept the risk, must not temporize in carrying out his decision to kill off Falstaff. There is no right way to do it, except publicly, vocally, and personally, bearing full responsibility for all consequences of the act. *He* must do it—and in the doing, hope that we will recognize our need to do it, too, so sanctioning him. The actor of Hal must feel all this and try with full conviction to persuade us of the rightness of his action, though not, I think, of the self-righteousness. To kill off Falstaff is an attempt to unify the realm, and (as the wider realm) the audience. It simply cannot succeed perfectly given the impurities intrinsic to the material. But as Hal addresses us through Falstaff, a clear mutual recognition of the impurities *is* possible. And that will be our final debt to Falstaff, who has forced the matter to this sad, illuminating crisis. If Hal performs the act with too few regrets or difficulties for our taste, subsiding too easily into the ritual role of Henry V, forgoing our full support, that too is part of the cost that he must be willing to bear. And it is part of our job to see and understand all this clearly.

The fact is, it is not so hard to let Falstaff go. William Empson speculates that the "triumph" of his creation was a major turning point for Shakespeare in that it liberated him from a dependency on aristocratic patrons, "marking a recovery of nerve after a long attempt to be their hanger-on."

> The point is not that he was like Falstaff but that, once he could imagine he was, once he could "identify" himself with a scandalous aristocrat, the sufferings of that character could be endured with positive glee. I am sure that is how he came to be liberated into putting such tremendous force into every corner of the picture.[12]

Whether this speculation is as sound as it is ingenious, it speaks to something we cannot help feeling in Falstaff, and that is the prodigious personal passion, free and unprecedented, that has gone into his creation. Somehow it is because of that enormous triumph that Shakespeare is able to abandon him in good dramatic conscience. Falstaff's death proceeds from his deep life.[13] And with his death there comes release from a burden well and honestly borne. It seems that the sheer relief of having imagined so full a creature as Falstaff allows Shakespeare to go past history, at least as the sort of obsession that has dogged him through eight successive plays. Empson thinks that "as a matter of trust from the audience, the triumph of Falstaff made possible the series of major tragedies." First, of course, Shakespeare must complete the Henriad as (presumably) planned. But now with the burden of the "other grief" lifted he is able to proceed in a newly lightened spirit, in a new vein altogether. Not surprisingly, he begins by addressing us in an ebullient new voice of confident recognition.

Part IV
Carrying Off History

11
Henry V

Arriving at *Henry V*, pilgrims are greeted outside by a genial host somewhat too colorfully, too hopefully dressed. Affably arch, he steers them indoors, begging elaborate pardon for the meager facilities but suggesting how to make the most from the little there is. He looks familiar. The respectable brother of Rumor perhaps? Distant cousin of Richard III? or of the Bastard? or even of Falstaff? A tribe of welcomers all. But this one lacks the family trait of obliqueness, of sly manipulation. He is so hearty and innocent—almost a buffoon in his openness, his narrow tastes, his explanatory zeal. He is an Englishman inviting Englishmen into an English house, to see the quintessential English play—and all without irony. When some of the pilgrims hang back, protesting that they are not, nor have ever been, true-born Englishmen, he earnestly misses the edge in their voice, reassuring them like a priest that if their spirits are only willing, then the play itself will gladly gentle them.

Never before in the histories has the audience been so openly solicited. Never before has it been assigned so explicit a role in the play. Indeed, what the Chorus says is so obvious that we may scarcely know how to accept it: we are at a play, and have an essential part in the making of the play. There is nothing new in this except the literalness. Throughout the history sequence, the relationship of audience to play has been growing steadily more complex. To be told now that it is just a simple, naked encounter after all is bewildering. Should we be embarrassed, or are we being beguiled by canny costuming?

Perhaps *Henry V* inaugurates the new Globe playhouse. Certainly a sensation of "public theater" rises from the play. The Earl of Essex could commission a clandestine performance of

Richard II; Henry IV, congenial to all environments but dependent on none, could be done in a chamber-theater as well as anywhere. But *Henry V* must be imagined as presenting itself to a genuine public.[1] This has nothing to do with the size of the imagined events, despite what the Chorus says—there are no battle scenes in the play, and besides, Shakespeare has never had trouble doing those—but it has everything to do with the role of the audience, without which the play would be felt to lack its animating element. For though any play implies and needs its audience, few have so deliberately built them in. Rumor addresses us as *any* audience in *2 Henry IV;* complex as our role is in that play, we have no specified identity as a company. But *Henry V* comes to us already full of its particular, scripted audience. The "audience" addressed by the Chorus is a part in the play that we are urged to fill.

No other Shakespearean play has so openly asked us to relinquish the myth of our individual solitudes. The special experience of a "ceremonial play" (Herbert Lindenberger's phrase) derives from the audience's awareness not simply of one another's presence at the performance, "but of the fact that others are *sharing* the same experience."[2] *Henry V* is clearly a "ceremonial play" in this sense. But just because the play is "public" and "rhetorical" in character does not mean it is only that, and just because we are aware of ourselves as a collective body, enacting a specific role in the play, does not mean we are absolved of our individual powers of attention. Indeed, our situation has become more complicated rather than less. To acknowledge the "public" modality of *Henry V* is not to define either the play or our role in it, but simply to acknowledge the crucial importance of our role. The nature of that role is the play's primary question, and one which only the play itself can answer.

Upon this question of the audience's role—who we are and how we are to respond—the critical tradition has mostly floundered. Granted, until recently the history of *Henry V* productions has done little to counteract the prevailing critical view of the play as fit chiefly for rousing ritual occasions. But the problem is not only historical. *Henry V* has proven a particularly embarrassing battleground for opposing warriors of stage and page, neither camp winning much glory in the contest. Theater-oriented criticism has tended to treat the play as Spectacle, or as a kind of colorful opportunity for overacting, while traditional literary criticism has been on the whole merely condescending, either blind or indifferent to values that express themselves best in performance.

The introduction to a recent edition of *Henry V* typifies the critical conventions that have so often crippled literary responses to the play. The editor's chief complaint is that the play is undramatic—that is, devoid of the conflict, struggle, and development that are so abundant in the earlier histories. Since Henry's status as "ideal king" is given from the outset (by the Chorus and Bishops), "he seems to be exempt from the condition of humanity: his important struggle—to establish his credentials for the exercise of regal power—is already won. . . . Despite the hardships he endures he is not really imperilled, and as we follow his exploits we have merely to await his predetermined triumph." Because Henry's character has been formed in the past (this reading implies), there is no authentic struggle in the present. Therefore the dramatic action is only the mimesis of a concluded struggle, the triumph at Agincourt being "predetermined" as it was not at Shrewsbury. For this studious editor, the dramatic present of *Henry V* consists of inflated theatrical effects, Shakespeare's attempt to enliven material naturally intractible to drama—a king too ideal, an action too epical. "He therefore has to try for grandeur—and to settle for the grandiose," and he therefore must have a Chorus to apologize for his failure.[3]

It is not this estimate of the play that concerns me—critics have both liked and disliked the play because they thought Hal the "ideal king," and they have both liked and disliked it because they thought the ideal either ironic or shabby. What interests me here are the widely shared assumptions underlying the editor's complacent stance toward the play. For though he speaks repeatedly of what "we" perceive and how "we" respond, this "we" is really quite oblivious to the theatrical situation as a live occasion.

Michael Goldman focuses his essay "*Henry V:* The Strain of Rule" precisely on the way the play transmits its live bodily energy to the public audience. In strenuous, athletic oratory, shared by the Chorus and Henry—each one exhorting his appropriate audience to *work*—the physical strain of performance itself produces a speech that makes for a "vital bond of pleasure that joins us to the play."[4] This is the sort of thing our editor seems unaware of. He hears none of the force or effort, none of the variety or contention of live voices. As "audience" he remains isolated and detached from such exertion and such pleasure, and so "unastonished" by the predictable ease of "ideal" Henry's successes. To him, the play's live action is only a hollow attempt to evoke the grandeur of a finished past, and so naturally there can be no vital commerce with the actors, who do their work in the present. As audience-of-one, really a solitary reader, he does not feel implicated in the play. He thinks it asks nothing of him, and therefore has nothing to give. But—and this is the rub—perhaps he fails to hear the language in which the request is made.

"If we think of the quality of our awareness as an intrinsic element in the work, or as intimately related to it," says E. A. J. Honigmann, "we have come a long way from the verbal icon."[5] Our editor, oblivious to his true role as audience, looking upon the play as just such a self-enclosed verbal icon, finds it incomplete, and sees no tension *in* it. But the moment we take up our role in *Henry V* and enter the play as audience, we can feel the tension struck up *between* us and the actors: the "strain of rule" is played out as the strain and pleasure, the risks and consequences of performance. This is what the Royal Shakespeare Company's production in 1975 demonstrated abundantly. An early review noted that, in terms of its conception,

> some clear lines have been laid down. Two assumptions of regal costume—the first, with awe and terror as he takes up the Dauphin's challenge to prepare for battle in France, the second with easy confidence after he has been bloodied and before the battle of Agincourt—show that Mr. Howard does not regard the putting aside of Falstaff as Hal's last step to maturity. . . . [The] whole foundation of this intelligent performance is of a man's attempt to forge himself in the painful fires of authority and battle. Witnessing a man's growth last night even caused me to wish that there was a fourth play to take Mr. Howard's Henry beyond even the wooing of Katherine.[6]

Clearly the RSC's audience was not being invited to share in a static celebration of the Star of England's "predetermined" success. Of course, this much could be said of any good modern production. But as the reviewer implies in his remarks about costuming, the RSC went a good deal further than earlier versions in seizing upon "theater" itself as the play's controlling metaphor: theater, that is, not as the epical pageant that so plagued productions of the play throughout the nineteenth and twentieth centuries, but as a live action unfolding intricately in time. Viewed in this way, with its fictive time intimately linked to its theatrical time, and hence to the pressure and quality of the audience's responses, the play looks very different from the grandiose thing, empty of struggle, growth, and therefore of life, that too many major scholars and critics have been in the habit of imagining.

Henry V is not a tough play in terms of its verbal or structural density; it *is* tough in the way it isolates the primary relationship of audience and play as it has operated through the history sequence, and in the steadiness and simplicity with which it allows that relationship to disclose its implications. The play makes not massive but unusual and delicate demands upon us, demands that I think critics— including myself—have been mainly oblivious of. Any play, insofar as it is a live performance, involves improvisation, and not merely on the actors' parts. But *Henry V* not only requires a vigorous improvisational relationship with its audience; it is also a play *about* such a relationship, and about the skills that are required by both parties to make it succeed.

Two morphological features control the terrain of *Henry V:* the conspicuous presence of the Chorus, the conspicuous absence of Falstaff. They are related like hill and valley—or better, like positive and negative charges upon the field of play.

The first point to be made about the Chorus is that he is unnecessary. Since he presents himself to us as absolutely necessary, as apologist for a play helpless to generate its own credibility, we begin with a silent contradiction. Of course *Henry V* is no more in need of choral aid than any other play; all are "inadequate" if the aim is to reproduce life without distortion. Shakespeare has dramatized an unusual command of such "inadequacies," however, and so we may take the Chorus as either ironic or ingenuous, or else as a dramatic character acting the role of the author's surrogate.[7] The point is that he is there because Shakespeare put him there, not because the material naturally requires him. His gratuitous, magniloquent presence bespeaks a powerful effort to start out fresh, like Henry himself, "in the very May-morn of his youth, / Ripe for exploits and mighty enterprises" (1. 2. 120–21). His first word, "O," is an agressive cipher, connoting both "Nothing" and the

"Foundation of All Possibilities." Under cover of a sigh for the deficiencies of drama, he asserts command of the dramatic occasion. Lamenting the meagerness of effects, he seizes control of all effects.

But to emphasize his voraciousness is to miss the dramatic occasion as surely as if we were to take his lament at face value. We have come to the theater, and he addresses us from the stage, asking us to join in defining the proper size of the event. We would be giddy-minded indeed if we failed to register the coyness of his wanting a "kingdom for a stage," of his contempt for the "flat unraised spirits" who must do all the acting. What we are here for and what the play is prepared to give us is neither epic nor puppetry, nor precious miniaturization. And so, rather than succumbing to the Chorus in awe, or else hooting him down like the audience of "Pyramus and Thisby," we must begin by meeting him *in* his rhetorical statement.

If we can believe the Chorus, we have the power not only to make the play, but to ruin it with the wrong responses. But granted that we are willing to play along, how do we go about it—what are the right responses? The opening address is crowned by an appeal to hear and judge "gently," echoing the earlier "pardon, gentles all." But this is easier said than done. For one thing, the Chorus's naked admission that " 'tis your thoughts that now must deck our kings" makes us naked, too; the natural response is to grab for the nearest self-protective posture: arrogant detachment or giddy acquiescence. Even if we do try bravely to assume the open-hearted stance the Chorus seems to ask, we will find ourselves buffeted by aggressiveness on one side, unctuous diffidence on the other. For he is not nearly so "clear" a figure as he first seems. At one moment he may seem quite transparent, guiding us into the play's interior; at the next moment he will seem wholly opaque, exulting in the color and music of his own rhetoric and steering us with a flourish through false entrances and irrelevant passageways.

The ambiguity inheres in our relationship with the Chorus, not in the Chorus himself as a character of complex motives or personality. Indeed, what is radically in question is his status *as* a character. To what extent is he "in" the play, as a member of the fictive company? The question can be settled only by the play itself, as we respond to him in action. That is because his role consists of indeterminacy of character, radical ambiguity, and hence vulnerability both to the company and to the audience. As our guide into the play, he is naturally isolated from the other actors.[8] But the problem then is how to maintain his roots in the play's fictive terrain. If he is so "strange" to that world that he loses the support of the fictive context, he may possibly lose ours, too. We may perceive him as supererogatory, a kind of rhetorical decoration. The actor, feeling gratuitous, may try to generate power by tearing a passion to tatters—to force his way on us precisely as Henry exhorts his soldiers to invade the breach: stretching sinews, setting the jaws, clenching the brows, and so on. He risks inadvertent parody.

Precarious balance is central to the role. The Chorus is foremost among the play's many go-betweens and peacemakers: Bardolph, Gower, Bates, Montjoy, Burgundy. In the purity of his role as go-between he focuses the real complexity of our relationship with the play. He projects the play's preoccupation with agency. And he enacts the risk undergone by the dramatic stranger, the traveler in the void between fictive world and theater world. In other words, he enacts the familiar role of the king in the history plays. In *Henry V* the two worlds of fiction and theater are represented by the "vasty fields" and the "wooden O": that is, the All or Nothing implied in the first prologue. They are imaginative abstractions, each existing only in silent opposition to the other. In the tension between them is the void—or the reality—of the play itself. Through the sequence of history plays it has been the distinctive and preeminent role of the king to establish the reality by risking the void.

So the Chorus crystalizes into sheer theatrical terms the essential dilemma of the history kings who would both control and be sustained by—be both "in" and not "in"—the fictive interior of the play. In particular he reflects Henry's dilemma: the need to be king on the one hand, and on the other a soldier in the army that is the expression of his own regal will. As soldier, the king would act; as king, the soldier would justify the grounds of action. But just as the Chorus cannot both midwife the play and inhabit it, Henry cannot both maintain the Cause and, like his soldiers, blindly find it thrust upon him.

At times the Chorus and Henry seem to be performing the split halves of a single role. Canterbury's praise of Henry's rhetorical skill might equally apply to the Chorus (1. 1. 38–50). The role is split, however, not between private and public phases, but between two analogous public parts, each confined to a carefully inscribed domain. The Chorus exhorts *us* to work our thoughts; Henry exhorts his troops to act. What the Chorus does for the play, Henry does for the war, which is to say, for the play's fictive core.

But to stress the likeness may be to overlook the odd fact of there being something to liken. The Chorus may crystalize the king's role into pure theatrical terms, but he exists in the first place because he is doing the job that, by all the logic and momentum of the previous plays, should naturally fall to Henry himself. He has assumed the king's hard-won role as shaper of the action, transmuter of historical fiction into living drama. To bring home the play to us the king in other histories has had to risk the stability of his role within the fiction. But in *Henry V* it is the Chorus who performs this task. In effect he is sacrificed to us so that Henry may safely act the wishful role of soldier in a context he is not responsible for. In projecting the war as an historical event. already justified by its success, the Chorus protects Henry from the need to worry unduly about the grounds of his action.

This view, however, implies a static conception of the play, in which the divided duties of king and Chorus are fixed and unchanging. This is not far different from the view of the Chorus as Shakespeare's mouthpiece, the product either of wise artistry (J. D. Wilson) or of desperate necessity (E. M. W. Tillyard, Herschel Baker). Essentially, it reduces the Chorus's role to a fancy Renaissance picture frame, within which Henry shines out as the "ideal king" inhabiting a risk-free environment. But if we respond to the Chorus's live performance, and therefore to the disturbing ambiguity of the role, and are therefore made nervous and self-conscious about our own crucial part in the play, then we will see him as part of the same dramatic world in which Henry resides. We will see their relationship as tense and kinetic, alive with the very effort of maintaining their separate domains. Chorus now becomes that side of the king which Henry would suppress, control, and force into the service of his ancestors: the *antic* side of the king. Not that the Chorus is antic in his behavior, but that he carries away from the king himself—and so expresses—the antic's potentially disruptive theatrical energy. And Henry, inhabiting a world that includes the antic Chorus, comes alive with an improvisational energy whose free expression he continuously labors to control. With immaculate machiavellian purpose he channels that energy toward the fulfillment of his will in the plot of the play. Both figures strike open, forthright, unambiguous postures, but regarded as a pair sharing the whole repertoire of a king's natural functions, they glow with the exertion such posturing costs.

The dramatic world is not a static landscape, but a highly charged system of events. Initially we are presented with a series of similes: the wooden O like the vasty fields, the Chorus like Henry, the play like the war. Likenesses are posed without the loss of original identities. But the effort of maintaining that simple structure is soon overcome by the pressure of the forward-moving drama and our increasingly hot part in it. The dramatic world turns kinetic and risky, shapes begin to melt and metamorphose, and the chaste relationships of the simile converge in the new, dynamic form of metaphor. War and play, Henry and Chorus, meet in us, the audience.

Falstaff—or rather his absence—gives the play its negative charge. The absence is notable not just because he had loomed so large in the earlier plays, but because Shakespeare so carefully reminds us of it at several key points now. The news of his illness intrudes somberly upon the farcical squabbling of his old followers (2. 1), and the Hostess's report of his death (2. 3) pierces through the public material of the play with unabashed and memorable feeling. His ghost is borne by the bereft, diminished pack of followers, who one by one are lopped from the play. Henry himself never speaks of Falstaff, but in the flush of his victory at Agincourt the ghost rises with characteristic mischievousness from the mouth of Fluellen. Some scholars think Shakespeare originally meant to bring Falstaff into the play. But it could never have held him except by demeaning him into something like his role in *The Merry Wives of Windsor.* As it is, the effect of excluding him while at the same time keeping us aware of the exclusion is twofold. It bequeaths the play's fictive domain wholly to Henry, eliminating any rivalry for control of the stage. And it renders that unrivaled command strangely hollow—a fantasy of absolute control rather than an achieved condition.

Significant action requires significant sacrifice. Truly to succeed his father's time rather than to repeat it, to redeem time from its mocking confinement in the infinite wooden O, and to create a future beyond the everplaying present, Henry must violently excise his past. Memory of former times must be absolutely wasted, the Manningtree ox gored, roasted, and consumed. Falstaff, the incarnate never-changing here-and-now, god of the one reality requiring no faith, the indisputable reality of the stage itself, is sacrificed for the hope of something different: a future different from the past.

The sacrifice gives access to a—possibly—blessed new world. The beginning of *Henry V* is charged with the tremulous sense of an ancient dream about to materialize with undreamt freshness. A new national hero, another Arthur, has arisen to recapture the true grounds of English unity, English glory. Destiny awaits his grasp, all he must do is *act*, and everything conspires to propel action in just one direction. There is no resistance, only wholehearted encouragement, and the action itself comes to him as naturally as flexing new muscles or as making thrilling speech. "Now Lords, for France. . . . Then forth, dear countrymen. . . . Cheerly to sea. . . . No king of England, if not king of France." The pursuit of "France" is the pursuit of England, or of "Englishness" in some essential if elusive sense. And war is understood as more than just another raid on foreign soil. War is the final performance by which the ultimate homecoming will be accomplished. War abroad is Henry's way of dreaming the ancient dream so intensely as to bring it into material being at long last, to finish up and fulfill English history. War will produce the future that could never be believable so long as Falstaff presided over the here-and-now. War, in *Henry V*, replaces Falstaff as the vehicle of performance.

Having declared the war, Henry orates swellingly:

> . . . Or there we'll sit,
> Ruling in large and ample empery
> O'er France and all her almost kingly dukedoms,
> Or lay these bones in an unworthy urn,
> Tombless, with no remembrance over them.
> Either our history shall with full mouth
> Speak freely of our acts, or else our grave,
> Like Turkish mute, shall have a tongueless mouth. . . .
> (1. 2. 226–33)

What an opening for Falstaff: bones and tombs, mouths, mutes, and everything gambled for fame. But everyone applauds, and no winkers or mockers intrude to hail "my royal

Hal . . . my sweet boy." Henry is soberly witty, but now the cause of wit is war, not Falstaff. Of course we may not miss the ironist: sufficiently giddy-minded (as Henry IV foresaw) we may cheer along as lustily as all the others. On the other hand, we may resist the easy pull of Henry's rhetoric, feeling the absence of Falstaff in the absence of real restraints upon the scene's action, the irrevocable plunge into war. From this perspective, "war"—Henry's dream of glory—is also his dream of dissociated action, of safe and presanctified violence. It is the equivalent of his waking up in *2 Henry IV* to find himself already king, having bypassed the need to make the painful transition for himself. For Henry, war would be what our "unastonished" editor thought it was, an effortless performance, a virtual fait accompli—in other words, a wish to vault over the whole interim process of the play, which consists of Henry's discovery of the need and cost of "sanctifying" the war himself.

The more sharply we preserve the memory of Falstaff, the better we will understand the meaning of war in the play. *Henry V* is not, after all, a play about war, not the jingoistic drum-and-thunder "action" play beloved by giddy-minded audiences and loathed by academic skeptics. It is a play about war as a metaphor for play, and its essential action is interior. The start-and-stop, thrust-and-doubt rhythm of the play is the rhythm of Henry's uncertainty and discovery.[9] Such a rhythm projects upon our attention a distinctly human process: a mind engaged with painfully real materials. *Henry V* is a play about a king who has run out of fathers and needs to create his own play—or ceremony—of unity: one that reaches out of "history" (which is what he is left with once Falstaff is excised) and manages to incorporate his future audience, us.

I said earlier that Falstaff and the Chorus were intimately if silently related, like negative and postive charges upon the field of play. Henry's last act in *2 Henry IV* was to banish Falstaff, his last utterance a command to the Chief Justice to "see performed the tenor of my word." If we think of *Henry V* as that performance, bloomed out of the head of Henry, the creator-king, it will be easier to see how its various figures are connected. The Chief Justice, briefly supplanting Falstaff, "performs" Henry's word and disappears: the "word" begins with the choral "O." The Chorus becomes Henry's new instrument, projection of his dreaming self, enabling Henry to enter his own laboring dream as chief actor. The Chorus is also Henry's means of reaching out to *us*—the means by which the private dream becomes the public reality.

In this sense the Chorus reincarnates the sacrificed Falstaff. A Falstaff "performed" upon according to Henry's instructions, confined offstage until his "conversations / Appear more wise and modest to the world"—given, you might say, a "staffectomy"—might well turn up as the straitened, near-buffoonish Chorus. If the same actor were to play both parts in successive productions of the *Henry* plays we would probably recognize the absent Falstaff in a few seemingly inadvertent and telling mannerisms: vestiges, so to speak, of the former life.[10] The shock of recognition—all the greater for there being no initial perception of the relationship—would bring the two powerfully into line, not as similar, but as oppositely charged characters. As theatrical impressario the Chorus has taken over one of Falstaff's crucial functions, the antic, but discharges it in a different way, to engage us in the creation of an heroical vision. Like Falstaff, the Chorus defines the theatrical arena in which Henry's acting will be mounted. But Falstaff both defined and undermined that arena by entering and leaving it at will. The Chorus redefines the interior action as heroical history and seeks to protect its purity by interposing himself as a buffer between the life of the stage and our naked reactions. But for all his zealousness and ideological narrowness, he is still a version of Falstaff in his essential function as agent of the action, the one who "sees performed the tenor of my word." Both of them have faint family ties with Puck in the past, Ariel to come. But like Puck, Falstaff thrives in the freedom of his mischief; like Ariel, the Chorus is tightly strapped to the machiavellian will of the master-dreamer.[11]

"There can be few plays that carry upon them more heavily than *Henry V* the weight of centuries of theatrical tradition," writes Sally Beauman.[12] But any play begins in a state of grace; *Henry V* does so with an emphatic spirit, trumpeted by the Chorus and taken up by the bishops in their hyperbolic adulation of a newly reborn Henry, "full of grace and fair regard." The play's beginning corresponds with that of Henry's as monarch of a new English dawn. For Henry as for the company and for Henry's fellows—brothers, peers, soldiers—everything is new, yet to be tested and learned. He is king, but what is that? Who are his people? How to govern, how to speak—

above all, how to act? Whatever else he does, he must certainly act: a play is action and forces response, and a king cannot be except by acting. In this sense the May-morn urgency enjoined on him by all concerned—bishops, brothers, counselors, and of course the Dauphin, who among the French is also straining for action—creates a situation like that in *The Tempest,* where everything conspires in readiness—men and nature, stars and heaven—to solicit Prospero's action.

Any action is dangerous, but especially regal action. The bishops' motives are plainly mixed, and war is urged for almost too many good reasons. Henry carefully insists on public justification of his cause—clearly he holds to the medieval distinction between just and unjust wars—and scrupulously subjects his instincts to rationalization by counsel. But none of this sober caution can mask the underlying excitement, the gathering exhilaration, the sense of *playing* at deliberation. Especially given the tedious restraint of the Archbishop's Salic Law speech, *we* are like greyhounds straining in their slips to get on with what the Chorus has promised. Once "resolved" by the Salic speech, Henry practices some royal magniloquence:

> France being ours, we'll bend it to our awe
> Or break it all to pieces. Or there we'll sit,
> Ruling in large and ample empery. . . .
>
> (1. 2. 225–27)

He tries to imagine being king of France, and his language tries out exotic images, but in fact he is practicing being king of England.

As Sigurd Burckhardt notes, the rationalized motive for the war occurs in the Salic Law speech, but the emotional trigger, both for us and for the onstage company, is the Dauphin's obligingly scornful gift of tennis balls.[13] Henry's zestful response is perhaps the first fully felt moment in the play. (It is the moment in Olivier's film when the raucus theatergoers are suddenly seized by the power of the fiction and fall into a charmed hush.) But if Henry is stung, he is stung into energetic display and release. He rises to the Dauphin's bait, in fact, as he once rose to Falstaff's. Neither the legal sanction nor the call to ancestral glory could draw him out with such dangerous power as the Dauphin's insinuation—very much in Falstaff's vein—that he is only playing at kingship as he had formerly played at heir apparency. Quite clearly Henry loves the challenge: it gives him the chance he craves to play for real. His speech is playful and deadly, witty and self-revealing:

> When we have matched our rackets to these balls,
> We will in France, by God's grace, play a set
> Shall strike his father's crown into the hazard.
>
> (1. 2. 262–64)

What makes it frightening is Henry's insistence on his own helplessness in the face of war, when it is so obvious that war is what he wants and needs. The exuberant anger gives us a more "real" Henry—more spontaneous, more complicated—than we got moments earlier in the persona of self-restrained magniloquence. But this Henry is a persona, too. He is still practicing, though now flirting with dangerous capacities in himself. Resolved on war, he will now "be like a king"; that is *perform* like one. To "be" a king he must have the luxury of a war that is forced on him by Fate, by Mars, by Nature, or by international politics: one that is imposed from without.

What we have is the myth of the Stranger Within, one version of which is *Oedipus Rex,* another "The Secret Sharer." Like Henry, Conrad's young captain is as well prepared as the Service could make anyone, but is still a stranger to self, crew, ship, and command. And like the captain, Henry must improvise his command as he goes. He tries out roles—he has a taste for extreme stances—but he is young, a performer. For the first time in his career he is without real or symbolic fathers and can choose as his models those "mighty ancestors" who had distinguished themselves in former French wars. Yet the freedom to choose these models also becomes a burden because Edward III and the Black Prince are heroes of the past, part of another order. In court, in rehearsal, and as bravado, they may suffice; they impel Henry into action. But soon he surpasses his need for them, for of course he must test his own adequacy. Therefore he puts himself in danger and frightens and confuses his friends, his army, and himself by the violence of his reactions to Scroop's treachery, to the siege of Harfleur, to Bardolph's petty theft. These disturbing dramatic moments are stations in Henry's internal odyssey.

Like the captain's journey, the war is Henry's dream, yet he must continue to discover its deeper reality if he is to wake up from it. Like the captain he must risk his command in order to gain it. What makes Henry fit to be tested for command is not only his past in *Henry IV*, but the intriguing gaps of character he evinces in the prologue phase of the enterprise. Amidst the calls to glory and ancestral honor Henry alone seems aware of the costs of war. But he cannot yet conceive of it except as an extension of himself and his glory: "Take heed how you impawn our person," he warns the rationalizers, and then adds, "How you awake our sleeping sword of war." The two lines neatly catch his odd, tense doubleness—the personal note, then the vivid threat purged of person, as if the sword itself might wake and act out its own violent destiny. In such an image the Hero, "our person," sleeps and wakes as Stranger, the invisible wielder of the implacable sword. The little drama is magnified later when, roused to passion by the Dauphin's gift, Henry envisions the reality of the destruction to come. First the Hero rises, summoning the rather shopworn sun-effect from *1 Henry IV:*

> But I will rise there with so full a glory
> That I will dazzle all the eyes of France, . . .

But then the invisible Stranger emerges, raining sourceless destruction:

> . . . for many a thousand widows
> Shall this his mock mock out of their dear husbands,
> Mock mothers from their sons, mock castles down;
> And some are yet ungotten and unborn
> That shall have cause to curse the Dauphin's scorn.
> (1. 2. 279–89)

This speech is surprisingly personal in its passion. He performs the destruction through the deadly wit of his speech ("mock" is a word for play-acting); reveals his willingness and ability to wage real, not just theatrical, war. Yet the speech is characteristically distanced from the real source of the passion. "But this lies all within the will of God," says the hero, backing off. Perhaps this glimpse of the violent stranger within makes the hero claim moral justification all the more stridently.

At this point Henry has little difficulty containing the stranger in the hero, the soldier in the king, the person in the myth. But as the play continues and leads into war, the contention of these personae grows more clamorous. He repeatedly denies responsibility for the war, yet the vehemence of the disavowal conveys the eloquence of struggle. At some level he is wrestling with himself to acknowledge the thing of darkness as his own. Then, before Agincourt, on his night of panic, he invokes for the first time the name of his father and acknowledges the guiltiness he has inherited. Weighted by the past he had thought he had abolished, Henry offers up his record of frantic attempts to pacify the ghost of Richard, even though like Claudius he knows such bargaining is vain. But the one name from the past he never utters, even by implication or by distant allusion, is Falstaff's. That he does not sets the limit to his willingness to acknowledge the vanity of his enterprise. To think of Falstaff now would be to stand outside the dream of the future and look upon it as one more way of killing time "till Falstaff come."

The play begins in May and moves into winter, the origin of May, developing its own imperatives, but also discovering its own conditions as it goes along. Within his dream Henry encounters a thickening and incontestable reality: the past the dream departed from, the dreamer's capacity for violence, the otherness of war and its actors, the costs of action itself. These things overwhelm his efforts to start out fresh, "ripe for exploits and mighty enterprises." But he must push into that weight of war and play if there is to be even a single moment of awakening into a genuine future.

Despite strenuous efforts, both Henry and the Chorus gradually lose control of their special domains. Through the first three acts the Chorus labors to maintain his hierarchical assumptions, appealing to the "gentles" among us to help keep the play highminded. Epic, after all, is the aristocrat's art, while a mere "play"—unexalted by the patronage and indulgence of gentles—is a hopelessly common affair. Thus he rhapsodizes about the "culled and choice-drawn cavaliers" in Henry's train but never recognizes the kinds of soldiers we actually see on stage. Yet his exertion on behalf of our credulity implies the competition. Though he appeals to us to "force a play," once we do begin to cooperate the play itself takes on a momentum that diminishes his control and even threatens to antiquate him altogether.

This process begins as early as act 2, before the crossing to France. "Now all the youth of England are on fire," he intones.

He digresses, however, to describe the conspiracy of Scroop et al. against Henry, then ends the speech with a flourish: "The scene is now transported, gentles, to Southampton." At Southampton we may expect to see Henry masterfully expose the traitors before a triumphant departure for France. But in fact we are "transported" only to rowdy Eastcheap, and the Chorus is forced to give up the stage to Bardolph, Nym, and Pistol. As the RSC plays the scene, the vaudevillian squabbling of the Falstaffians is carried out upstage while war preparations are mimed downstage. Upon this "front cloth" act, the news of Falstaff's illness intrudes, bringing to the scene a sudden reminder of mortality and of sobering reality. Then the Hostess's mordant judgment—"the king has killed his heart"—makes a mute connection between Henry's sacrifice of Falstaff and the mounting momentum of war. War is gathering power, not from the remote and heroic images the Chorus would impose upon us from his stockpile of epic effects, but from the native comic energies of the stagelife itself. The play's real roots lie in Eastcheap, not Olympia, and overriding the Chorus, it takes its own natural time to "transport" us to Southampton, and thence to France. Nevertheless the war, spawned by the play, has already begun to dominate the rhythms of the play with its own somber logic.

Pistol, Nym, and Bardolph are native growths of the stage. Transported to France, they shrivel and fall away, victims of a war that usurps the stage with the force of a metaphor unrestrained: the "sleeping sword of war" with no Falstaff to call it lath. Unprotected by Falstaff, his followers are, so to speak, forced through the breach by Henry, the fodder of his dream of English unity. By contrast, the professional soldiers Fluellen, Jamy, Gower and Macmorris are bred not by the stage but by its fiction, the war itself, though they exist quite independently of its cause. They are brought forth once the crossing to France has been made and the fictional reality has taken hold upon the stage. For a while, before the Eastcheapers begin to fall away, the two groups compete in their vividly contrasting styles of theatrical presence. When they are thrown together (as in 3. 2), the stage crackles with a kind of unpredictable energy quite different from that generated by Henry or the Chorus. The captains and the Falstaffians, in other words, represent two kinds of dramatic spontaneity neither of which the Chorus, in his attempt to control the play through external models, can admit. But they are precisely the kinds of life that Henry must learn to acknowledge and to unify without suppressing, if he is to make his private dream of unity a public reality.

The stubborn charm of actual stage-life necessarily breeds doubts about the heroic ideal it presumably represents. The stage life is so palpable, after all, and the ideal so ghostly. On the live stage we are presented with numbers of fractious characters, highborn and lowlife, captains and commoners, Chorus and king, all converging upon the wooden 0 from different imaginative sources. We are presented, indeed, not just with characters, but with a diversity of live bodies, the actors themselves in the process of assuming their characters. Though this is true of any play, *Henry V* actively exploits the truth. The reality of actors needing to be unified in a company projects the inner reality of national elements needing to be unified in a country. On both levels the war—as the form of dramatic action and as the internal fiction—will be both the means to this unity and a demonstration of it. But this unity will not be achieved by thrilling calls to nationhood, brotherhood, or English honor. Unification cannot be imposed; it is the central process of the play itself. The fact is that Henry must learn how to command, not a war, but a play.

The hero's first test abroad comes in his encounter at "girded" Harfleur (3. 1). Faced with the threat of chaotic retreat, Henry responds with a powerful rhetorical performance. According to Alan Howard, "Playing the ['Once more unto the breach'] speech full tilt is like trying to run 440 yards uphill in an opposing wind. It is an amazing performance, an audition for himself in front of his men that must pay off: their backs are literally to the wall." Howard emphasizes the urgency of the situation—the army is in retreat and, as we learn shortly, is sick, dispirited, battered. To this occasion Henry rises with the "huge reserves of spirit, and energy" that he has always been able to bring to "moments of extreme physical test" (*RSC*, p. 144).[14]

Through sheer performing exertion Henry succeeds; he forces his army back through the breach, brings about the parlay, and hence the surrender of Harfleur. But this very style of "success" opens up problems that it is not able to deal with. In Henry's voice we (and presumably the soldiers) hear the effort, the sheer willfulness, and we respond to that, but nervously.

We have heard this rousing will often before in the histories, though it has never sounded out so purely. The images it selects to express itself now are those of acting: imitation, disguise, lend, let, try out. But Henry seems to be instructing actors how to *parody* parts: "Stiffen the sinews . . . lend the eye a terrible aspect . . .let the brow o'erwhelm it . . . set the teeth, and stretch the nostril wide." This is the kind of acting Hamlet instructs the players *not* to do. Here, bad acting equals good soldiering.

Another dissociation occurs between the orderliness of the language and the effect it seeks, namely furious activity. Though the performance itself is athletic and exciting, yet it remains rhetorically calm:

> In peace there's nothing so becomes a man
> As modest stillness and humility,
> But when the blast of war blows in our ears,
> Then imitate the action of the tiger: . . .
>
> (3. 1. 3–6)

Decorum governs the speech, peace and war each requiring its appropriate kind of performance. Furthermore, the imagery of "blast of war" displaces the source of the warring from Henry himself, who of course is sounding the blast at this very moment. The artifice of the speech echoes the hierarchical class principle that Henry evokes when he separates his audience into "you nobles" and "you yeomen." He patronizes both groups as "dear friends" as easily as he used to adjust his style to any occasion in *Henry IV*. The "nobles" he tries to inspire by invoking their heroic fathers; he would not name his own in this connection, of course, but rather his more appropriate ancestors, Edward III and the Black Prince. The yeomen he asks to be true to their "pasture"—and rather awkwardly sees "noble lustre" in their eyes, a nervous equivocation in the theme of nobility.

Henry's performance here is of a kind sufficient in *1 Henry IV:* his heroics, the all-too-ready resort to elaborated literary images, may not have convinced Henry IV during the interview scene, but he was willing to pretend to be convinced for the sake of their mutual political needs. Now giddy minds may applaud the performance at the breach but what comes through is the greenness of this performing mode in a military (as against a courtly) situation: the sense of Henry himself imitating an external, readymade model of command. By definition, the military situation is new, both for Henry and—despite the appeal to heroic ancestry—for England. To be in France now means to be in unfamiliar terrain. For Henry that terrain is also the unexplored realm of his kingship, far removed from the role of a gallant prince and heir apparent.

The Chorus has exhorted us to "work, work your thoughts," and Henry has exhorted his troops to "stiffen your sinews," and so forth. Now we get a revealing interlude. First come the Falstaffians, Bardolph's urging of Pistol and other cowards ("On, on, on, on, on! to the breach") an obvious parody of Henry. Then Fluellen's crass "Up to the breach, you dogs" shows the brutality underlying Henry's flattery of his "dear friends" whom he pictures straining like "greyhounds in the slips," eager to "close the wall up with our English dead." This literalizing of heroic metaphor was Falstaff's job in earlier plays; here it falls to whatever scabrous lifeforce may assert itself. In their strongly diversified characters and voices, the Falstaffian remnants and the multinational captains who now burst into the play function all together to resist the specious unity celebrated and performed by Henry's "to the breach" style. In the case of Pistol, Nym, and others, Henry's speech does not work, because of either their denseness, cynicism, or simple resistance to wartime rhetoric. In the case of the captains the speech is irrelevant. They hardly need urging to fight; the trouble is that their professional readiness has nothing of "noble lustre" in it and makes a mockery of Henry's dream of an England gloriously united in *his* cause.

Against this background of resistance Henry makes his ultimatum to the Governor of Harfleur: surrender or be savagely wasted (3 . 3). The scene repeats the siege of Angiers in *King John,* with the key issues sharpened tenfold. If the Governor resists, "licentious wickedness" will break loose; the city will be trampled, wives and daughters raped, old men and children mercilessly slaughtered. And none of this will be Henry's fault, since this is war and these are soldiers, and once released they are hounds of hell. As in *King John,* the dominant image in this brutal address is rape—both as a metaphor for attack and as a literal consequence of rampage.

As a rhetorical performance the speech naturally invites comparison with the exhortation at the breach.[15] That was the "uphill" performance, rousing resistant troops to assault through elevating imperatives: "On, on, you noblest English. . . . Dishonour not your mothers. . . . Be copy now to men of grosser blood." This is the "downhill" counterpart, the unstrapping of restraints upon a plunge:

> What rein can hold licentious wickedness
> When down the hill he holds his fierce career?
> (3. 3. 22–23)

The energy of the speech is tumultuous rather than athletic. The speaker keeps insisting that his control is on the edge of slipping away, implying that the only rein ("reign"?) is the rhetorical control of the plunging form itself:"What is it then to me . . . What is't to me . . . Therefore, you men of Harfleur . . . If not. . . ." The rhetorical form is the vehicle of sanction, allowing Henry to play "soldier . . . in my thoughts" and surrender the role of king and controller. The straining greyhounds of the breach become the hellish hounds of lust and unfettered violence. The reified "blast of war" that "blows in our ears" becomes the rape of "shrill-shrieking daughters" and cloud-breaking howls of mothers. War, as an occasion for the performance of English nobility, becomes "impious," a horror over which Henry, either as king or as man, has no control whatsoever. The tiger to be imitated at the breach here swallows the actor completely.

However the scene is played, it is one of *Henry V*'s most disquieting moments. (No wonder that Olivier, in his idealizing film, left it out altogether.) In the RSC production Henry stands downstage and speaks directly to the audience. We are the Governor of Harfleur, we are the raped ones, absorbing the full force of Henry's assault. But we are also intimate witnesses of its cost to Henry. From this vantage the performance reveals itself as an interior action, a crucial moment in Henry's heroic dream. The English troops, sick and desolate, are hardly up to another assault, let alone the fury that Henry threatens. But the speech is not really a bluff. To meet the test of this situation Henry has got to "play" at war-making more realistically than ever before. He has to find in himself the emotional resources for a rhetorical performance that will actually suffice to stop the battle. Like a Method actor, he must reach into himself to discover the reality of the war he is waging, to sound his own capacity for monstrous violence.

And so the soldiers he had bid play beasts at the breach he now becomes himself: "A name that in my thoughts becomes me best" (l. 6). *Soldier* is his chosen role, and in that role it is he who plays out a beast, "the blind and bloody soldier" pursuing its lusts without inhibition. "If I begin the batt'ry once again, / I will not leave the half-achievèd Harfleur" (7–8). It is a highrisk performance. Played to us at close quarters, the intimacy might be almost too intense. No buffering, solicitous, semipersonal Chorus now, but Henry himself exhilarating and threatening us directly. At the same time he hazards himself almost recklessly. Could he carry out the threatened rape if he had to? He generates the power to convince the Governor, us, and himself that he could. But in doing so he risks becoming what he threatens, a merciless "hand / Of hot and forcing violation," a thing "with conscience wide as hell," its human mind removed.

Does the tiger swallow the man? The performance works, after all, because it *is* frightening. To what extent is Henry's insistence on his own blamelessness a controlled effect, to what extent an ingrained necessity of character—the hero replying to the swaggering stranger within? From our position as Governor, one of the more disturbing aspects of the speech is the dissociation of form from the emotional frenzy it expresses. Despite the sheer force of the assault, it is difficult to locate the speaker himself. The arch metaphorical constructions give the impression of a learned mind in control of the occasion (the hero). But then the euphemisms peppering the speech give just the opposite impression (the stranger). Threats of mowing down virgins like grass, or defiling the "locks" of "shrill-shrieking daughters" might be artful fillips of cruelty, or else an odd flinching on Henry's part: to the Governor he might well seem dangerously unreliable—a smiling terrorist, possibly psychotic, to whom, for reasons entirely his own, certain unpredictable words are taboo.

The performance also makes large demands on us, in our roles both as Governor and witnesses. Indeed, what makes the moment compelling is precisely our part in it. Crucial and costly as it is to Henry, it is not a moment of tragic self-discovery, but rather one of intense theatrical complicity, a fusion of feeling between him and us. Under great pressure, Henry improvises greatly; we too must improvise our responses. The moment is intimate and complex to a degree that those old views of Henry as either stupid chauvinist or Christian hero could not contemplate. In such a moment we are led across a threshhold of theatrical experience; we move from a position outside of the event to one within it. Witnessing the event, we become part of it; and so its significance is changed. "Kindly to judge" comes to mean "to judge our kind."

The moment caps an effort that has carried unbroken through the Chorus, the breach, the comic-violent interlude. Now the Governor's surrender precipitates an immense relief that quickly gives way to emotional desolation. Henry instantly gives orders for mercy and announces plans to "retire to Calais," "The winter coming on, and sickness growing / Upon our soldiers." He has achieved a seemingly real triumph, but the mood is bleak. Some crucial point seems missing—a test of the cause for which this moment has been suffered. The demands on Henry's playing skill have been enormous, he has met them with a characteristic sense of gravity and consequence, yet all the while the nature of the play itself has been changing. It has been a costly performance, and now the future seems more uncertain than ever.

The loaded sequence in 3. 6 (after Harfleur) dramatizes this sense of swiftly thickening complexity. Pistol pleads with Fluellen to intervene in the punishment of Bardolph, who has "stol'n a pax." Fluellen refuses, then when Henry enters tells him that "one Bardolph, if your majesty know the man," has been, or is about to be, executed. In case Henry could possibly have forgotten him, Bardolph is described in detail. The king's single response is harsh: "We would have all such offenders so cut off." Then he goes on, in what has become a familiar pattern, to generalize and moralize this action by proclaiming a new policy of "lenity" toward the enemy:

> . . . And we give express charge that in our marches through
> the country there be nothing compelled from the villages,
> nothing taken but paid for; none of the French upbraided
> or abused in disdainful language; for when lenity and
> cruelty play for a kingdom, the gentler gamester
> is the soonest winner.
>
> (3. 6. 104–9)

This is a complex situation. If we did not know Bardolph or associate him with Henry's past and particularly with Falstaff, we might well react as we would expect the Chorus to: Henry's policy, however stern, is enlightened, modern, courageous, and befitting this mirror of Christian kings. Rapacious armies, after all, were one of the worst scourges of medieval warfare, since they depredated not the enemy's armies but farms, villages, and civilian populations. The Chorus, speaking from the fixed future, can see Henry's "justice" as part of the full picture. He knows Henry as an established legend, model of Christian virtues. For him, then, the scene becomes one of a series of exemplary tableaux.

The actual drama, however, makes more complex demands on us. It shows us Henry *becoming* king just as it shows us the reality of actors, lowlifes, and soldiers. And from the soldiers' point of view—those yet to be "gentled" by this action—Henry's "lenity" *is* cruelty, or at best the arbitrary act of Majesty. The sickness and desolation of the army has been emphasized in the previous scene (by the French) and will be reemphasized a moment later by Henry to the French herald, Montjoy. Under the circumstances, to execute Bardolph for pilfering a church and then to moralize this justice by suspending the soldiers' traditional rewards of pillage—often their only rewards for risking lives in a game of aristocrats—then, adding insult to injury, to require them to behave like gentlemen to the enemy: all this might well demoralize an army to the point of mutiny.

For us, after Harfleur, Henry will seem neither sanitized by history nor so blithely unfeeling as he must look to his troops. For one thing, the decorum he would enjoin upon his soldiers is a matter now of inward values, unlike the exclusively exterior behavior he had urged at the breach. In the figure of the "gentler gamester," the meaning of "gentle" is undergoing metamorphosis (though characteristically, the pragmatic note enters, too). For if commoners are now asked to behave like gentlemen, it follows that gentlemen will have to acknowledge their kinship with commoners. The war, if successful, will render class distinctions, if not obsolete, then arbitrary.

So our sympathies are divided and tested. We can see that Henry's policy of "lenity" to the enemy is vital to his hopes for unity among the English. If each soldier were allowed his private reward of pillage for joining a king's cause that he never hopes to understand, let alone share, then "unity" could be at best a patriotic pretense. Therefore Henry asks the soldiers to give up their traditional rewards and to commit themselves to *his* cause, which is the nobler cause of nationhood. He asks them in effect to help transfigure the mere occasion of war from a game of aristocratic glory into something mutually meaningful. And yet it is clearly not enough for Henry to insist that high and lowborn are all in this together. Having repudiated the soldiers' part in the traditional plot of medieval warfare, he must also repudiate the king's part. Thus to Montjoy, before his army, he openly refuses the king's traditional prerogative of being ransomed for high stakes if captured. This decision is a crucial one for Henry, yet there is no suggestion in the text that it wins him any credit with his troops. Later, on Agincourt eve, Bates will express a presumably widespread doubt among the soldiers: would not a king, he wonders, promise to forego the rule of ransom in order to win his soldiers' loyalty? Who would know if he were to break that promise, and who would challenge him if he did?

Thus, though we see Henry moving toward a new kind of unity, we also see him moving through a harshly revealing isolation. The RSC dramatized the experience in a remarkable way. When Montjoy enters he catches Henry at a bruised moment, fresh from Bardolph's execution, feeling the antagonism of his troops, frightened by the volatility of his own feelings, and for perhaps the first time in his life finding no performing resource available. This is his first scene since his exhaustion of performances at Harfleur. Addressing Montjoy but keenly conscious of its effect on his troops, Henry at first flounders, trying out old roles, old sallies of wit and bravado, before settling his mind about the ransom. But the soldiers cannot see the significance of his decision. They watch from the inverted "canopy"—the stage-representation of the muddy fields, of the sickness and squalor of this war. Henry, roaming the stage "almost 'out of frame,' caught between the spectators on the canopy (his army) and the spectators in the audience . . . wrestled with his dual problem of king and actor: whether to continue." Or, rather, *how* to continue, since he must continue to act one way or another. In the end "he decides to step firmly into the scene. He returns to his soldiers. He commits himself to them" (*RSC*, p. 165). But they are not yet committed to him, and he finds himself bitterly alone. For he has also renounced his privileged relationship with us and committed himself to the interior life of the play: to the reality of actors, soldiers, and the war.

The dreamer relinquishes control of the dream. And the play goes into its freest, deepest, and most powerful moments.

The Chorus in act 4 seems somewhat gentled himself, almost pensive as he evokes a "ruined band" "low-rated" against the "confident and over-lusty French." His sympathies are chastened by the reality of war, his class assumptions less automatic. The "poor condemnèd English, / Like sacrifices, by their watchful fires / Sit patiently and inly ruminate / The morning's danger" (22–24). For the first time he shows himself to be aware of the significance of outward signs instead of their mere inadequacy: "and their gesture sad, / Investing lank-lean cheeks and war-worn coats, / Presenteth them unto the gazing moon / So many horrid ghosts" (25–28).

This more sensitive vision forces the Chorus to come up with a corresponding vision of the "royal captain." Working hard, he tries to evoke sympathy for an idealized version of Henry-as-brother, inspiring his troops by his presence, so that "every wretch, pining and pale before, / Beholding him, plucks comfort from his looks" (41–42). But this is a spurious sentiment, just the kind of self-gratifying fantasy of control that Henry must repudiate. Once again, the Chorus urges us to envision a scene ("A little touch of Harry in the night") quite different from the one we actually get.[16] As he goes among his troops, troubled and disguised, Henry in effect rejects the dream version of the scene asserted by the Chorus. At the level of the fiction occupied by the soldiers ("wretches," the Chorus calls them) mere "looks" and shows have lost what potency they ever had. Henry must go into the fiction and generate a unifying spirit from inside. It is the necessity implied by the myth of the secret sharer.

Henry goes into the heart of his dream of command. There, in the most personal scene of the play (4. 1), all the play's impersonality, all that Henry habitually assigns to God or War, and that the Chorus assigns to History or Mars, recoils upon Henry the dreamer. Assuming the disguise of a plain soldier ("A name that in my thoughts becomes me best"), the king "plays dead" in order to come awake. Meeting Pistol, he hears himself spoken of with the irreverent affection of a Falstaffian.

But Pistol's impression of the king as a "bawcock, and a heart of gold, / A lad of life, an imp of fame . . . the lovely bully" (4. 1. 45–48), resounds with impertinent nostalgia: he knows only Hal of "the former days," and has no way of recognizing Harry le Roy of these days. Both present and absent, Henry moves on then to overhear Fluellen and Gower arguing, Fluellen preoccupied as always with the "ceremonies of the wars, the cares of it, and the forms of it, and the sobriety of it, and the modesty of it" (72–74). This is an artist's solicitude for the relationship of craft and form, medium and ideal, and Henry is impressed: "There is much care and valor in this Welshman" (82). He has just reminded Pistol that he too is a Welshman, and Fluellen's care echoes later in the Ceremony soliloquy, where Henry bitterly weighs the costs of tending his own great craft, of keeping the ceremonial watch of kingship.

Henry moves deeper into the night, where neither he nor we have been before. The encounter with Williams, Bates, and Court (83 ff) sounds out the obscured interior of the play's martial rhetoric and strikes the most distinctive note of all. The scene discloses the quiet reality, not of clowns or captains or of any previous acquaintances, but of "soldiers." They are not heroes: they will fight for the king without much believing in him and are content that the justice of his cause, if any, is "more than we should seek after." But certainly they are not "wretches," though they are fearful, nor are they the rapacious demons of Henry's fantasy at Harfleur. There is obviously nothing fantastic about them, and nothing distinctive except the indisputable stability of their presence. He would never have met such men before—neither in his sportive days nor in his sunny days of heroism—since they are workaday men, invisible in any drama of higher colors. Nor could he ever have conjured them up in his fancy. And yet they are the central stuff of his enterprise. What shakes Henry is the unshakable substance of the men, the stubborn privacy by which they shelter themselves from his manipulating intelligence, even now as he sits among them as a "soldier." It is not his argument that they resist: with a little prodding they consent to his key contention that "every man's soul is his own" and that the king's responsibility, however great, is not increased by the weight of individual consciences. What they resist is his style, peremptory and elaborate, by which he attempts to win their sympathy for the "absent" king. But the king's name inspires no awe, no affection, no deep belief, and only a habitual kind of loyalty. If the king is indeed "but a man, as I am," why then, that is *his* business as it is every man's: all are alone, all free and self-responsible. It earns him no special favor that what he must worry about in his private conscience is a battle in which thousands of men like Williams and Bates overwhelmingly stand to get killed. Henry's disguise provides, then, no easy way for him to knot up his two personae, soldier and king, into a tolerable whole; and indeed he comes close to blowing his cover. When he flashes in exasperation at Williams, "Your reproof is something too round" (192), it is the offended king speaking, not the soldier.

Conceivably, the agreement to quarrel with Williams after the battle is not so shallow a king's game as it seems, since Henry at the moment feels dissociated from all his roles, strong in none. Baffled by the autonomy of the soldiers, who are therefore not "his soldiers" at all, he cannot really be responsible for their private ceremonies of guilt or innocence, courage or cowardice. Yet their very independence burdens him all the more with the need for a "just cause," an overarching Ceremony in which the soldiers may respectfully participate and very likely die. Clearly such a cause would be the stronger, its chances for success the better, for the voluntary commitment of numerous strongly centered men. But how to solicit such commitment? The king's responsibility for the war is untransferable exactly as each subject's responsibility for his own soul is untransferable, yet the war is a collective action, too, and the king cannot prosecute it by the exertion of his will alone, as if the actors were the playthings of his fantasy.

The debacle launches Henry into his one really private moment in the play. Like his other set speeches, the soliloquy (216 ff) has a conventional rhetorical form (the topic now is the King's Sleepless Watch) but as usual, the protective form discloses a turbulence within. Henry needs rhetorical control here because he stands alone on stage at his most critical moment of all. When he put on Erpingham's robe earlier, he allowed himself to relax into prose and out of the vigilant conventionalities of the public verse of Henry the Fifth.[17] Now, dislocated by his encounter with the soldiers, detached from his familiar identities of soldier and king, he is vulnerable to both hysteria and epiphany. The clenching back into verse at this point conveys both possibilities. As the speech rolls on through its devices, releasing long-suppressed passions, it reveals Henry groping for anchorage among a staggering gush of resentments. Though extravagant with self-pity, the soliloquy sharply illuminates his "twin-born" condition.

Loosened from familiar roles, afloat among feelings he has never been able to deal with except through performance, Henry divides like a dreamer simultaneously aware of himself as dreamer and the dreamed one. On the one hand his vision expands hugely; he sees himself not as a king fighting God's ordained battle, but as *the* king, in whom others reside fearfully—yet like children, protected, and hence not really or finally fearful. He surveys the entire realm of his creation and assumes responsibility not just for this battle, this war, but for his kingdom. He absorbs the Chorus's function, securing the boundaries that enable his subject-children to sleep, work, and play—his actors, in other words, to act.

On the other hand the enlarged vision is matched by an outraged cry at the loss of sentient selfhood it entails. For the watch of Ceremony is sustained by the king's continuously absenting himself from his realm, though a spectacular shadow of the king will continue to walk the public stage. Ceremony, as Henry grieves, is empty and powerless, has no substance or reality of its own; and when it is worshipped it is misconstrued as its own shadow. Henry scorns the props and shows of ceremony, but he cannot repudiate invisible Ceremony itself, which requires total vigilance and allows no relaxation. Like the playwright, he achieves design by removing himself from his work. He justifies his realm by conferring "place, degree, and form," by spinning out of his own life the living context in which others' acts participate and bear meaning.

Henry howls in protest of what this watch must cost him. Never till now has he seen his role as so hopelessly vast. "We must bear all," he cries, be "subject to the breath / Of every fool" (19–21); "What infinite heart's ease / Must kings neglect that private men enjoy!" (22–23). He does not think of the fearful private soldiers he has just encountered, but fantasizes bitterly about the "wretched slave, / Who, with a body filled, and vacant mind, / Gets him to rest, crammed with distressful bread" (254–56). And again: "The slave, a member of the country's peace, / Enjoys it; but in gross brain little wots / What watch the king keeps to maintain the peace" (267–69). This caricature is Henry's fantastic opposite—and the image suggests the impotence he feels now as ceremonial king, sole keeper of the watch. He is like a natural man of action whose own hands seem suddenly to be floating out of reach. He sees the true extent of his domain, and the vision appalls him. What he needs is a son, a Hal (a bawcock, an imp of fame) to act for him as he once acted for his father (and, in the bright dawn of this play, as he set out to act for his ancestors and for the Chorus). The hysteria reveals itself in the confusion of the personified image of Ceremony (the personification itself being Henry's characteristic way of distancing rowdy impulses). At first Ceremony is all that distinguishes a king from other men, but within a few lines it has become the king's tormentor, a besetting fantasy of royalty itself:

> . . . No, thou proud dream,
> That play'st so subtilly with a king's repose.
> I am a king that find thee; . . .
>
> (4. 1. 243–45)

Finally comes the perplexing climax to the piling-up of "thrice-gorgeous" Ceremony's signs, instruments, and powers, none of which "can sleep so soundly as the wretched slave."

The impression of clarity in this speech comes from the sustained cry of pain beneath the suave topic of the King's Complaint. Henry is bidding a panicky farewell to the personal life he had always kept apart from his public image—a farewell, that is, to Hal, lad of life whom Pistol had recently extolled and who emerges now only in the note of sharp, intuitive protest at his absorption in the role of Henry the Watcher. For of course Henry has no idea of backing away from this role. He may shudder at the prospect of reentering the world from this suspended moment and taking up the burden he has envisioned here, but he will certainly do it. Part of what he sees here, after all, is that the burden is his own choice. He does not attempt to transfer responsibility to God or destiny; does not complain that the crown has thrust itself upon him devouringly (as he told his father it had in *2 Henry IV*). So if the responsibility costs him "himself," his heart of gold, that is part of his choosing, too. Henceforth, his appearances as Harry, good fellow, soldier, brother, bluff lover, indeed his role as leading man, will all have a deliberate quality to them that his earlier career full of performances never had. The roles will not be felt expressions of live, interior selves so much as royal artifacts, though capable of compelling dramatic power.

What Henry gropes for in the soliloquy is not tragic insight into his own nature, but rather poise: the balance of faculties that will enable him to take and inspire prosperous action, to direct a masterful performance by the company. The poise eludes him in his stance as put-upon king; but then, after an interruption by Erpingham, the tension breaks and he falls to his knees for a prayer. The tone shifts inward, and Henry is seized with a critical terror, intense and personal. Not his ancestors, but his father comes to mind—and with it, his guilt, the past, the futility of acting to "waste the memory of the former days." Though he does not think of Falstaff, for one moment he is Hal, "the lovely bully," caught in the old dream he had declared himself forever wakened from. Like Richard himself, he is king by sequence and succession (if not by *fair* sequence), which is to say by virtue of that old dream; as with Claudius all the energy of repentance, the attempts to pay off the past, are useless, the effects of the succession in hand. The play by which Henry would so waste the past turns it up as fresh as ever, just as it turns up the reality of his soldiers. Nothing is granted him, no advantages of succession, as his father had hoped, of fate or of future. History will not justify him, instead he must justify history. He must do it all, "we must bear all." The futility throws him nakedly upon himself; at that point he hears "my brother Gloucester's" voice calling "my liege!" and he returns to his familiar role. He will not look back or return to this dark moment; he will never again be so contemplative, cast his vision so wide from so still a center, or regard himself with such ironic understanding. The moment will live, but not in his consciousness; it will make him a lighter man and a better king. From Agincourt he will emerge something like the legend that the Chorus celebrates.[18]

The play shows us Henry becoming the legendary king, and it shows us Agincourt becoming "Agincourt." Once he emerges from his nighttime trial, Henry can go on to play whatever onstage role the plot requires from him—not hypocritically, but effortlessly, because he is absolved now of the need to reconcile inward and outward forms of self. The bouyancy of his St. Crispin's speech conveys this sense of selfless performance. The role is all—to maintain the country's "peace."

As Agincourt creates "Henry Fifth," he creates "Agincourt," which in retrospect stands as a resounding triumph, but in the dramatic process is more complex. "Agincourt" is the heart of a war that is the test of a company's ability to unify itself. The unity must come from within, a process of private individuals entering into a mutual action that grows into something strange and admirable: a successful battle against overwhelming odds, a drama more compelling than the "history" it supposedly subserves. Emerging from his trial, Henry seems to understand that the traditional arguments for a just war, exercised upon Williams and Bates, have become irrelevant. Instead, the action must justify itself by the poise of its execution and its power to change its participants, now and afterwards—by its power, in other words, as drama. Henry relinquishes himself into that action, which is to say that he forgoes the king's ransom—and the action comes alive.

Our part in this process is likewise crucial. One trouble with Herbert Lindenberger's provocative analysis of *Henry V* as a "ceremonial play" is that it ignores the element of process.[19] He assumes that such a play brings together a preformed audience, one which already exists by virtue of sharing the experience that the play celebrates. This is the Chorus's assumption in the beginning: "you all *know* the real Henry, the real meaning of Agincourt, and need only call up images from that experience in order to animate this play into epic." This corresponds to Henry's assumption in the beginning as well—that he need only act in order to seize what is already given as his, the reality dreamt so vividly that it seems to preexist. What he discovers as he sallies into that dreamscape is the need to earn the unity he had assumed was there—to compel it by the force of his own commitment, to make it shine out, and so to create its audience. On Agincourt eve he understands that everything must be done—that nothing new and worth having is inherited, and that "history" is literally created by the play at Agincourt.[20]

The St. Crispin's speech (4. 3) differs in thrust and spirit from earlier performances. It is energetic but not athletic, strenuous but not self-exhausting. Its force resides in its literalness, its recognition that the grounds of the action lie not elsewhere, in England or in history, much less in some plan of God's, but rather here-and-now, on this stage at this hour among this limited band of brothers, this company of actors. The action is a ritual action: it does not represent history, it makes history. Hereafter history will consist of remembering and imitating this moment. The scene's capacity to generate the wider waves of meaning and color, to move audiences, is grounded in its self-acceptance *as* drama. Therefore, Westmoreland is not to wish one more soldier among us, nor is any to be constrained who is among us unwillingly.

The Crispin fellowship is to be signified by blood—the blood that is itself gentled by this action. There is no compulsion, rather each man's soul is his own, and the fellowship is carried by each man and joined ceremonially. Now Henry's refusal to be ransomed ("They shall have none, I swear, but these my joints," 4. 3. 123) is understood not as a promise but as an act. His speech bodies forth the ceremony—and this is the real meaning of *ceremony*, that which forms the men into a ritual at once exclusive and expansive. For clearly the "band of brothers," while it pointedly excludes those "gentlemen in England now abed [who] Shall think themselves accursed they were not here" (64–65), just as pointedly includes us who are *not* abed, and who *are* here, in the power of its pleasure. Its power, generated internally, shines out superfluously, spilling over in the theater, to claim us, too, as part of its ritual action. We do not simply celebrate it retrospectively as part of a tradition from which we inherited our gentleness, and hence our status in the theater, but we participate in the action and are gentled *by* it. We earn our role as *Henry V*'s scripted audience.

Having journeyed inside the public role of "king," Henry now conveys his faith to the others: "All things are ready, if our minds are so." This line is the key—soul and mind perfectly poised for penetration of the world of action. How else could an army outnumbered more than five to one literally "go through" the massive enemy unscathed? Shakespeare, unlike his sources, eschews any mention of military tactics.[21] What enables the English to win the battle is morale, an internal spirit of unity. The battle is a mental operation, not a military one. There are no external supports—for once, not even an appeal to God.

"Agincourt" is carried then by a strictly emotional and dramatic logic. It could have been won in no other way, not by any amount of Breach bluster or "royal captain" sentiment. But it still comes as a surprise to realize that no battle is represented on the stage in this most martial of plays. The entire action is "represented" by one vaudevillian bit of comic-realism involving Pistol, LaFer, and the Boy (Falstaff's old page): true things minded by their mockeries indeed. The implication certainly is that if we know what Agincourt is, then there is no need to try to "represent" it.

Yet if we are gentled, if this action is our own, we are very quickly reminded of its cost. For the war is enacted by the throat-cuttings as well as by the comic mockeries. Usually it is the Boy (and later, under Henry's orders, LaFer) who are killed to "represent" the slaughter of innocents. This is a harsh test of our commitment to the integrity of the fiction—and so I take the textual confusions, seemingly deliberate, as to Henry's motive and the proper sequence of events.[22] The war is real if the gentling is, and Henry is as ruthless as he is committed—as ready to act in this way, if required, as in any other. If we have been committed to the action of discovery in the play then we will know that the brutality must be carried out in full knowledge of its gravity: war accepting its conditions, Henry determined to end it, but content to act directly to do so. Surely this settles the lingering question from Harfleur. Having sounded there his own capacity to act violently, he proceeds to do so here. But there is no conflict between stranger and hero any longer, just right action. No excess of self-knowledge cripples this soldier, just the necessary kind to shape his actions toward an end. "I was not angry since I came to France / Until this instant" (4. 7. 50–51). This is less the remark of a man wondering about his own feelings than a leader carefully inscribing the benchmarks of history-in-the-making.

In the first wake of victory, before Henry even knows he is victorious, Fluellen compares him with Alexander, "in his rages, and his furies, and his wraths, and his cholers, and his moods, and his displeasures, and in his indignations" (32–34)—he seems to have trouble getting the comparison past such violent qualities—and in his "killing" of his companion: and here Gower supplies the name Fluellen has forgotten, "Sir John Falstaff." Henry has been absent from the stage, has receded from the personal figure presented to us in the night scene, and his motives and feelings and thoughts have been screened from us as if he were just a historical figure. So to hear Falstaff's name at this point, in this context, makes the severest test of our sympathies yet and casts the coldest light upon Henry at the moment of his triumph. Then the prisoners' throats are cut—LaFer's perhaps, on stage. We could not have more graphically brought home to us what the sacrifice of Falstaff has made possible: this action, this glory. The blood of slaughter is inseparable from the blood of gentling. Now, once the whole Agincourt action subsides and passes, what is it? Can it be made good, made worth the sacrifice? Can its power be extended to transfigure the whole occasion of the play itself?

The burden of the final act is to transfigure war into peace. But everywhere we are shown how costly, ephemeral, and artificial that peace is. Pistol's humiliation, for instance, is a sour business underneath the comedy. The last of the Falstaffians (the others all in their own ways wasted, like the Hostess, by "malady of France"), Pistol limps home in a grim parody of the legend of Agincourt, pimp, thief and war-whore trading as best he can upon his battlescars. But we are not encouraged to dwell on such ironies. The mood of act 5 is signaled by the Chorus, who enters laboring for peace, mediating between benign surface and disquieting substructure, dissipating the intensity of Agincourt through a blander, more comprehensive focus. Thus, in his prologue, he first takes us outward, giving us the epical "historical" perspective on Henry's triumphs; but then he hastens, rather awkwardly, to redirect us toward the stage itself. Clearly, despite his lip service to the "huge and proper" life of things, his own allegiances have shifted to the stage life. Here, he seems to say, is where we must fashion the peace.

But the task of making peace will be exactly as light or heavy as the war has been real. When Montjoy asks Henry, after Agincourt, for "charitable license . . . To book our dead, and then to bury them," he typically adds the need "To sort our nobles from our common men." It is an habitual, traditional distinction, a reflex of the hierarchical order that the French have come to symbolize. The reason he needs to "sort" the classes out comes clear with luminous irony in the image that follows:

> For many of our princes, woe the while!
> Lie drowned and soaked in mercenary blood.
> So do our vulgar drench their peasant limbs

> In blood of princes, and their wounded steeds
> Fret fetlock-deep in gore and with wild rage
> Yerk out their armèd heels at their dead masters,
> Killing them twice.
>
> (4. 7. 70–77)

Montjoy etches a bitterly realistic picture of self-strangled distinctions—peasants, princes, steeds, all convulsed in gore and mud, in death, rage, and reflex violence. Henry surely understands that the mordant ironies are those of war itself, not just of the French part in the war. Until Montjoy goes on to tell him, Henry does not even know that he has won, or that the English have come off so lightly. Then, when he hears, it is suddenly all over.

Much of the play's power derives from the disclosure of the reality of war at the heart of its own metaphor of war. "Reality" is the perception of what appears to lie outside the manipulated form of the play, and which the play's dramatizing intelligence seems to encounter rather than to conjure. Such inadvertent encounters test and strengthen, but also alter the original design. Henry, too, at the heart of his dream, encounters an intractible "reality" in the persons of the soldiers on Agincourt eve. To accept and understand this reality is crucial to his success at unifying his band of brothers the next day. The burden of the King's Cause must be fully reckoned: to pursue the future means to become weighed down in the present; to act upon a dream means to become heavy in the action. Agincourt succeeds because Henry commits himself to the present action, and the future thus flows from the moment rather than vice versa. But at once comes the need for cutting throats. The bog does not dissolve; rather, a new past, a new burden, has been created, a new sort of muck has been bred. The play bears no illusions about the glories of successful war.

To go forward in the face of such knowledge lays a special burden upon the future. The meaning of the goal changes as one hacks one's way toward it. If one embraces war to get to peace, the peace must be made worth the warring. Now although Henry does weigh the burden of the King's Cause, neither he nor anyone else ever questions the sufficiency of the cause once the bishops have provided him with the reason that permits him "in right and conscience" to "make this claim." France equals England: Henry simply and obdurately maintains this equation as his sanction for the absolute need to act toward the future. *There,* in the future, justification will be achieved, paradoxes squared. In the future the past will be recreated in the light and image of the new-won Present. Time will, in effect, be mastered by the artist-king, whose mission is to redeem it and keep history from turning tragic.

Shakespeare himself has no such investment in the justification of history. Deep within Henry's dream, he is working, not to mock or repudiate Henry, but to encompass him. He is working to carry off history and come loose at last from the structures of medieval hierarchicalism that dominate his material and thwart his drive toward genuine tragic form. Yet he does not proceed by exclusion or repression, but by seeing "history" through. That is the reason for *Henry V*'s peculiar equanimity. By "playing dead" to its own heightened activity, allowing the metaphors of historical process to declare themselves freely, the play calmly illuminates the historical mode of drama in its "purest" form. Beneath its turbulent surface, the history play is a masculine mode that thrives by expunging its own and threatening its enemy's women, and that licenses a specially fabricated creature called a "soldier." War, the pure heart of this pure "history," sanctions just those libidinal displacements that mutely rack and complicate the other womanless plays—the history plays that suffer the sexual conventions they inherit.

This is a heavy load to lay upon the final scene of the final history play. And yet, to transfigure war from waste to recreation is its chief burden. Its tone is announced by Burgundy, an elaborately new figure conjured up just for this occasion, who claims to have "labored / With all my wits, my pains, and strong endeavors / To bring your most imperial majesties / Unto this bar and royal interview" (5. 2. 24–27). The RSC gave over his role to the Chorus, who has indeed labored with art and strong endeavor for a peaceful ending, and who might well be felt to have earned his place among the participants. In effect he now urges Henry to extend his gentling action from his "band of brothers" to include the opposition. But for all his highmindedness, the political realities of the peace show plainly beneath the courtesies and attestations of "brotherhood." Katherine, says the Victor, is "our capital demand, comprised / Within the fore-rank of our articles" (96–97). Her submission to Henry is the chief price of peace for this savaged garden, "fertile France." "Some of you," he suavely underlines his point, may

> . . . thank love for my blindness, who cannot see many a fair French city for one fair French maid that stands in my way.

And Charles, king and father, agrees to pawn his daughter for the peace:

> Yes, my lord, you see them perspectively, the cities turned into a maid; for they are all girdled with maiden walls that war hath never entered.
>
> (5. 2. 303–9)

Of course war is entering now. But the conquering soldier must also submit to possible transformation in this encounter. Some critics see the whole exchange as a cynical political charade, but I do not think it is. True, Shakespeare underscores the political framework that renders Henry's success as a wooer forgone; but the wooing scene itself, as the theatrical tradition attests, carries far greater force and charm than what is strictly necessary to satisfy political ceremonies. Clearly, Henry means to succeed in his new role as suitor and throws himself upon the isolation of performance to win by wooing what he has already won by waste.

Henry has shown himself to the French as worthy of his heroic ancestors, famed for their adventuring in France. The French have now witnessed in him the same wondrous passage from wild youth to awesome power that the bishops celebrated in the beginning. To them, as to the bishops, the change is miraculous because they have not been privy to the experience Henry has undergone in the play itself, his immersion in the transforming processes of the dramatic event. The French can now only submit to the heroic conquerer, shaking their heads in surprise, but it is as himself—the true *English* king, not just a new Edward III or any other version of the golden-vizarded strongman—that Henry must woo and win Katherine. He does not woo as a political courtesy, or for his personal esteem, but in order to make a public act personal. He assumes the role of the vulnerable English suitor in order to imbue the Peace with "English" values, and in his own person to recreate the ruined past as "the best garden in the world."

So the wooing scene recapitulates the play's central action. The vehicle shifts from war to courtship, but in the miniature as in the major, a boundary is secured, a theatrical area defined, and a forgone conclusion put out of mind in order to make the interior action—the action of becoming—significant. And not only to Henry and Kate, for the scene finally must thrive with us. In the symbolic act whereby Henry represents himself as suitor for Kate's free consent, the whole course of the war is to be "made good." The artist-king would make the scene itself so good that it would overwhelm its conditions, overflow its boundaries, and reverse original relationships by *causing* the Peace, the genuine peace, rather than flowing from it—precisely in the style of Agincourt, and of powerful theater generally.

Yet Katherine resists Henry's need for transformation. The play after all has propagated life, not puppets, and not phantoms of Henry's self-gratifying wishes. Williams, earlier, pressed to take gold in settlement of his quarrel with Henry, refused to dignify Henry's effort to redeem the night's deception. And now Katherine, though she is "won," is not deeply or finally won, but only provisionally (as Berowne wins Rosaline in *Love's Labor's Lost,* not within the span of the play, but afterwards, offstage). Yet precisely because she resists, the scene generates its own real, and limited, charm; and we feel that what Henry achieves he achieves truly, because Katherine is real in her resistance as well as her acquiescence. Her adventuresome spirit and sensuality have already been well established—she has been learning English, especially its names for the body, all along. Once she and Henry are alone, therefore, their scene takes on some of the autonomous density of real space in which real people improvise a delicate new relationship. The action proceeds comically through incommunication toward understanding. At first (98–119) Henry is glib, tries "deceits" and a wooer's verbal maneuverings ("An angel is like you, Kate"). Next (121–30) he falls back upon overdirectness ("I know no ways to mince it in love"). Finally (132–65), still meeting taciturn resistance, he is provoked into the necessity of an all-stops-out performance of himself as plain soldier-as-wooer. *Mutatis mutandi,* Henry risks exposure and ridicule as he had in outright performances like that at Harfleur. He produces heat, and Katherine seems both attracted and entertained (for example, 184–85). In the end, having plucked her consent, he insists on the kiss, because "nice customs curtsy to great kings" and "we are the makers of manners, Kate" (260–63): a light but sober statement of eminence, of himself as the promulgator of models now, not vice versa.

But Henry's success, however substantial, is clearly muted—not the kind of thrilling theatrical moment that sweeps all conditionals off the stage. Behind the entire scene stands the humorlessly vigilant Watcher-king. Agincourt was the magic moment when that detached watchfulness broke and diffused itself into the action. But afterwards the magic fades, and to "be" king henceforth requires from Henry an unremitting effort of performance: not antic, self-revealing outbursts, but symbolic roles that he must struggle to make adequate to his enlarged sense of history. Like all kings, he knows the ephemerality of action, for on Agincourt eve he has had intimations of all-leveling time. And against such reality, signifying moments must be set up and maintained.

Therefore, though Agincourt has gentled the warrior for wooing, the wooing cannot be more than a performance, however ardent, and the wooer cannot be more than a symbolic role. For the Watcher-king will risk no failure as Shakespeare's real lovers do.[23] And without that willingness to hazard all for nothing, recreation can at best be partial, mixed. The whole last movement of the play settles into this mode of muted success. Nothing is allowed to undermine the sense of peace that comes with a just job of completion, but nothing obscures our view of the vigilant art that maintains it. Cushioned barriers are up. Between English and French, Henry and Katherine, and to some extent the play and the audience, we are aware of an amiable pretense mutually agreed upon. Between us and the actors nothing intimate is risked; the Chorus has distanced us and widened our view. All Falstaffians, captains, and soldiers are gone, and no intrusive stagelife contradicts the general sense of benignity. And we, accepting it, have been gentled by our participation. Waking from a dream at Agincourt, we now find ourselves in another, and quite pleasant, dream of peace.

Are we being softened, rocked to sleep, lulled and charmed? Is that what "to gentle" really means—to waste *our* memory of the arbitrary origin of this war? This "cause" is not *our* cause: the idea of reclaiming "England" by way of France is an obsession of late-coming Francophiliac aristocrats. Regarded coldly, the old mystic quest for nationhood reeks with the instincts for territory, possession, exclusion, control. "History," after all, is made by altering memories, wasting reality, idealizing the past. Look again at that genial Chorus, exhorting us to make our giddy minds "the quick forge and working house of thought." *His* thought! What we need is Falstaff.

But after all, *Henry V* refuses to trumpet glory, except to the incorrigibly giddy-minded. For many Elizabethans, to whom the idea of nationhood itself was new, the angst that the play inspires must have come through fresh and sharp. For *Henry V* clearly celebrates both the power and the emptiness of the national dream.[24] To act, however greatly, is to incur guilt and responsibility: Henry, the actor, learns this. In all the history plays the pursuit of the golden future is dogged by the shadow of the past, and the drama is the quintessential form of the continuing effort to subsume, waste, and recreate that past. Yet Shakespearean drama, skeptical always of its own obsessive motives and its own most powerful means, preserves a record of its own "wondrous" processes. In *Henry V* the ending is controlled by a vigilance that supersedes Henry's and that reveals itself through the effort of its restraints. Katherine as a hope to fulfill the future that Henry envisions is quite uninspiring, whatever else her charm, not because Shakespeare might not have drawn her more complexly, but because the play submits to the "facts" of the chronicle, which gives no warrant for inspiration. For the "future" itself brings this cycle, as it brings Henry's England, round merely to Henry VI—as the Chorus dutifully, helplessly, as if with immense reluctance, acknowledges in the Epilogue. Shakespeare refuses to waste the meaning of *what's coming,* and he refuses the temptation to mythologize, even within the compass of chronicle "facts," by staging a festive ending. Instead, all festivity is unceremoniously shunted into the Choral narrative.[25]

To lull us into a soothing dream of peace, our memories like so many cattle swaying into the abattoir of history, then to bludgeon us with a festive myth of consummation—this Shakespeare will not do. Yet if he will not cheapen the commitments underlying the arduously shaped concepts of "gentling," "ceremony," and atonement, how *are* those commitments to be honored?

The RSC clearly perceived our part in the general struggle toward identity, form, and unity. We are addressed throughout the play in many ways, sometimes quite directly, as when Henry speaks to us as the Governor of Harfleur. Later, when the French king, Charles, emerges from his lethargy in 3. 4 to trumpet the French response to Henry's challenge, he appears in his gold armor, vigorous, to deliver his tirade directly to us, who thus become his warlords. He represents the "aroused warrior-might of France" (*RSC*, pp. 157–58), the lords of the old regime, and in ritually naming them he is also naming us: conscripting us in the national effort to "bar Harry England," the upstart, the vassal. The moment is arresting, and it has power of persuasion clearly akin to Henry's own. Throughout the play, then, "we" are spoken to not as a block of fixed predilection, but as a multitude, diverse, confused, shifting and unsettled in our sympathies; as "gentles" or as wretches or as soldiers; as educated, having read the story; as French power, custodians of a venerable hierarchical order; as tenaciously ironic survivors of Falstaff; and as many other, fleeting personae as well.

Shakespeare pulls away from a festive strategy of unification as much out of respect for our separate realities as from a similar respect for his stubborn material. But just as he would transform that material, he would surely transform us, too, into something other than the sum total of our parts. He offers to engage us in a ceremony that unites us and, if we are willing, changes us, through an acceptance of our diversities. Of course we come to the theater half-willing to shed them. There we are offered a role as "audience," a role prefigured *in* the play but one that, we discover, assumes that we reach it from a thousand different sources, motives, and levels of response: the mirror-image of Canterbury's moral of the bees, that "many things, having full reference / To one consent may work contrariously" (1. 2. 205–6). What makes this nonfestive ceremony "work" are the improvisational nimbleness and the stubborn resistances of all its participants, onstage and off. If we are to be transfigured by this experience, fused into an audience, our differences overborne and our separate derivations forgotten, it will occur in a theatrical moment shining back with a power we ourselves have helped to generate.

To refuse festivity without falling into black irony is the trick of the play's clear-eyed insouciance. The blunted ending has sanctioned the disappointment that so many impatient, usually academic, critics have felt in the play. *Henry V* had always disturbed me by its passivity, its willingness to submit to the given and "play dead" to its governing conditions. But regarded "perspectively," as Charles says, through the freshness of a production like the RSC's, the play comes alive in its very willingness to risk its own conditions. In taking that open-eyed risk it achieves great natural bouyancy, winning its freedom by reaching an equipoise with those conditions rather than selling out to them. In the end, much rests with us, with our judgment, perception, and kindness. The play does not assert itself, nor does it go limp with false effacement. It remains extraordinarily vulnerable in the pureness of its middle mode. To understand this, one must be willing to take the first step into the play, nakedly refusing the old temptation to dress it up in chauvinistic robes and mind-numbing dioramas, and intensely but openly imagine it in fresh, unencumbered, undetermined performance.

"Gently to hear, kindly to judge": these are haunting Shakespearean words. Ultimately they have much the same force, *gens* and *kindred* meaning "one." This is of course what the theater aspires to do for and to us, and what we go to the theater for. Implied in the pact is the promise and danger of a fabulous power. If the play can get our consent from the beginning and induce us to give up our quotidian selves, and can both honor and overcome our multiplicity and our natural resistances, then it can possibly overpower history itself. To destroy history and finally to carry it away, Shakespeare must make an extraordinarily intimate yet delicate appeal to us. We are asked to make the dream of the play our own dream, to share its burdens and pleasures—but then to enlarge it, justify it, rescue it from the meanness that all such dreams, left to themselves, must shrink to. Across the improvisational line embodied by the Chorus, we are being wooed to exchange our lives with the life of the play—to fill it up with ourselves before it recedes from us into an irredeemable past. And from this act we are to receive ourselves. *Henry V* in this sense is a "ceremonial play" because it boldly commits itself to our capacities to understand and be changed by it.

Conclusion

After such a tremendous journey, what a sad shock it is to end up at the beginning, to be brought round merely to *Henry VI* again, "which oft our stage hath shown." I said before that the fundamental motive of the histories was the need to make a future. But the cycle—because that is what the sequence has turned out to be—looks like a wheel of endless dreams in which the dreamer strives to come awake, waking from one quasi-reality into a sharper one, but the last a mere return to the first. Is there to be no future—no way off this island after all? Is nothing really changed?

In the end of *The Tempest* everyone is released to whatever future awaits. Prospero's wonderful and terrible fabrications are over; he can do nothing more. Though he knows that nothing will last and that all the works of time and change may finally be only illusion, nevertheless the adventures on the island have made the future (as against a despairing repetition of the past) possible. Now he puts himself in our hands, asking for his off-island future, too, as Duke of Milan and as mortal man. With our hands and breath, then, we dissolve the island, leaving not a rack behind.

Except of course for Caliban, whose fate like everything else about him remains ever-vexing and profoundly ambiguous. In the beginning he had been conjured forth from his hard rock and made to "Speak!" by a variety of abusive names: slave, tortoise, hag-seed, earth. He enters cursing (as Prospero warned), yielding no "kind answers," and proceeds to reaffirm himself as the "abhorrèd slave," vile and unnurturable, who had exiled himself from Prospero's kindness by trying to rape Miranda, and even now must continually be "prevented." Clearly Caliban is brought forth as the outsider, the other, against which the circle of human kindness can be closed. Only after he has been displayed and then thrust violently back into his hard rock is Miranda ready to encounter Ferdinand, her off-island prince—to recognize him instantly as her future, her *kind*.

Prospero does not create Caliban, but he does shape the relationship, making him the ground for Ariel's spectacular performances. In the end, once all the other shows are played out, the playwright-wizard acknowledges that this base fabrication is "mine" as well. Endowed with Prospero's speech, Caliban has been forever transposed from mere brutishness: finally there are no answers that are not "kind." Whatever he was before Prospero came, he has since been awakened, questioned, made to speak, brought into relationship. He has been *dramatized* as ground—maintained just outside the human circle, a source both of danger and of prodigious earthy energy.

In other words, he is "mine" but also "not mine"—strange as well as family. His origins are still in him, therefore his fate. Unlike Ariel, he instinctively resists Prospero's loving force, and therefore insures his own continued bondage. This indeterminacy is essential to him. He is manifestly unfinished, unrecreated: half-man half-beast, full of murder and music, never sure why he suffers or if he wakes or dreams. And now, as the others depart, he must surely be left behind, island-bound, though forever, somehow, suing for grace. For him *now* there seems no imaginable resolution. He remains in transit; in the end, the others all released to their own unknown and private worlds, Caliban can only stay with us, vexingly in ours.

From the Temple Garden scene in *1 Henry VI* we saw how the action branched into two futures: the fixed future that is foreknown because from our exterior vantage it is already cemented as the past; and the interior drama, the artist's and our existential journey through the self-generating sequence itself. Could the second drama change the significance of the first? Or could it only end by affirming its implacability? Could history be changed? (Could Caliban change, despite Prospero's despair of the "unnurturable" slave?)

Futility sits deep in the bone of the histories—most poignantly when it seizes those figures who are most fiercely and complexly committed to the justification of their lives in time. We view them through a darkened glass, straining for brilliance, for endurance, against the obscure certainty of failure. We see them even in the flower of zestful enterprise, full of the power to change the world and make history, already doomed to it, already tinted with the deadly chill of nostalgia. The weight of our foreknowledge seems to extend itself into the world of the play, like the lead that sits upon Richard III's sword, or the pall that descends upon the Bastard in the dark as he hears of the advent of "Prince Henry."

1 Henry VI ends with Suffolk "bereaving [Henry] of his wits with wonder," "breeding love's settled passion in [his] heart": an easy conquest by the brazen use of "wondrous rare description." *Henry V* by contrast ends on the king's complaint that "having neither the voice nor the heart of flattery about me, I cannot so conjure up the spirit of love in her, that he will appear in his true likeness." The distance from Suffolk's success to Henry's failure measures what Shakespeare came to understand about the true costs of poetic speech. Now he refuses to intervene on Henry's behalf (as he did on Richard II's), refuses to redeem the drama through a poetry of greater persuasiveness than Henry can be imagined to have gained from his own depth of experience and complexity of feeling. Henry lacks the poetry of persuasion (what he scorns as the "voice of flattery") because he is unwilling or unable to hazard his place in a temporal design—to give up the future for the sake of an incandescent performance *now.* Though he has had a disturbing midnight vision, he insists on believing in time, in continuity, in Henry VI—the son whom he imagines presiding in power and glory over the garden of peace secured by his warrior father. Committed to this dream of the future, unwilling to gather his power in the present, Henry V must coerce and command his love; however he may soften the necessity with charm and epic verve, he must be content with an image of love, a poor "likeness" rather than the thing itself.

Henry IV ends his life on that mixed note of hope, guile, and anxiety that characterizes his whole career. Even as he attempts to distill the motives of his life and death, to purify the meaning of succession, he betrays the lack of faith, the hard-rock pragmatism that has always been the mark of both his success and his failure:

And now my death
Changes the mode, for what in me was purchased
Falls upon thee in a more fairer sort,
So thou the garland wear'st successively.

> Yet, though thou stand'st more sure than I could do,
> Thou art not firm enough . . .
> Therefore, my Harry,
> Be it thy course to busy giddy minds
> With foreign quarrels, that action, hence borne out,
> May waste the memory of the former days. . . .
>
> (*2 Henry IV* 4. 5. 198–215)

He sues for grace, but goes to his death (in the "Jerusalem" Chamber) enslaved to the vanity of redemptive time. There can be no change of mode, except, perhaps, rhetorical: Henry V is bound to the wheel of time no less than was his father. The succession is not a fulfillment of the past, a transformation of machiavellian theater into something of great constancy, but an attempt to replace the "former days" in our short and giddy-minded memories with more of the same, only brighter and more gorgeously costumed. In this pragmatic dependency on the idea of king-as-machiavel, lodged in time, having no choice but to labor in the murky zone where time and character assume each other's features, the kings express the nature of the history mode of drama itself: intrinsically effortful, distrustful of the unknown, never really able to abandon its coercive, contentious, compulsively verbal self to the possibility of free creation beyond the control of its own voices.

Like Caliban, endowed with speech yet knowing only how to curse and so insure his bondage, "history" once roused by the dramatist from its unquickened status as "times deceased" turns out to be at best only half-redeemable. Despite the hopes it raises when met with great imagination, despite its occasions of lyricism, sensual beauty, heroic exertion, in the end it remains doggedly impure, half wild and obscure, half unexpressed and inexpressible. It resists the gratification of fulfillment or even completion, festive or tragic. And though like Caliban it can sometimes hear the deep and healing, melancholy music calling it to lose itself to wonder, hence to recreation, it never does or can submit wholeheartedly.

Not surprisingly, the inability of the histories to really "change the mode" involves the curious distortion of its women—*their* inability to alter the masculine nature of the plays by an enduring, consequential presence. With few exceptions—Hotspur's Kate a notable one—they are marginal or twisted types, whores or witches, ciphers or harridans. In the early plays they are loud, tormented, haranguing; in the later ones, they turn up in the underground, but otherwise have dropped into silence or out of sight altogether. They cannot take root in the ground of the plays, and that is because—as *Henry V* makes clear—the ground of the histories is female, and she is desecrated and denied even as she is courted. Henry's true mistress is not French Katherine, but the true mistress of all the histories, the ideal of "England" herself. No wonder that Henry VI should be the wispy issue of Henry V and his stand-in lover. For her, great virgin ghost of desire, have all yearning, combative energies been roughly deployed through the chimerical landscape called "history." They are returned not vivid and replenished, but abstract half-realized figures, anxiously willing their own illusions of coherence, forced to warm themselves upon a worked-up passion as their only—and losing—defense against her indifference. She exhausts without fulfilling; she never comes herself but sends her clouded agent, time; she is never really there, but always in the future, beckoning, eluding, punishing; she is the vanity of kings, for whom they act and for whom they die ungratified. Like his predecessors, Henry V remains desperately in bondage to this consuming ideal, obsessed with securing the motives of action in an unassailable Cause, with planting his Truth in the ground of her Reality. He cannot let her go, even though this ghostly fiction, as long as she retains her obscure and chilling power, inhibits the free submission to other stranger, truly recreative kinds of power.

One source of the melancholy that we feel in these plays is Shakespeare's "intensely dramatic perception," as Wylie Sypher puts it, "that the course of history has been nothing but a masquerade [performed] against the vast backward and abysm of time. For Shakespeare has the new Renaissance consciousness of the infinite, the opening of illimitable distances like the blue backgrounds in paintings by Leonardo or Patinir or Herri Met de Bles, like a world dissolved, like Prospero's visionary horizon against which we are transient dreamwork. For Shakespeare history can seem to be one more illusion. This is his dramatic reply to Machiavelli, who lacked poetry."[1]

But if he felt this he also felt the existential grip of history. His ability to evoke the infinitely receding background that renders human endeavor futile is matched by the intensity of his feeling for its desperate foreground reality: the pain and strife and lift of being alive on the historical stage, even if it *is* only a passing show rounded by an impenetrable sleep. Shakespeare looks down sadly on his show of kings trapped in the illusion of time, refusing to coerce his material, his characters, but not serenely detached. He has gone through the cycle himself, has translated himself into his characters, traced out both the succession of kings and the succession of plays in the sequence, not from a position of philosophical distance, but on his pulse as an artist. Sinking into his materials, he has allowed the most life-filled and farreaching fictions to flower out of the bare rock of the times decreased, until it seems that all the possibilities of "English history"—all the truth and reality it has to offer, all the "kind answers" it has to yield to his increasingly evocative questions—have been exhausted.

Like Prospero, master-dreamer, he has urgently stepped down into his own insular dreamwork, the vanity of his own art. He creates the awesome fictions that allow his characters to declare their true natures; he himself is seeking out the truth of his relationship to them and to his own powers. Shakespeare is looking for the otherness in his own vision of the past—to imagine it so fully that it takes on life and begins to speak, not in the voice borrowed from its master, but in its own. To discover what is truly "mine" and what is "not mine," what he controls and fabricates, and what he cannot control and redeem; to be roused to genuine anger, the bitterness of the knowledge of failure, to strike the limits of his transforming powers: this is necessary in order for him as artist to free himself from the vanity of his own art, from bondage to the ideal mistress "England," whom he has undertaken to serve as no man ever did before, and to win as no one ever has. To break the grip of that fiction of a redeemable Past—the idea of an "England" fully recreated as a body of dramatic art, rich, strange, and admirable—Shakespeare, like Prospero, finally has to do what Henry and all his predecessors are unable to do: to let it go.

The clear-eyed equanimity of the end of *Henry V* expresses a calm farewell to English history, like Prospero's measured rites of conclusion at the end of *The Tempest*. In one sense *Henry V* as a whole is a ritual of farewell, a carrying-across of strictly homebound "English" history to a wider, stranger world—"histories" both more profoundly personal and more awesomely remote. Having made the final crossing steadily, Shakespeare is freed to explore the mythic past that has been his deeper subject all along.

"In the beginning," D. H. Lawrence begins a cosmogony myth, then pauses: "there never was any beginning, but let it pass. We've got to make a start somehow."[2] Shakespeare chooses to start with the death of Henry V—and he necessarily begins as an outsider, a stranger approaching a formidably closed world of times deceased, yet a world whose very presence *out there* exerts a powerfully intimidating hold on the present. By the time he has come round again to that beginning, acknowledging even the choice of beginnings "mine," he has exchanged his life with that of the past, has filled it with his consciousness, his unstinted and incomparable imagination. Like Oedipus, he has claimed that past from the gods, appropriated it from its otherness, and now, full of unimaginable new powers, he heads into an unknown future.

But the history itself, has it been changed? How can it not be, since it exists always and only in terms of relationships, only in the *figuring* of the times deceased? Shakespeare has brought the dead past into a living relationship with us; and, having been through the cycle, we are changed. As we take our leave upon calm seas—Prospero's last charge to Ariel before he is released—we can look back to see *Henry V* returning into *Henry VI.* But now the whole process is quickened with our consciousness: that once-impersonal past is now part of us and we are part of it. Under auspicious gales, we bear it with us into open seas.

Notes

My text throughout is *William Shakespeare: The Complete Works*, gen. ed. Alfred Harbage (Baltimore, Md.: Penguin Books, 1969). Individual editors are as follows: for *1 Henry VI*, David Bevington; for *2* and *3 Henry VI*, Robert K. Turner and George Walton Williams; for *Richard III*, G. Blakemore Evans; for *King John*, Irving Ribner; for *Richard II*, Matthew W. Black; for *1 Henry IV*, M. A. Shaaber; for *2 Henry IV*, Allan G. Chester; for *Henry V*, Alfred Harbage.

Introduction

1. The picture of Shakespeare as an active historical thinker (rather than ideologue, mythographer, or dramatic chronicler) emerges in two comprehensive studies of the histories: Robert Ornstein, *A Kingdom for a Stage: The Achievement of Shakespeare's History Plays* (Cambridge, Mass.: Harvard University Press, 1972); and Moody E. Prior, *The Drama of Power: Studies in Shakespeare's History Plays* (Evanston, Ill.: Northwestern University Press, 1973). Both stress the range and variety of Shakespeare's sources and influences; Ornstein in particular sees the history plays as the most innovative work of Shakespeare's first decade of playwriting. A more probing study of the two-way relationship of the dramatist to his intellectual climate is Wilbur Sanders, *The Dramatist and the Received Idea* (Cambridge: At the University Press, 1968). Some of the others (aside from those specified in notes below) who have helped shape my ideas both about Shakespeare as historical thinker and about historical thinking in general, are L. F. Dean, *Tudor Theories of History Writing* (Ann Arbor: University of Michigan, 1974); G. R. Elton, *The Practice of History* (New York: Crowell, 1967); F. J. Levy, *Tudor Historical Thought* (San Marino, Calif.: Huntington Library Publications, 1967); Nancy S. Struever, *The Language of History in the Renaissance* (Princeton, N.J.: Princeton University Press, 1970); Hayden White, *Metahistory: The Historical Imagination in Nineteenth-Century Europe* (Baltimore, Md.: Johns Hopkins Press, 1973).

2. Herbert Lindenberger makes the most sustained and comprehensive attempt I know of to define the special nature and province of the history play, Shakespearean and otherwise. Especially noteworthy (for Shakespeare studies) is the fourth chapter, "The Historical World as Imaginative Place," pp. 95ff., in *Historical Drama: The Relation of Literature and Reality* (Chicago: University of Chicago Press, 1975). See also "The Early 1590's and the Changes of Heroic Song" in *The Tiger's Heart: Eight Essays on Shakespeare* (New York: Oxford University Press, 1970), where Herbert Howarth explicitly distinguishes Shakespeare's manner of historical search from the Spenserian mode of mythologizing. Shakespeare's contemporary dramatists, insofar as they were inter-

ested in English history, tended to approach it either fancifully (romance in Greene's *James IV*, tragic occasion in Marlowe's *Edward II*), or else submissively, like the anonymous "dramatizers" of chronicle material.

3. I have derived the terms *antic* and *machiavel,* though very obliquely, from Sigurd Burckhardt and Michael Goldman. In his seminal essay, "The Poet as Fool and Priest," in *Shakespearean Meanings* (Princeton, N.J.: Princeton University Press, 1968), Burckhardt sees Shakespeare as acting in his plays through two voices—one, the "fool" who "wantons" words, detaching them from their quotidian contexts, throwing them into a crisis of multiple and conflicting meanings, and in fact threatening them with meaninglessness; the other, the "priest," who redeems the word in a transcendent meaning that gathers all the others into it. This is a superb and powerful conception, and one to which I am deeply indebted. At the same time, I believe it works best in the tragedies and comedies, plays that do resolve themselves, and less well in the histories, whose ethos is irresolution itself, a deep-rooted resistance to endings, and indeed a survival instinct for pressing on toward a future that ultimately is embodied in *us,* in our active presence in the theatrical occasion. For this special emphasis I have borrowed from Michael Goldman, again obliquely. In *The Actor's Freedom: Toward a Theory of Drama* (New York: Viking Press, 1975), Goldman describes how the Elizabethan dramatists deployed in a new combination the dramatic values implicit in two conventions—Senecan rhetoric and Machiavellian plotting—to develop the Revenge genre. "It is only when revenge is hit upon as the source for a complete play that the dramatic possibilities of Seneca's rhetoric (scarcely exploited in his own plays) are released on the stage. . . . As Seneca's rhetoric allowed feeling to come thrusting out in performable aggression, so the machiavellian interest in manipulating the world—that is, in plotting—allowed that aggression to make itself felt in a large, comprehensive flow of action. The revenge plot enabled a single actor's flow of aggression to shape an entire, very complicated play" (p. 99).

I am also mindful of James L. Calderwood's idea of the "duplexity" of the dramatic experience: *Shakespearean Metadrama* (Minneapolis: University of Minnesota Press, 1971). He also employs this idea to good effect in "*1 Henry IV:* Art's Gilded Lie," *English Literary Renaissance* 3 (1973): "mimesis" and "theatrics" are "two dimensions of drama . . . each devoted to its own brand of truth, its own species of reality or unreality" (p. 135).

Finally, my understanding of the antic as a kind of fool owes a general debt to two books: Enid Welsford, *The Fool: His Social and Literary History* (London: Faber and Faber, 1935), and William Willeford, *The Fool and His Sceptre* (Evanston, Ill.: Northwestern University Press, 1969).

4. See, for instance, Willeford, *The Fool and His Sceptre* p. 18: "The fool reverts to the chaotic lump when he has turned his back on it too long. But *our* having turned our backs to it too long is the precondition of his appearance. The fool turns us around."

Chapter 1

1. E. M. W. Tillyard, *Shakespeare's History Plays* (London: Chatto and Windus, 1944); Lily B. Campbell, *Shakespeare's "Histories": Mirrors of Elizabethan Policy* (San Marino, Calif.: Huntington Library Publications, 1947); J. P. Brockbank, "The Frame of Disorder—*Henry VI,*" in *Stratford-Upon-Avon Studies 3: Early Shakespeare,* ed. John Russell Brown and Bernard Harris (London: Edward Arnold, 1961); H. T. Price, *Construction in*

Shakespeare (Ann Arbor: University of Michigan Press, 1951); Robert Ornstein, *A Kingdom for a Stage: The Achievement of Shakespeare's History Plays* (Cambridge, Mass.: Harvard University Press, 1972).

2. For this reading of *The Merchant of Venice* I am indebted to Sigurd Burckhardt, *Shakespearean Meanings* (Princeton, N.J.: Princeton University Press, 1968), pp. 206–36; and to Kirby Farrell, *Shakespeare's Creation* (Amherst: University of Massachusetts Press, 1975), pp. 141–62.

Chapter 2

1. *1 Henry VI* has been notoriously hounded by questions of its authorship and its place in the sequence. In his introduction to the *Arden* edition of the play (London: Methuen, 1962), Andrew S. Cairncross discusses the subjects exhaustively, and I am content with his—and by now the overwhelmingly favored—conclusions that the play does indeed come first, and was authored primarily if not exclusively by Shakespeare. See also Robert Y. Turner, *Shakespeare's Apprenticeship* (Chicago: University of Chicago Press, 1974), especially the introductory chapter. Critics increasingly seem willing to accept the idea that Shakespeare was indeed capable of designing and executing a sophisticated trilogy in *Henry VI.*

2. My "viewing" of the play has been aided by, among others, Barbara Hodgdon, "Shakespeare's Directorial Eye: A Look at the Early History Plays," in *Shakespeare's "More than words can witness": Essays on Visual and Nonverbal Enactment in the Plays,* ed. Sidney Homan (Lewisburg, Pa.: Bucknell University Press, 1979); G. K. Hunter, "The Royal Shakespeare Company Plays *Henry VI," Renaissance Drama* 9 (1978); Carol McGinnis Kay, "Traps, Slaughter, and Chaos: A Study of Shakespeare's *Henry VI* Plays," *Studies in the Literary Imagination,* 5 (1972); Homer D. Swander, "The Rediscovery of *Henry VI," Shakespeare Quarterly* 29 (1978); and David Daniell, "Opening Up the Text: Shakespeare's *Henry VI* Plays in Performance," in *Drama and Society,* ed. James Redmond (Cambridge: At the University Press, 1979).

3. A number of critics have described this "shadowless" style, among them J. P. Brockbank, "The Frame of Disorder—*Henry VI,*" in *Stratford-Upon-Avon Studies 3: Early Shakespeare,* ed. John Russell Brown and Bernard Harris (London: Edward Arnold, 1961), and F. W. Brownlow, *Two Shakespearean Sequences* (London: Macmillan & Co., 1977), p. 23. I have dealt with it in a somewhat different context in " 'Art and Baleful Sorcery': The Counterconsciousness of *Henry VI, Part I," Studies in English Literature* 15 (1975).

4. Edward Berry, *Patterns of Decay* (Charlottesville: University Press of Virginia, 1975), pp. 17–20.

5. H. T. Price, *Construction in Shakespeare* (Ann Arbor: University of Michigan Press, 1951). "Others" would prominently include Brockbank, "The Frame of Disorder."

6. Jonas A. Barish, "The Antitheatrical Prejudice," *Critical Quarterly* 8 (1966): 337. A little later Barish describes the antitheatrical prejudice as deriving from "a conservative ethical emphasis in which the key terms are those of order, stability, constancy, and integrity, as against a more existentialist view that prizes exploration, process, growth, flexibility, variety and versatility of response. In the one case we seem to have an ideal of stasis, in the other an ideal of movement; in one case an ideal of rectitude, in the other an ideal of plentitude" (p. 342).

7. Hall supplies elaborate motivation for the Somerset-Plantagenet quarrel, which

Shakespeare obviously could have used had he wanted to. As it is, the quarrel in the play is clearly made the cause rather than the effect of the dynastic rivalry. I deal with this scene at length in "Art and Baleful Sorcery" (see n. 3 above).

8. Knowingly or not, Shakespeare inherited from Holinshed's *Chronicles* a confusion of two different historical Mortimers.

9. "The characters in the plays are all living, all unaware, within a web of significance which connects individual actions. The law of cause and effect is always operating, but the individual, having lost his hold upon moral realities because of pride, selfishness, or weakness, cannot see beyond the moment." Robert K. Turner, Introduction to *2 & 3 Henry VI* in *The Complete Works*, p. 475.

10. James Joyce, *Ulysses* (New York: Random House, 1961), p. 190.

Chapter 3

1. *The First Part of the Contention Betwixt the Two Famous Houses of York and Lancaster* is now generally accepted as a "bad quarto" of *2 Henry VI*—i.e., a memorial or reconstructed version. Robert E. Burkhart argues in *Shakespeare's Bad Quartos* (The Hague: Mouton, 1975) that the so-called bad quartos were really adaptations of the originals for provincial touring performances. The most eloquent dissent from the general consensus is that of C. T. Prouty, *The Contention and Shakespeare's 2 Henry VI* (New Haven, Conn.: Yale University Press, 1954).

2. The lines are not strictly comparable since those in *The Contention* are clearly butchered. My general point remains unaffected, however.

3. Robert Ornstein, *A Kingdom for a Stage: The Achievement of Shakespeare's History Plays* (Cambridge, Mass.: Harvard University Press, 1972), p. 46: "As so often before, sorrow is Henry's refuge. Imagining himself the helpless dam, he weeps as much for his loss of Gloucester as for Gloucester himself."

4. York's obsessive, synecdochic self-reference (i.e., to himself as *hand, heart, tongue, eye,* and so on) is usefully summarized by A. C. Hamilton in *The Early Shakespeare* (San Marino, Calif.: Huntington Library Publications, 1967), pp. 41–42. And James L. Calderwood finds the hand-arm imagery to imply York's "fragmentary existence and uncompleted nature: in his own view of himself he is a part seeking its whole, a hand without the body which only kingship can give it. At the same time, the hand imagery suggests a radical limitation of York's character" ("Shakespeare's Evolving Imagery: *2 Henry VI*," *English Studies* 48 [1967]).

5. Carol McGinnis Kay, "Traps, Slaughter, and Chaos: A Study of Shakespeare's *Henry VI* Plays," in *Studies in the Literary Imagination* 5 (1972): 15–16.

6. C. L. Barber, *Shakespeare's Festive Comedy* (New York: Meridian Books, 1963), p. 13.

7. Barbara Hodgdon (see chap. 2, n. 2, above) discusses Shakespeare's uses of public and private perspectives in establishing continuity among scenes and characters.

Chapter 4

1. The people of the *Henry VI* plays, "though violent . . . are, in a deeper sense, all strangely passive: they are at the mercy of circumstances and their uncontrolled selves. More—they inevitably end by handing over the control of their country to the tyrann-

ous Richard III, who explicitly renounces all 'soft laws' of 'nature' . . . with a considered philosophy of egotism, saying 'I am myself alone.' . . . He at least makes some sense of this chaos—for awhile" (G. Wilson Knight, *The Olive and the Sword* [London: Oxford University Press, 1944], pp. 10–11).

2. *Puppetry* is Brockbank's term—see n. 7 below.

3. Ronald Berman, "Fathers and Sons in the *Henry VI* Plays," *Shakespeare Quarterly* 13 (1962): 494.

4. E. M. W. Tillyard, *Shakespeare's History Plays* (London: Chatto and Windus, 1944), p. 190. And Robert K. Turner, Introduction to *2 & 3 Henry VI* in *The Complete Works,* p. 475: "The implication of the historical accounts becomes, in fact, something of an embarrassment to the plays themselves . . . no well-defined protagonist was at hand, and the allegorical figure of England was too vague to serve as an agent of dramatic concentration."

5. Other examples of this play-idiom abound—e.g., 4. 3. 33–34, 48–50; 5. 1. 23–41.

6. Edward Berry (*Patterns of Decay* [Charlottesville: University Press of Virginia, 1975], pp. 68–72) sketches various ways of accounting for Richard's abrupt emergence in 3. 2. Tillyard, among others, sees it as a case of Shakespeare's reviving interest, in anticipation of Richard III.

7. Richard "becomes the conscious embodiment of all the drives—moral, intellectual and physical—that elsewhere show themselves only in the puppetry. Translating into theatrical terms, we might say that when he takes the stage for his first exercise of the soliloquy-prerogative he inherits from York . . . his language shows him capable of playing the parts of York, Clifford, Edward, Margaret or Warwick. All their energies are made articulate . . ." (J. P. Brockbank, "The Frame of Disorder—*Henry VI,*" in *Stratford-Upon-Avon Studies 3: Early Shakespeare,* eds. John Russell Brown and Bernard Harris [London: Edward Arnold, p. 97).

Though York (at least in Part II) is more than simply "dogged" as Brockbank describes him, as a play-consciousness he is of course rudimentary when compared with his son. His playmaker's instinct leads him to withhold himself—literally—while deploying a surrogate in Cade. By contrast, we might say that Richard arises out of the roles to which the others are reduced. Also, in much the same manner in which York "creates" Cade, Richard "creates" himself.

8. "Shakespeare's mock-heroics have come of age . . . [Richard's] aspiration to outdo the celebrated Greeks and their modern apologist gives a final, ironic turn of the screw to the humanistic pursuit of fame and honor. . . . Richard can turn the very formulas of rhetorical invective to his own advantage, arguing that it is precisely those qualities which make a man despicable in the world of copybook humanism that best qualify him for an earthly crown" (David Riggs, *Shakespeare's Heroical Histories* [Cambridge, Mass.: Harvard University Press, 1971], p. 137).

9. Berry, *Patterns of Decay,* p. 72.

10. Obviously Richard does not abolish the convention itself, merely its gratuitousness.

Chapter 5

1. William Willeford, *The Fool and His Sceptre* (Evanston, Ill.: Northwestern University Press, 1969), p. 163. For my use of the terms *antic* and *machiavel,* see the Introduction to this study, pp. 14–15.

Chapter 6

1. Michael Neill presents a brilliant argument for a basically anguished Richard who "sublimates his tearing consciousness of inner formlessness by concentrating on its outward image, which he creates as something outside himself, a shadow" ("Shakespeare's Halle of Mirrors: Play, Politics, and Psychology in *Richard III*," *Shakespeare Studies* 8 [1975]: 99–129). The essay is highly stimulating, and I am much indebted to it even though my own argument takes a different direction.

2. Among other things, Margaret parodies the writer of history plays who would stand detached and objective before his materials. Some critics take her quite seriously as an efficacious playwright-surrogate; e.g., A. C. Hamilton, *The Early Shakespeare* (San Marino, Calif.: Huntington Library Publications, 1967), pp. 193–94. Any view of *Richard III* as taking an ironic stance toward its morality "scourge-of-God" structure is indebted in some degree to A. P. Rossiter's title essay in *Angel With Horns*, ed. Graham Storey (London: Longmans, Green, 1961).

3. Robert B. Heilman so imagines in his essay, "Satiety and Conscience: Aspects of *Richard III*," in *Essays in Shakespearean Criticism*, ed. James L. Calderwood and Harold E. Toliver (Englewood Cliffs, N.J.: Prentice-Hall, 1970).

4. Cf. Wilbur Sanders, *The Dramatist and the Received Idea* (Cambridge: At the University Press, 1968), pp. 72–75.

5. Peter Brook, *The Empty Space* (New York: Avon Books, 1968), p. 54.

6. "Moral sentience" is Heilman's term ("Satiety and Conscience," p. 138). Norman Rabkin does believe that Richard achieves such moral sentience during his night at Bosworth: see his *Shakespeare and the Common Understanding* (New York: Free Press, 1967), p. 251. For the term *terrific* and the specific likening of actor to *ghost* I am indebted to Michael Goldman, *The Actor's Freedom* (New York: Viking Press, 1975), pp. 7, 27–29, passim.

7. William B. Toole, "The Motif of Psychic Division in 'Richard III'", *Shakespeare Survey* 27 (1974): 21–32.

8. Cf. Goldman, *Actor's Freedom*, pp. 13–15.

9. Theodore Weiss in "The Anarch Supreme," *The Breath of Clowns and Kings* (New York: Atheneum, 1974), deals cogently with the bond of breath between Shakespeare and Richard on pp. 165, 199.

Chapter 7

1. The dating of *King John* is notoriously uncertain. E. A. J. Honigmann (in the Arden edition [London: Methuen, 1954]) is one of the few who argue for *The Troublesome Raigne* as the reduction from Shakespeare's play, rather than as his chief source, which means that *John* would predate 1591. Most scholars place it somewhat earlier than *Richard II*, around 1595; a few, later.

2. Eugene M. Waith reviews the play's theater history in "*King John* and the Drama of History," *Shakespeare Quarterly* 29 (1978): 192–211.

3. Edward Rose, "Shakespeare as Adapter," pp. xvi–xvii in *The Troublesome Raigne of John, King of England, Parts I and II*, ed. Charles Praetorius, 2 vols. (London, 1888).

4. John R. Elliot, "Shakespeare and the Double Image of *King John*," *Shakespeare Studies* 1 (1965): 64–84.

5. Among those who do see the play as a dramatized contention of principles of "right" and "strong possession" is William Matchett in "Richard's Divided Heritage in *King John,*" *Essays in Criticism* 12 (1962): 231–53. Though I disagree with Matchett on this and other points, I appreciate his essay as one of the few serious defenses of the play's aesthetic unity. Three others are worth noting: Adrien Bonjour, "The Road to Swinstead Abbey," *English Literary History* 18 (1951): 253–74; James L. Calderwood, "Commodity and Honour in *King John,*" *University of Toronto Quarterly* 29 (1960): 341–56; and Sigurd Burckhardt, "*King John:* The Ordering of This Present Time," in *Shakespearean Meanings* (Princeton, N.J.: Princeton University Press, 1968). Burckhardt's is the only study I know that treats the play as artistically self-conscious, and I am, here as elsewhere, deeply in his debt.

6. In TR, for instance, the Bastard's animosity toward Austria is emphatically explained by the prominence of the lionskin Austria wears, which he is supposed to have taken from Richard I, the Bastard's father. Similarly, the Bastard has a romantic interest in Blanch, which he is forced to relinquish to the Dauphin, thereby inflaming his motive for revenge.

7. The verbatim line, according to Burckhardt ("*King John,*" p. 118), is Melun's at 5. 4. 42: "For that my grandsire was an Englishman." Shakespeare invents no new scenes outright and omits only four of TR's, though he cuts and adds liberally within individual scenes.

8. I have been persuaded by Honigmann's reading of line 215 in his Arden edition. He restores the Folio's "comforts" for Rowe's more generally accepted emendation, "Confront your city's eyes," explaining: "Fl was rejected since irony was said to be out of place. As John's speech is full of innuendo, of over- and under-statement, the *winking* of this very line being playful, as though the gates are no stronger than eyelids, we return to Fl" (p. 33). With Caroline Spurgeon in the background, Honigmann analyzes the pervasive imagery of "body outrage," blinding, rape, and bastardy-fornication under the general head of "imagery of oppression" (pp. lxi–lxv).

9. Emrys Jones notes that "as they fight, the opponents become drained of force—as if activity itself were unreal." See *The Origins of Shakespeare* (Oxford: Clarendon Press, 1977), p. 246.

10. In the one production I have seen—at the Stratford Festival, Ontario, in 1974—the Citizen stood on the balcony, upstage center, looking down upon the kings and their retinues deployed around the arc of the stage.

11. Samuel Johnson saw the pun on "match" in line 447:

> This union shall do more than battery can
> To our fast-closèd gates; for at this match,
> With swifter spleen than powder can enforce,
> The mouth of passage shall we fling wide ope,
> And give you entrance; . . .
>
> (2. 1. 446–50)

But he did not like it. "I am loath to think that Shakespeare meant to play with the double of *match* for *nuptial,* and the *match* of a *gun.*" Indeed.

12. I have discussed this seduction scene is an earlier chapter (pp. 80–81).

13. I use these "Part 1" and "Part 2" divisions only for convenience of reference, since I summarized the structure earlier. Acts 1–3 are usually broken into five scenes averaging 300 lines each. (Honigmann, in the Arden *John,* splits 2. 1 into two scenes

and consolidates the usual 3. 2 & 3 quite sensibly.) Acts 4–5 contain ten scenes, averaging 110 lines.

14. Honigmann finds "the spectacle of Hubert threatening to blind Arthur to be the most exciting picture of the play." (Arden *John,* pp. lx–lxi) He emphasizes the ingenuity of Arthur's appeal to Hubert's pity. Sigurd Burckhardt thinks that Arthur's language, uniquely free of ideological baggage, becomes the standard against which Shakespeare measured the rhetorical values in the rest of the play. He quotes M. M. Reese *(The Cease of Majesty)* to the effect that in the torture scene "Shakespeare deliberately refused this issue" of a debate between duty and conscience as he found it in TR. Burckhardt then comments: "[Shakespeare's] Arthur never once employs the argument of higher authority and more terrible sanctions. . . . [His pleading] is directed entirely at Hubert the man, designed to awaken in him that sense of compassion which, once admitted, will render him incapable of the cruel act" ("*King John,*" pp. 121–22).

15. According to Emrys Jones, after Arthur's death the Bastard experiences a "moment of vision": "For the first time the true darkness is acknowledged" (*The Origins of Shakespeare,* p. 254).

16. The whole passage: 4. 2 "fakes the sequence of events more cleverly than perhaps any other part of the cannon. John's new coronation (1) and the rumored death of Arthur (85) took place in 1202; the landing of the French (110) in 1216; the death of Eleanor (120) in 1204; the death of Constance (122) in 1201; the Peter of Pomfret episode (131) belonging to the year 1213; the five moons (182) to 1200; practically the whole span of John's reign being crammed into one scene and made to seem simultaneous, for the dramatic advantage of heaping up John's troubles and omens of misfortune" (Honigmann, Arden *John,* p. xxxi).

17. A. P. Rossiter, *Angel With Horns and Other Shakespeare Lectures,* ed. Graham Storey (London: Longmans, Green, 1961), p. 43.

18. Sir Edmund Chambers's ordering, and most revisions of it, would put—between *Richard III* and *King John—Venus and Adonis, The Rape of Lucrece,* early sonnets, *Love's Labor's Lost,* and possibly *Romeo and Juliet* and *A Midsummer Night's Dream.* Robert Y. Turner, in his energetic rethinking of the whole question of *Shakespeare's Apprenticeship* (Chicago: University of Chicago Press, 1974), would put, after *Richard III, A Comedy of Errors, Titus Andronicus, The Taming of the Shrew, The Rape of Lucrece, Two Gentlemen of Verona, Love's Labor's Lost, Romeo and Juliet*—all before *Richard II,* though Turner does not commit himself on *John,* being tempted by Honigmann's argument for a much earlier dating (predating TR, 1591).

Chapter 8

1. Analyzing syntactical patterns, Stephen Booth argues that Richard becomes theatrically and verbally frustrating from the point in 1. 3 when he throws down the warder. See his "Syntax as Rhetoric in *Richard II,*" *Mosaic* 10 (1977): 91–94.

2. Wilbur Sanders, *The Dramatist and the Received Idea* (Cambridge: At The University Press, 1968), p. 173.

3. A. P. Rossiter, *Angel With Horns and Other Shakespeare Lectures;* ed. Graham Storey (London: Longmans, Green, 1961), p. 26. Stephen Booth locates the stylistic change from 3. 2 on in the syntax. "Richard [as before] makes one lengthy, extravagant, self-indulgent speech after another, but with very few exceptions, he makes them in

straightforward syntax. His conjurations tend still to be *senseless*, but they make what sense they have *for* us" ("Syntax as Rhetoric," 97).

4. Burke notes that "every attempt [by Richard] at coercing by prayer [i.e., magical verbal efficacy] is promptly countered by an adverse turn in the objective situation." Quoted by James L. Calderwood in *Shakespearean Metadrama* (Minneapolis: University of Minnesota Press, 1971), p. 151.

5. Peter Ure, ed., *King Richard II*, The Arden Shakespeare, 5th ed. rev. (London: Methuen, 1961), pp. lxvii–viii.

6. See Sanders, *Dramatist*, pp. 163–64. Sanders here is describing what he considers a "deliberately cultivated texture of moral and motivational opacity in the drama." Ultimately, as the patient reader will see, I consider this opacity the most interesting symptom of the dramatist's unresolved struggle with his material.

7. Lois Potter, "The Antic Disposition of Richard II," *Shakespeare Survey* 27 (1974): 36.

8. The idea of Bolingbroke as "grim Necessity," the shadowy future, is also conveyed by the queen's dream. She bears, she insists, an inward grief that is nameless. When news arrives of Bolingbroke's return, she understands that *this* is the child of her apprehensions (2. 2).

9. In 3. 3 at Flint Castle, Bolingbroke enters with "drums and colors." But the mass of his power surely has to be imagined as waiting offstage, rather than fully represented on. He makes a *show* of power that, in terms of sheer theatrical flare, is eclipsed by Richard's show of acquiescence.

10. Ure, Arden *Richard II*, p. lxxi.

11. I am in debt to Kirby Farrell, *Shakespeare's Creation* (Amherst: University of Massachusetts Press, 1975), for this concept of the "king of shadows." See, for instance, p. 111.

12. Calderwood (*Shakespearean Metadrama*, pp. 175 ff) refines upon a critical tradition, originating with G. Wilson Knight, that sees Shakespeare, in Richard's soliloquy, reflecting upon the poet's task of creating verbal order out of a fallen verbal cosmos. I would only emphasize that parody by its nature cuts both ways, and that Shakespeare is also showing what a poet-dramatist *cannot* do: i.e., "hammer it out." Richard's creative method shows, as Parker Tyler puts it, how his "poetic metaphysics has matured in duress rather than in free choice; though Richard's instinct is poetic, he remains a king rather than becomes a poet" ("Phaethon: The Metaphysical Tension Between the Ego and the Universe in English Poetry," *Accent* 16 (1956): 30).

13. Exton is the at-long-last materialization of our wishes. He appears in 5. 4 after the semicomic public business of 5. 2 and 3, while the interior pressure for resolution builds up. But Richard has emerged ever since 1. 3 as the one we want and need to kill. Possibly even earlier: the play's first scene "pushes each member of its audience toward being his own Pierce Exton—impatient to hear a decisive assertion in a muddle of indecisive verbal gestures" (Booth, "Syntax," p. 89).

14. In almost all the other histories, Shakespeare counterpoises the ceremonial or ritual styles with scenes of boisterous, anxious, or even revolutionary commoners. In *Henry V*, the Chorus will stoutly refuse to acknowledge the existence of the comic ruffians whom the play, nevertheless, allows to take the stage in scene after scene.

15. Leonard Barkan, "The Theatrical Consistency of *Richard II*," *Shakespeare Quarterly* 29 (1978).

16. In a study of *Richard II*'s imagery, Richard Altick years ago showed how verbal self-consciousness constantly emphasizes the illusion of two worlds *(intensional* and *extensional)* and hence the artificial nature of the play as a verbal, poetic construct. What is perceived as artificial can also be perceived as illusory. ("Symphonic Imagery" in

Richard II, PMLA 42 [1947]: 339–65; reprinted in the Signet *Richard II,* ed. Kenneth Muir [New York: New American Library, 1963], pp. 199–234. See especially pp. 213–14). Ultimately, it seems to me, the leading question of the play concerns the source of its insistent ceremoniousness—or perhaps, as I have suggested, the stubborn obscuring of that source within the play.

Chapter 9

1. In the two parts of *Henry IV* . . . the effects [of Richard II's self-destructive acts] are exploded to create an entire dramatic world and the many various characters who inhabit it" (Alvin B. Kernan, "The Henriad: Shakespeare's Major History Plays," in *Modern Shakespearean Criticism,* ed. Alvin B. Kernan [New York: Harcourt, Brace, and World, 1970], p. 253).

2. It is the various strengths of a stirring world, not deficiences, which make the conflict in *1 Henry IV,"* writes C. L. Barber in *Shakespeare's Festive Comedy,* (Princeton, N. J.: Princeton University Press, 1959), p. 203. Edward Pechter adds, "But it works the other way around as well, the conflict makes for the strengths" ("Falsifying Men's Hopes: The Ending of *1 Henry IV," Modern Language Quarterly* 41 [1980]: 218).

3. A. R. Humphreys has a good analysis of this speech in the introduction to his revised Arden edition of the play (London: Methuen, 1961), p. 1xii.

4. "The prose in which [Hal] explains why time is nothing to Sir John is wonderfully leisurely and abundant, an elegant sort of talk that has all the time in the world to enjoy the completion of its schematized patterns" (Barber, *Shakespeare's Festive Comedy,* p. 199).

5. G. R. Hibbard has deftly set out the features that make for the great originality of *1 Henry IV*. Having touched on its quantum increase in new vocabulary, its proliferation of new characters and the intricate interplay among them, the abundance of prose, the amount of sheer invention, the dramatic structure—scenes related "like a series of shifting planes, corresponding to the way in which reality presents itself to us in the actual business of living"—Hibbard comes to what he considers Shakespeare's "break-through" in dramatic speech: Hotspur's "unpoetic" poetry, "its responsiveness to the tones of the speaking voice, and its predilection for imagery that is exact and down to earth. . . . It is a verse that bespeaks the man. . . ." (p. 9); and of course Falstaff's prose, which is infused with the qualities we would ordinarily associate with poetry. One of the implications of this is that an original audience would have felt itself in the presence of something new and unpredictable, especially in historical drama. See " 'Henry IV' and 'Hamlet,' " *Shakespeare Survey* 30 (1977): 1–12.

6. For ideas about audience collaboration I am especially indebted to Thomas Whitaker, *Fields of Play in Modern Drama* (Princeton, N. J.: Princeton University Press, 1977): e.g., "For those who are discovering their roles, and for those who are responding to the actor's gestures of discovery, a play is a collaborative miming that is lifted moment by moment into the light of the attention" (p. 16).

7. James Joyce, *Ulysses* (New York: Random House, 1961), p. 193.

8. Shakespeare picks up "pick-thanks" directly from Holinshed but suppresses his allusion to the "malicious rumours" of Hal's parricidal bloodthirstiness that these same smiling pickthanks spread. In the parallel scene in Part 2, of course, the parricide theme bursts violently through; but even in Part 1 there is at least one curious outcropping. In

the very midst of the ritual of proof and acknowledgement of son by father in 5. 4, Henry cannot help adding, perhaps rather coyly, that Hal by his "fair rescue . . . showed thou mak'st some tender of my life." But Hal's response is truly startling:

> O God, they did me too much injury
> That ever said I heark'ned for your death.
>
> (50–51)

He proceeds vehemently to deny his guilt by insisting that he *could* have let Douglas kill the king had he wanted him dead. In view of the earlier suppression of the pickthanks' "rumours," and of its sheer gratuitousness here, the outburst is eloquent.

9. John Russell Brown, ed., *Shakespeare in Performance: An Introduction Through Six Major Plays* (New York: Harcourt, Brace, Joranovich, 1976), p. 167.

10. The most influential piece of psychoanalytic criticism of the father-son relationship—an approach that necessarily posits a particular past—is Ernst Kris, "Prince Hal's Conflict," *Psychoanalytic Quarterly* 17 (1948): 487–505. Others are J. I. M. Stewart's "The Birth and Death of Falstaff," in *Character and Motive in Shakespeare* (London: Longmans, Green, 1949); Philip Williams' "The Birth and Death of Falstaff Reconsidered," *Shakespeare Quarterly* 8 (1957): 359–65 (William's perspective is in part anthropological); and M. D. Faber, "Falstaff Behind the Arras," *The American Imago* 27 (1970): 197–225. But see my discussion of *2 Henry IV*, where the issues crystallize as they never really do in Part 1.

11. Some, like John Danby, think of Hal/Henry V as a "whitewashed" Richard III (*Shakespeare's Doctrine of Nature* [London: Faber and Faber, 1949], pp. 90–91). Harold C. Goddard argues from this perspective eloquently and at length in *The Meaning of Shakespeare*, vol. 1 (Chicago: University of Chicago Press, 1951), pp. 161–214.

12. Daniel Seltzer, "Prince Hal and the Tragic Style," *Shakespeare Survey* 30, (1977): 22.

13. Edward Pechter, "Falsifying Men's Hopes: The Ending of *1 Henry IV*," pp. 225–26.

14. Brian Vickers, *The Artistry of Shakespeare's Prose* (London: Methuen, 1968), pp. 114–17.

15. Pechter (See n. 13 above) argues for the essential ambiguity of *1 Henry IV*—i.e., a play that induces a pleasurable "civil war" in *us*, exciting our mutually exclusive rages for order and chaos. Another recent study, reaching similar conclusions, is Elizabeth Freund's "Strategies of Inconclusiveness in *Henry IV, Part 1*," in *Shakespearean Comedy: Theories and Traditions* ed. Maurice Charney (New York: New York Literary Forum, 1980), pp. 207–16. Both studies acknowledge debts to Richard Lanham's *The Motives of Eloquence: Literary Rhetoric in the Renaissance* (New Haven, Conn.: Yale University Press, 1976).

16. Sigurd Burckhardt's reading of this scene, like so much else in his work, has been seminal: see "Swoll'n With Some Other Grief: Shakespeare's Prince Hal Trilogy," in *Shakespearean Meanings* (Princeton, N.J.: Princeton University Press, 1968), pp. 147–49. James L. Calderwood follows his lead in some interesting directions. He imagines Falstaff giving us a conspiratorial wink on "nobody sees me" (l. 25). See *Metadrama in Shakespeare's Henriad* (Berkeley: University of California Press, 1979), p. 71.

17. For an excellent exploration of the essential openendedness of the history play, see David Kastan, "The Shape of Time: Form and Value in the Shakespearean History Play," *Comparative Drama* 7 (1973).

Chapter 10

1. Like "tiring" above, "mock" has theatrical connotations.

2. Sigurd Burckhardt, *Shakespearean Meanings* (Princeton, N.J.: Princeton University Press, 1968), p. 160.

3. Cf. James L. Calderwood, *Metadrama in Shakespeare's Henriad* (Berkeley: University of California Press, 1979), p. 129: *2 Henry IV* "has the name but not the substance and vitality of its predecessor. . . . Having parasitically fed on a dramatic order already largely used up, it has called order itself in question." Much as I respect Calderwood's reading, it should be clear in the following pages where I disagree with him. *2 Henry IV* has its own, not its predecessor's, substance, vitality, and form.

4. See Burckhardt, *Shakespearean Meanings,* p. 159.

5. Freud sees the familiar "rescue fantasy" as a "defiance" of the father—i.e., a "squaring of accounts" ("A Special Type of Choice of Object Made by Men," in *Complete Psychological Works,* [London: Hogart Press and the Institution of Psychoanalysis, 1957], 11:172). Later clinical theorists such as Karl Abraham see it precisely as an inversion of the deeper Oedipal-parricide wish: see his "The Rescue and Murder of the Father in Neurotic Phantasy Formations," in *Clinical Papers and Essays in Psychoanalysis,* ed. Hilda Abraham, trans. Hilda Abraham and D. R. Ellison (New York: Basic Books, 1955), 2:68–75. See chap. 9, note 8, above.

6. As I mentioned above in chap. 9, note 10, any reading of the play employing psychoanalytic perspectives is indebted in some measure to Ernst Kris. In "Prince Hal's Conflict," Kris argues that Hal seeks out morally unimpeachable action as a way of resolving an Oedipal conflict; that is, he spends energies that would otherwise seek parricidal form and at the same time avoids intimacy and hence contamination by his father's stain of "regicide": taboo to Hal because it evokes living parricidal urges of his own. Perhaps Kris argues too narrowly, but in retrospect it seems true that Hal, in Part 1, contrives a scenario—an "action," a plot—whereby he can credibly play out a formal relationship to his father and hence at least partially absorb those obscure but vital energies that now, in Part 2, threaten all the more forcefully.

7. For this speech some editors (e.g., Holland, Signet *2 Henry IV*) follow the Folio, which regularizes the jagged lines. I prefer Allan G. Chester's use of the Quarto (in the Complete Pelican edition). A. R. Humphreys follows the Quarto as well in the Arden edition.

8. Quoted by Humphreys in his note on the speech in Arden *2 Henry IV,* p. 150.

9. On this displacement of the parricide-wish onto the crown, see Philip Williams, "The Birth and Death of Falstaff Reconsidered," *Shakespeare Quarterly* 8 (1957): 361–62.

10. See Burckhardt, *Shakespearean Meanings,* p. 162; also Norman N. Holland on the absorption of Hal "to the role of hero-king, while Falstaff is engulfed by a mythic significance that demands his rejection and death" (Signet ed., [New York: New American Library, 1965], p. xxxviii).

11. Edward Berry, "The Rejection Scene in *2 Henry IV,*" *Studies in English Literature* 17 (1977): 218.

12. William Empson, "Falstaff and Mr. Dover Wilson," *Kenyon Review* 15 (1953): 261–62.

13. I take Falstaff's rejection as the equivalent of his death, whatever temporary plans Shakespeare might have had to extend him into *Henry V.* On that subject I have something more to say in the following chapter.

Chapter 11

1. Both *Henry V* and the Globe are generally dated 1599. G. P. Jones has recently revived the old argument for an original "chorusless" *Henry V*, represented by the Quarto text. He takes the Chorus not as the voice of public theater, but as the means of adapting the play for court entertainment, one of whose characteristics was the flattery of the audience. See " 'Henry V': The Chorus and the Audience," *Shakespeare Survey* 31 (1978): 93–104. My own view is obviously very different.

2. Herbert Lindenberger, *Historical Drama* (Chicago: University of Chicago Press, 1975), p. 81. Lindenberger analyzes *Henry V* as representative of the "ceremonial play," i.e., a play that eschews unity in the text for "unity in the events and in their traditional meaning," which is "overwhelmingly public in character," relatively uncomplex in language and idea, but strong on the nonverbal elements of drama. It seems to me that Lindenberger gives away far too much in order to fit *Henry V* to this type, but he oversimplifies in a refreshing and fruitful direction.

3. Herschel Baker, *The Riverside Shakespeare*, gen. ed. G. Blakemore Evans (Boston: Houghton Mifflin Co., 1974), pp. 931–32. I am using Baker as representative of an academic stance toward the play too familiar to need much documenting. For instance, E. M. W. Tillyard found *Henry V* a great falling-off (*Shakespeare's History Plays* [London: Chatto and Windus, 1944]), and J. D. Wilson defended it (*The New Cambridge Shakespeare: King Henry V* [London: Cambridge University Press, 1947]) but both saw Shakespeare as *needing* the Chorus to fit his material for the theater. But also see note 7 below.

4. Michael Goldman, *Shakespeare and the Energies of Drama* (Princeton, N.J.: Princeton University Press, 1972), p. 58.

5. E. A. J. Honigmann, *Shakespearean Tragedy and the Mixed Response* (Newcastle upon Tyne: At the University Press, 1971), p. 7.

6. Charles Lewsen, from a review in *The Times* reprinted in *The Royal Shakespeare Company's Centenary Production of Henry V*, ed. and with interviews by Sally Beauman (Oxford: Pergamon Press, 1976), p. 249. Hereafter, unless otherwise noted, this book is abbreviated in the text as *RSC*.

7. Without detailing the many conflicting readings of the Chorus, let me suggest three more or less representative approaches: (a) "For what the Chorus said is Shakespeare's own opinion." J. D. Wilson, *Shakespeare's Histories at Stratford, 1951* (New York: Theatre Arts Books, 1952) p. 5; (b) "But who said [the choruses] are Shakespeare? . . . 'Me Chorus' is plainly not the author." H. C. Goddard, *the Meaning of Shakespeare* (Chicago: University of Chicago Press, 1951), 1:216; (c) ". . . he is the author's surrogate . . . . What he does 'honestly' apologize for through the Chorus is his inability to render on stage the destructiveness of war. . . . If there is a subtle irony in the Chorus' innocent manner, it is directed, not so much against Harry and his men, as against the audience." Robert Ornstein, *A Kingdom for a Stage* (Cambridge, Mass.: Harvard University Press, 1972), pp. 186–87. Ornstein implies that the audience of "gentles" wants a spectacle of slaughter, and will not get it: it is *they* who need true gentling.

As usual, the variety of responses ought to suggest the obvious, namely that the seeming simplicity is an artistic effect, a device that actually stimulates varied and ingenious responses.

8. "You're very much on your own, of course; in a way it's a very lonely part—you're separated to an extent from the rest of the action . . . it makes you rather vulnerable. If you make any kind of mistake there's no one else playing with you to

help you retrieve yourself" (Emrys James, speaking of his role as Chorus in the RSC production noted above, note 6, p. 62. This valuable book includes the working text of the play, an introduction by the director, Terry Hands, interviews with the designer, composer, and many of the actors, and running commentary on the text by Hands, Alan Howard (Henry), and others.

9. Terry Hands and Alan Howard describe this start-and-stop rhythm of the play in *RSC*, pp. 15–25 and 55–56.

10. I know of no production that deliberately transmuted Falstaff into the Chorus. The RSC's sequence of *1 & 2 Henry IV* and *Henry V*, however, did cast the same actor (Emrys James) as Henry IV and the Chorus. "One was given the quite remarkable impression that the old king had been rewarded miraculously with his own deep wish: 'Not an eye / But is a-weary of thy common sight, / Save mine, which hath desired to see thee more.' (3. 2. 88–89)" (Samuel Crowl, "The Long Goodbye: Welles and Falstaff," *Shakespeare Quarterly* 31 [(1980]: 370).

11. "Now, in the choral prologues of *Henry V*, Shakespeare has elevated Falstaff's revolt against the play into an official principle of the play. Over and again the Chorus makes Falstaff's divisive point about the purely theatrical and inadequate nature of what sets itself up as true history." J. L. Calderwood, *Metadrama in Shakespeare's Henriad* (Berkeley: University of California Press, 1979), p. 176.

12. *RSC*, p. 9.

13. *Shakespearean Meanings* (Princeton, N.J.: Princeton University Press, 1968), p. 192 n.

14. Michael Goldman also stresses the sheer athleticism of the Breach speech in his *Shakespeare and the Energies of Drama*, pp. 62–63.

15. For example, see D. A. Traversi, *An Approach to Shakespeare* (Garden City, N.Y.: Doubleday Anchor Books, 1969), 1:268–69. Traversi emphasizes the different distribution in the two speeches of the running "conflict between control and passion" in Henry's character.

16. The "discrepancy" is not always noticed by critics, and it can certainly be rationalized, but the question is, why bother? The Chorus, in his habitual manner, clearly seems to be introducing the scene to come rather than narrating different events than those dramatized. By breaking the Chorus's speech into three separate parts and playing the nightscene directly after line 47 ("A little touch of Harry in the night"), the RSC heightened the contrast between "the kingly exterior the Chorus describes, and the Henry we see." (*RSC*, p. 175)

17. "For the audience, the usual lack of concision, meter, and pace gives Harry a new voice, helping to realize the new range of his thought and feeling which may well embody some of their own incipient comments on the action. As the soldiers move off and Harry is alone, the dramatic focus will be, for the first time, potentially intense and deep" (J. R. Brown, *The Signet Classic Shakespeare: Henry V* [New York: New American Library, 1965], p. xxx).

18. "There is no Henry, only a king. . . . I think Shakespeare was profoundly interested in this particular study. Not, indeed, by the character, for there is no character, but by the singular circumstances of its disappearance" (Una Ellis-Fermor, *The Frontiers of Drama* [London: Methuen, 1945], p. 46). But I think the play dramatizes that disappearance.

19. Lindenberger, *Historical Drama*, pp. 79–81. See note 2, above.

20. Richard Lanham is instructive and, indeed, eloquent on the rhetorical (nonlinear, noncausal) relationship of *history* and *drama*, especially as it operates in *Henry V*.

See his *The Motives of Eloquence* (New Haven, Conn.: Yale University Press, 1976), for instance, pp. 192–93.

21. Shakespeare "omits any mention of tactics such as the stakes which protected the English archers from the French cavalry. All the chroniclers attributed victory to Henry's tactics, but not one gets a mention in the play apart from the killing of the prisoners, which has a special non-military importance. The work of raising morale is, in Shakespeare's presentation, Henry's essential contribution to the victory" (Andrew Gurr, " 'Henry V' and the Bees' Commonwealth," *Shakespeare Survey* 30 [1977]: 65–66).

22. The question is: does Henry order the cutting of prisoners' throats in reprisal for French atrocities, or merely out of anger that they continue to resist being defeated? In 4. 5 the French rally desperately. At the end of 4. 6 Henry hears alarums:

> The French have reinforced their scattered men.
> Then every soldier kill his prisoners!
> Give the word through.
>
> (36–38)

At the beginning of 4. 7 Fluellen and Gower attribute the slaughter to Henry's righteous anger at the French brutality. J. H. Walter (Arden *Henry V* [London: Methuen & Co., 1965]) ignores Henry's first order and notes of Gower's remarks: "This is the result of the rally led by Bourbon" (p. 124 n). This is obviously a selective reading of conflicting "evidence." The Folio remains benignly silent on the "truth." The RSC, like any production, had to choose their selection according to their best interpretation of the play. Reluctantly, they chose to show Henry's order as a reaction to the French slaughter of the boy.

23. Cf. Ornstein, *A Kingdom for a Stage,* p. 198: "If Harry's wooing lacks the tender humor and intimacy of Hotspur's moments with Kate, it is because the conquerer of Agincourt cannot, even in his 'passion,' forget his royal self." And Goldman, *Energies of Drama,* p. 73: In the wooing, "the king really has to *play* at being the man; he is in a sense affecting a 'humanity' perfectly appropriate to his position and his audience."

24. Cf. Norman Rabkin's reading of *Henry V* as radically ambiguous—i.e., "requiring that we hold in balance incompatible and radically opposed views each of which seems exclusively true. . . . The clash between the two possible views of the world of *Henry V* suggests a spiritual struggle in Shakespeare that he would spend the rest of his career working through" ("Rabbits, Ducks, and *Henry V,*" *Shakespeare Quarterly* 3 [1977]: 295–96). Peter B. Erickson also deals perceptively with the ambivalence of style and mood in *Henry V,* showing how Shakespeare manages to probe, dramatically, the very ideal that he celebrates epically. See " 'The Fault / My Father Made': The Anxious Pursuit of Heroic Fame in Shakespeare's *Henry V,*" *Modern Language Studies* 1 [1979–80]: 10–25.

25. See Burckhardt's remarks on the deliberately nonfestive ending in *Shakespearean Meanings,* pp. 199–200.

Conclusion

1. Wylie Sypher, *The Ethic of Time* (New York: Seabury Press, 1976), pp. 26–27.
2. D. H. Lawrence, *Fantasia of the Unconscious* (New York: Viking Press, 1960), p. 63.

Works Cited

Abraham, Karl. *Clinical Papers and Essays on Psychoanalysis.* Edited by Hilda Abraham. Translated by Hilda Abraham and D. R. Ellison. 1st. ed. Vol. 2. New York: Basic Books, 1955.

Altick, Richard. "Symphonic Imagery in *Richard II.*" *PMLA* 42 (1947): 339–65.

Baker, Herschel. Introduction to *Henry V* in *The Riverside Shakespeare,* edited by G. Blakemore Evans. Boston: Houghton Mifflin Co., 1974.

Barber, C. L. *Shakespeare's Festive Comedy: A Study of Dramatic Form and Its Relation to Social Custom.* Princeton, N.J.: Princeton University Press, 1959; Cleveland, Ohio, and New York: Meridian Books, 1963.

Barish, Jonas A. "The Antitheatrical Prejudice." *Critical Quarterly* 8 (1966): 329–48.

Barkan, Leonard. "The Theatrical Consistency of *Richard II.*" *Shakespeare Quarterly* 29 (1978): 5–19.

Berman, Ronald S. "Fathers and Sons in the *Henry VI* Plays." *Shakespeare Quarterly* 13 (1962): 487–97.

Berry, Edward I. *Patterns of Decay: Shakespeare's Early Histories.* Charlottesville: University Press of Virginia, 1975.

———. "The Rejection Scene in *2 Henry IV.*" *Studies in English Literature* 17 (1977): 202–18.

Blanpied, John W. " 'Art and Baleful Sorcery': The Counterconsciousness of *Henry VI, Part I.*" *Studies in English Literature* 15 (1975): 213–27.

Bonjour, Adrien. "The Road to Swinstead Abbey." *English Literary History* 18 (1951): 253–74.

Booth, Stephen. "Syntax as Rhetoric in *Richard II.*" *Mosaic* 10 (1977): 91–94.

Brockbank, J. P. "The Frame of Disorder—*Henry VI.*" In *Stratford-Upon-Avon Studies 3: Early Shakespeare.* Edited by John Russell Brown and Bernard Harris. London: Edward Arnold, 1961.

Brook, Peter. *The Empty Space.* New York: Avon Books, 1968.

Brown, John Russell, ed. *Shakespeare in Performance: An Introduction Through Six Major Plays.* New York: Harcourt, Brace, Jovanovich, 1976.

Brownlow, Frank Walsh. *Two Shakespearean Sequences: "Henry VI" to "Richard II" and "Pericles" to "Timon of Athens."* London: Macmillan Co., 1977.

Burckhardt, Sigurd. *Shakespearean Meanings.* Princeton, N.J.: Princeton University Press, 1968.

Burkhart, Robert E. *Shakespeare's Bad Quartos: Deliberate Abridgements Designed for Performance by a Reduced Cast.* The Hague: Mouton, 1975.

Calderwood, James L. "Commodity and Honour in *King John.*" *University of Toronto Quarterly* 29 (1960): 341–56.

———. "*1 Henry IV:* Art's Gilded Lie." *English Literary Renaissance* 3 (1973): 131–44.

———. *Metadrama in Shakespeare's Henriad: "Richard II" to "Henry V."* Berkeley: University of California Press, 1979.

———. *Shakespearean Metadrama: The Argument of the Play in "Titus Andronicus," "Love's Labour's Lost," "Romeo and Juliet," "A Midsummer Night's Dream," and "Richard II."* Minneapolis: University of Minnesota Press, 1971.

———. "Shakespeare's Evolving Imagery: *2 Henry VI.*" *English Studies* 48 (1967): 482–93.

Campbell, Lily B. *Shakespeare's "Histories": Mirrors of Elizabethan Policy.* San Marino, Calif.: Huntington Library Publications, 1947.

Crowl, Samuel. "The Long Goodbye: Welles and Falstaff." *Shakespeare Quarterly* 31 (1980): 369–80.

Danby, John. *Shakespeare's Doctrine of Nature: A Study of King Lear.* London: Faber and Faber, 1949.

Daniell, David. "Opening Up the Text: Shakespeare's *Henry VI* Plays in Performance." In *Drama and Society,* edited by James Redmond. No. 1. Themes in Drama. New York: Cambridge University Press, 1979.

Dean, Leonard F. *Tudor Theories of History Writing.* No. 1. University of Michigan Contributions in Modern Philology. Ann Arbor: University of Michigan Press, 1974.

Elliot, John K. "Shakespeare and the Double Image of King John." *Shakespeare Studies* 1 (1965): 64–84.

Ellis-Fermor, Una Mary. *The Frontiers of Drama.* New York: Oxford University Press, 1945.

Elton, Geoffrey Rudolph. *The Practice of History*. New York: Crowell, 1967.

Empson, William. "Falstaff and Mr. Dover Wilson." *Kenyon Review* 15 (1953): 213–62.

Erickson, Peter B. " 'The Fault / My Father Made': The Anxious Pursuit of Heroic Fame in Shakespeare's *Henry V*." *Modern Language Studies* 10 (1979–80): 10–25.

Faber, M. D. "Falstaff Behind the Arras." *The American Imago* 27 (1970): 197–225.

Farrell, Kirby. *Shakespeare's Creation: The Language of Magic and Play*. Amherst: University of Massachusetts Press, 1975.

Freud, Sigmund. *Complete Psychological Works.* Edited by James Strachey. Translated by James Strachey in collaboration with Anna Freud, assisted by Alix Strachey and Alan Tyson. London: Hogarth Press and the Institute of Psychoanalysis, 1953—. Vol. 11, "Five Lectures on Psycho-Analysis, Leonardo da Vinci, and Other Works," 1957. The Standard Edition.

Freund, Elizabeth. "Strategies of Inconclusiveness in *Henry IV, Part I*." In *Shakespearean Comedy: Theories and Traditions,* edited by Maurice Charney. New York: New York Literary Forum, 1980.

Goddard, Harold C. *The Meaning of Shakespeare.* 2 vols. Chicago: University of Chicago Press, 1951.

Goldman, Michael. *The Actor's Freedom: Toward a Theory of Drama.* New York: Viking Press, 1975.

———. *Shakespeare and the Energies of Drama.* Princeton, N.J.: Princeton University Press, 1972.

Gurr, Andrew. " 'Henry V' and the Bees' Commonwealth." *Shakespeare Survey* 30 (1977): 61–72.

Hamilton, A. C. *The Early Shakespeare.* San Marino, Calif.: Huntington Library Publications, 1967.

Heilman, Robert B. "Satiety and Conscience: Aspects of *Richard III*." In *Essays in Shakespearean Criticism,* edited by James L. Calderwood and Harold E. Toliver. Englewood Cliffs, N.J.: Prentice-Hall, 1970.

Hibbard, G. R. " 'Henry V' and 'Hamlet'." *Shakespeare Survey* 30 (1977): 1–12.

Hodgdon, Barbara. "Shakespeare's Directorial Eye: A Look at the Early History Plays." In *Shakespeare's "More Than Words Can Witness": Essays in Visual and Non-Verbal Enactment in the Plays,* edited by Sidney Homan. Lewisburg, Pa.: Bucknell University Press, 1979.

Honigmann, E. A. J. *Shakespearean Tragedy and the Mixed Response: An*

Inaugural Lecture Delivered Before the University of Newcastle upon Tyne on Monday 8th March 1971. Newcastle upon Tyne: At the University Press, 1971.

Howarth, Herbert. *The Tiger's Heart: Eight Essays on Shakespeare*. New York: Oxford University Press, 1970.

Hunter, G. K. "The Royal Shakespeare Company Plays *Henry VI*." *Renaissance Drama* 9 (1978): 91–108.

Jones, Emrys. *The Origins of Shakespeare*. Oxford: Clarendon Press, 1977.

Jones, G. P. " 'Henry V': The Chorus and the Audience." *Shakespeare Survey* 31 (1978): 93–104.

Joyce, James. *Ulysses*. Modern Library Edition. New York: Random House, 1961.

Kastan, David Scott. "The Shape of Time: Form and Value in the Shakespearean History Play." *Comparative Drama* 7 (1973): 259–77.

Kay, Carol McGinnis. "Traps, Slaughter, and Chaos: A Study of Shakespeare's *Henry VI* Plays." *Studies in the Literary Imagination* 5 (1972): 1–26.

Kernan, Alvin B. "The Henriad: Shakespeare's Major History Plays." In *Modern Shakespearean Criticism: Essays on Style, Dramaturgy, and the Major Plays*, edited by Alvin B. Kernan. New York: Harcourt, Brace, and World, 1970.

Knight, George Wilson. *The Olive and the Sword: A Study of England's Shakespeare*. London: Oxford University Press, 1944.

Kris, Ernst. "Prince Hal's Conflict." *Psychoanalytic Quarterly* 17 (1948): 487–505.

Lanham, Richard. *The Motives of Eloquence: Literary Rhetoric in the Renaissance*. New Haven, Conn.: Yale University Press, 1976.

Lawrence, D. H. *Psychoanalysis and the Unconscious* and *Fantasia of the Unconscious*. Viking Compass Edition. New York: Viking Press, 1960.

Levy, Fred Jacob. *Tudor Historical Thought*. San Marino, Calif.: Huntington Library Publications, 1967.

Lindenberger, Herbert. *Historical Drama: The Relation of Literature and Reality*. Chicago: University of Chicago Press, 1975.

Matchett, William. "Richard's Divided Heritage in *King John*." *Essays in Criticism* 12 (1962): 231–53.

Meyerhoff, Hans, ed. *The Philosophy of History in Our Time: An Anthology*. Garden City, N. Y.: Doubleday Anchor Books, 1959.

Neill, Michael. "Shakespeare's Halle of Mirrors: Play, Politics, and Psychology in *Richard III*." *Shakespeare Studies* 8 (1975): 99–129.

Ornstein, Robert. *A Kingdom for a Stage: The Achievement of Shakespeare's History Plays.* Cambridge, Mass.: Harvard University Press, 1972.

Pechter, Edward. "Falsifying Men's Hopes: The Ending of *1 Henry IV.*" *Modern Language Quarterly* 41 (1980): 211–30.

Potter, Lois. "The Antic Disposition of Richard II." *Shakespeare Survey* 27 (1974): 33–41.

Price, Hereward T. *Construction in Shakespeare.* Ann Arbor: University of Michigan Press, 1951.

Prior, Moody E. *The Drama of Power: Studies in Shakespeare's History Plays.* Evanston, Ill.: Northwestern University Press, 1973.

Prouty, C. T. *"The Contention" and Shakespeare's "2 Henry VI."* New Haven, Conn.: Yale University Press, 1954.

Rabkin, Norman. "Rabbits, Ducks, and *Henry V.*" *Shakespeare Quarterly* 28 (1977): 279–96.

———. *Shakespeare and the Common Understanding.* New York: Free Press, 1967.

Reese, Max Meredith. *The Cease of Majesty: A Study of Shakespeare's History Plays.* New York: St. Martin's Press, 1961.

Riggs, David. *Shakespeare's Heroical Histories: "Henry VI" and Its Literary Tradition.* Cambridge, Mass.: Harvard University Press, 1971.

Rose, Edward. Introduction to *The Troublesome Raigne of John, King of England, Parts I and II,* edited by Charles Praetorius. 2 vols. London, 1888.

Rossiter, A. P. *Angel With Horns and Other Shakespeare Lectures.* Edited by Graham Storey. New York: Theatre Arts Books, 1961.

The Royal Shakespeare Company's Centenary Production of "Henry V": For the Centenary Season at the Royal Shakespeare Theatre. Edited and with Interviews by Sally Beauman. Oxford: Pergamon Press, 1976.

Sanders, Wilbur. *The Dramatist and the Received Idea: Studies in the Plays of Marlowe and Shakespeare.* Cambridge: At the University Press, 1968.

Seltzer, Daniel. "Prince Hal and the Tragic Style." *Shakespeare Survey* 30 (1977): 13–27.

Shakespeare, William. *The Complete Works.* Edited by Alfred Harbage et al. Baltimore, Md.: Penguin Books, 1969.

———. *The First Part of King Henry IV.* Edited by A. R. Humphreys. 6th ed. rev. The Arden Shakespeare. London: Methuen and Co., 1961.

———. *King John.* Edited by E. A. J. Honigmann. 4th ed. rev. The Arden Shakespeare. London: Methuen and Co., 1954.

———. *King Richard II.* Edited by Peter Ure. 5th ed. rev. The Arden Shakespeare. London: Methuen and Co., 1961.

———. *The Life of Henry V.* Edited by John Russell Brown. The Signet Classic Shakespeare. New York: New American Library, 1965.

———. *Richard II.* Edited by Kenneth Muir. The Signet Classic Shakespeare. New York: New American Library, 1963.

———. *The Second Part of King Henry IV.* Edited by Norman N. Holland. The Signet Classic Shakespeare. New York: New American Library, 1965.

———. *The Second Part of King Henry IV.* Edited by A. R. Humphreys. Rev. ed. The Arden Shakespeare. London: Methuen and Co., 1966.

Stewart, J. I. M. *Character and Motive in Shakespeare.* London: Longmans, Green, 1949.

Struever, Nancy S. *The Language of History in the Renaissance: Rhetoric and Historical Consciousness in Florentine Humanism.* Princeton, N.J.: Princeton University Press, 1970.

Swander, Homer D. "The Rediscovery of *Henry VI.*" *Shakespeare Quarterly* 29 (1978): 146–63.

Sypher, Wylie. *The Ethic of Time: Structures of Experience in Shakespeare.* New York: Seabury Press, 1976.

Tillyard, E. M. W. *Shakespeare's History Plays.* London: Chatto and Windus, 1944.

Toole, William B. "The Motif of Psychic Division in 'Richard III'." *Shakespeare Survey* 27 (1974): 21–32.

Traversi, Derek A. *An Approach to Shakespeare.* 3d ed. rev. 2 vols. Garden City, N. Y.: Doubleday Anchor Books, 1969.

Turner, Robert Y. *Shakespeare's Apprenticeship.* Chicago: University of Chicago Press, 1974.

Tyler, Parker. "Phaethon: The Metaphysical Tension Between the Ego and the Universe in English Poetry." *Accent* 16 (1956): 29–44.

Vickers, Brian. *The Artistry of Shakespeare's Prose.* London: Methuen and Co., 1968.

Waith, Eugene M. "*King John* and the Drama of History." *Shakespeare Quarterly* 29 (1978): 192–211.

Weiss, Theodore. *The Breath of Clowns and Kings: Shakespeare's Early Comedies and Histories.* New York: Atheneum, 1974.

Welsford, Enid. *The Fool: His Social and Literary History.* London: Faber and Faber, 1935.

Whitaker, Thomas R. *Fields of Play in Modern Drama.* Princeton, N.J.: Princeton University Press, 1977.

White, Hayden. *Metahistory: The Historical Imagination in Nineteenth-Century Europe.* Baltimore: Johns Hopkins University Press, 1973.

Willeford, William. *The Fool and His Sceptre: A Study in Clowns and Jesters and Their Audience.* Evanston, Ill.: Northwestern University Press, 1969.

Williams, Philip. "The Birth and Death of Falstaff Reconsidered." *Shakespeare Quarterly* 8 (1957): 359–65.

Wilson, John Dover. Introduction to *King Henry V.* The New Cambridge Shakespeare. New York: Macmillan Co., 1947.

Wilson, John Dover, and Worsley, Thomas Cuthbert. *Shakespeare's Histories at Stratford, 1951.* New York: Theatre Arts Books, 1952.

Index

013887